THE
Phoenix
AND THE
Spider

*A Book of Essays about some Russian Writers
and their View of the Self*

RENATO POGGIOLI

HARVARD UNIVERSITY PRESS · Cambridge · 1957

THE
Phoenix
AND THE
Spider

For Renata and Silvia

Foreword

The two main heroes sharing the spotlight in this book are Vasili Roza-nov, one of the few Russian writers of stature still little known in the West, and Leo Tolstoy, perhaps the greatest among Rozanov's elders, who spread forever the glory of his name to all the corners of the world. Yet, it is the lesser known and less great of the two who suggested the central idea of this book, running through its fabric like a single thread. That thread is the common theme of all the essays collected in this volume, as well as their general purpose, which is to convey the Russian view of the psyche as re-flected in a few classical and modern masters of Russian prose.

Even though they were written at different times, these articles take the shape of a cycle, and form a whole. The series opens with two landscape views of Russian realism, and unfolds as a gallery of literary portraits, cover-ing a hundred-year span, from the first third of the nineteenth century to the first third of the twentieth. As already implied, no poet is included, at least as such, within this circle, nor are the subjects of these profiles ex-clusively storytellers and novelists. Of the nine figures represented, only five belong to the central tradition of Russian fiction (Tolstoy, Dostoevski, Goncharov, Chekhov, and Bunin), while the other four are an essayist and writer of aphorisms (Rozanov), two letter-writers (the poet V. Ivanov and the critic and historian M. Herschensohn), and, finally, a Soviet author (I. Babel).

The first two essays, one panoramic in character, the other using the particular perspective of Dostoevski's work, are a double attempt to describe the peculiar psychological climate of Russian realism. Both of them treat that climate as a general, rather than as a specific, situation: as a common and abstract background, or rather, as a vague backdrop on a still empty stage, where many major or minor actors of the Russian literary drama will in turn play their concrete roles and utter their unique words. The aim of these two pieces is to propose many parallel, and even contrasting, interpretations of what Russian realism stands for; yet, to quote from Marianne Moore's famous poem, the reader should consider all those interpretations as but "imaginary gardens — with real toads in them."

In each imaginary garden the real toad may be either the author or the work; more frequently, the character that the work depicts; at times, all of them at once. Yet in every case the real toad is a view of man. And almost always, as happens in fairy tales, it ends by changing forever into a nobler creature, into a more ideal being. Thus, to give one example, what the essay on Goncharov and his masterpiece ultimately proves is that, while taking *l'homme moyen sensuel* as its point of departure, Russian realism finds its point of arrival in the realization that the average sensual man is spiritual as well, and not so average at that.

Goncharov is one of the masters of Russian classical realism; the same lesson can be learned from three lesser writers, who exemplify in typical fashions the later naturalistic, decadent, and impressionistic trends of Russian realistic fiction. The unexpected conclusion of the Chekhov essay is that the magic of art and feeling may transform into a new, youthful Psyche even the plainest soul. The paradoxical outcome of the Bunin study is the recognition that that impassive craftsman, that detached observer of the material and brutal side of life, wrote his masterpiece only when he yielded to "the spirit of music," and chose for once to sing, as Tolstoy would have said, not from the throat, but from the chest. The unexpected result of the Babel piece is that all his tales on revolution and war reveal, beyond the iron law of historical necessity, a more inspiring and consoling code, inscribed on "the magnificent grave of the human heart."

The analysis of the letters which Vyacheslav Ivanov and Mikhail Herschensohn sent each other across the same room, and from "opposite corners" of the mind, seems at first hardly to fit within the framework of this book. The text which is the object of this analysis was written in a spirit of controversy, as an intellectual debate between two men holding contrary views and taking opposite sides of the issue. As for the issue itself, it concerns nothing less than the mission and the message of the Russian revolution. One could say that in this controversy Ivanov speaks with Nietzsche's voice, and Herschensohn, with Rousseau's. Yet the total effect of their debate is that of a superior harmony: in the end, this argument about history resolves all its contradictions, and changes into a dialogue about ultimate values and eternal things. By their respective attempts at reconciling culture with religious tradition and with social change, Ivanov and Herschensohn serve equally well the loftiest demands of the Self.

Nobody, in Russia or elsewhere, has ever asserted the demands of the

Self as consistently and forcefully as the man who suggested the double emblem that has become the title of this volume. In return, I have devoted to him an essay which may be considered the cornerstone of the whole work. That essay quotes in full and discusses at length an aphorism by Rozanov claiming that even the most impure human soul is phoenix-like, burning in its own fire, and from its ashes reborn. Yet, notwithstanding this fabulous view, Rozanov proved the supreme value of the Self *ad absurdum,* by insisting on the absolute validity of even the most vulgar and trivial of its demands. Unlike Ivanov and Herschensohn, he formulated them not by heeding the dictates of the spirit, but by listening to the urgings of his all too human instincts, to the promptings of his foolish and capricious heart. He produced all his works and thoughts by spinning them from his own inner matter, from the humblest and lowest levels of his psyche. If this book were the fable at which its title seems to hint, then its moral would be that "each soul is a Phoenix," as Rozanov said; yet the crux of the matter is that it fell to the Spider to utter that noble and luminous truth.

If Rozanov lived and worked like a spider, Tolstoy lived and worked like a bee; and, unlike Rozanov, he tried to reconcile the lower and higher demands of the Self. His main purpose was indeed to transform both of them, to use a Kantian formula, into the "maxims of a universal law." Tolstoy's redeeming ambition was bound, however, to remain unfulfilled, because of a lifelong conflict between his mind and his heart. This is why in his case I have put aside the tools of criticism, and taken up those of biography instead. The essay on Tolstoy, which is the longest of the book, is also the only one turning its light on the man rather than on the creations of his pen. In brief, its subject matter is not literary psychology, but psychology *tout court.*

This is perhaps the place to explain the device I have contrived in order to draw my own version of Tolstoy's likeness. As implied in its title, this portrait represents him in a borrowed dress and in an assumed pose. In brief, it reflects Tolstoy's historical figure in the distorted mirror of a famous literary character. That character, who is Molière's Alceste, is treated as if he were Tolstoy's archetype. This means that I have taken up a Jungian concept, which strictly speaking belongs to the field of collective psychology. While others have already applied that concept to the fields of anthropology and mythology, I have gone further, and extended its use to the domain of biography, and of individual psychology as well.

This parallel between Tolstoy and Alceste could not have been developed without continuous reference to Molière's comedy, as well as to Tolstoy's works. While all passages quoted from the latter, and from many other sources, were given as translated, often by other hands, it was unthinkable to quote from *The Misanthrope* except as written by Molière. Yet, since this book is addressed to the lay reader, I felt that Alceste's lines should be followed by an English version of them. Luckily for all concerned, including, we dare say, the American public, the poet Richard Wilbur published, while these pages were still being written, his verse translation of *The Misanthrope* (Harcourt, Brace and Company), which is not only the first successful rendering into English of a French classical play, but a masterpiece on its own account, destined to remain in the annals of American letters. I am deeply grateful to the translator and to his publisher for permitting me to quote from that great comedy not only in Molière's alexandrines, but also in Richard Wilbur's couplets. I have done so except in a few cases, when a more literal version than Wilbur's was required.

While the most sizable and important contributions here are wholly new, some of these pieces have already appeared in print. My thanks for allowing them to be reprinted go to the University of Oregon Press for "The Tradition of Russian Realism," which appeared originally in *Comparative Literature*, III, 3 (Summer 1951), in a special issue devoted to realism, and edited by Harry Levin; to Kenyon College for "Dostoevski, or Reality and Myth," an abridged version of which was published in *The Kenyon Review*, XIV, 1 (Winter 1952); to the University of Syracuse Press for "On the Works and Thoughts of Rozanov," printed for the first time in *Symposium*, IV, 2 (November 1950); and finally, to Harvard University Press for "The Art of Ivan Bunin," already published in *Harvard Slavic Studies*, vol. I (Spring 1953), and for "A Correspondence From Opposite Corners," which was included in volume XX of "Harvard Studies in Comparative Literature," as part of a series of essays by several writers, which were collected and edited under the title *Perspectives of Criticism* (Cambridge, 1950) by Harry Levin.

I must finally address a more personal word of thanks to all those who made possible the publication of this book, from Mrs. Aida Blender and Miss Johanne Hirshson, secretaries of the Department of Comparative Literature at Harvard, who respectively typed the manuscript and read the proof, to those members of the staff of the Harvard University Press, especially Mrs. Paul Mendez, who helped me to make my English far better than it could otherwise have been.

R. P.

CONTENTS

THE
Phoenix
AND THE
Spider

The Tradition of Russian Realism

I N a history of Russian literature written by the Polish critic and scholar Aleksander Brückner, there is an important passage which is too long to quote entirely but can be summed up in not too many words. In the years before 1848, says Brückner, there appeared in Russia that school of writers of the forties who created the classical period, or golden age, of their national literature. Their tradition derived "in a straight line" from Pushkin and Gogol, but they learned also from the modern writers of the West, especially from the French Balzac and George Sand and to a lesser extent from the English Dickens. Brückner goes on to say that no other literature has ever produced, in an equally short time, so many outstanding figures. He remarks that virtually all of them broke into print between 1845 and 1847, and were granted the privilege of seeing their early writings appraised by the critical genius of Belinski. All of them, except Tolstoy, were born between 1812 and 1823, and died between 1876 and 1883; Tolstoy was the youngest of the group and survived even its latest members by the span of half a century. One of them was a poet (Nekrasov) and another a dramatist (Ostrovski), but all the others were writers of imaginative prose, novelists and storytellers. With the exception of Dostoevski, all of them were born and remained more or less disaffected children of the landed gentry. To supplement Brückner's statement, I may add that the majority of them sprang from the same region in central Russia, which lies to the south of Moscow, around the provincial capital of Tula, not far from which Tolstoy was born. Brückner concludes by laying down a series of generalizations about the common traits of their literary work, from the standpoint of both style and content; but while doing so he never mentions the term "realism" in his characterization of that group of writers, most of whom are traditionally labeled Russian "realists." [1]

There are several things to be learned from this survey. First of all, we

learn that there are obvious chronological and historical, cultural and psychological, social and political, geographical and even regional ties, besides the
purely literary ones, connecting such writers as Aksakov, Turgenev, Goncharov, Saltykov, Dostoevski, Tolstoy, Leskov, and *tutti quanti*. We learn,
furthermore, that they are the Russian classics par excellence — a conclusion
which Western literary opinion is all too ready to accept, against the best
judgment of its Russian counterpart. The present essay, however, is concerned with those writers not because they are "classics," but because they
are "realists." The first task of these pages is then to reconcile the apparent
contradiction in Brückner's statement that they derive "in a straight line"
from Pushkin and Gogol, a "classic" and a "realist" who are excluded from
their group. The second task is equally determined by what is implied in
Brückner's statement. The chronological limits he draws, as well as the
names he omits, suggest that the Polish critic fails to apply his own realistic
label to the nonetheless realistic masters of the following generations, for
instance, Chekhov and Gorki, not to speak of an author like Ivan Bunin,
who, as will readily be admitted, belongs to a different breed.

Before opening this inquiry, it is better to accept the position of Brückner
at its face value. In his literary history, which is the standard work in English, Prince Mirsky separates the "age of Gogol" from the "age of realism,"
and deals with Chekhov and Gorki in the chapters following an introduction entitled "The End of a Great Age." [2] In his book of essays on European
and Russian realism, the Hungarian Marxist critic Georg Lukács quite
significantly fails to deal directly with Gogol, and treats him merely as the
subject matter of investigations by those whom he calls the leaders of Russian
democratic criticism. It is perhaps even more significant, even if such an
omission is due to reasons of quite a different order, that Lukács finds no
place in his book for the "idealistic" genius of Dostoevski, whose absence
is made more meaningful by the compulsory presence of Gorki, as the
master of "socialist realism." But, when ideological considerations cease to
operate, literary discrimination starts working again; and it is on the strength
of critical considerations that, along with Gogol, Chekhov is excluded too. [3]

The double task of this essay is, then, to define the two sets of relations
which distinguish Russian realism from romanticism and from naturalism.
Such a definition will test Brückner's affirmation that the Russian classical
realists derive "in a straight line" from Pushkin and Gogol, and will help to
determine in what sense they differ from both late realists and naturalists,
in Russia and abroad. The critical tradition of nineteenth-century Russia

denied the romantic label to Pushkin on the basis of his "realism," while several recent critics, especially the Formalists, have denied him the same label on the basis of his "classicism." And, in at least one case, the denial has been effected by using the epithet "classical" not only as a standard of judgment but also as a historical concept, by which to assess the esthetic standards of an age previously considered as devoid of any lasting artistic merit. Thus Boris Eichenbaum reinterpreted Pushkin by showing how great was his debt to his immediate predecessors, and by re-evaluating the Russian literature of the eighteenth century, all too often discredited under the derogatory label of pseudo-classicism:

Pushkin's admirers are wrong when they try to exalt him by regarding his appearance on the horizon of Russian poetry as an unexpected one. Pushkin is not the beginning, but the end of the long road traveled by Russian poetry in the eighteenth century. . . . Having absorbed all the poetic traditions of the eighteenth century—a century so rich in activity and achievement for Russian art—Pushkin was able to create a high canon, classical in its equilibrium and apparent facility. He had no followers, nor could he have any, because art cannot live on a canon alone.[4]

This denial of the existence of a Pushkinian tradition is a commonplace; what is paradoxical is the affirmation that this was due not to what was new but to what was old in Pushkin's work. In reality, part of the Pushkinian heritage remained alive, and affected the development of Russian literature more than Eichenbaum and the critics sharing his view are prepared to admit. Notwithstanding their view, and however strange it may seem, what remained alive was not the romantic but the eighteenth-century strain of Pushkin's art. And this was not merely due to what one might call Russia's "cultural lag." As a matter of fact, it is exactly this conservative side of Pushkin's genius that has been all too often confused with his supposed "realism."

The ambiguity of his position does not make Pushkin less of the romantic, which, historically speaking, he was; rather, it makes him a complex figure of whom one could say, as Friedrich Schlegel once said of Goethe, that he was at the same time the Shakespeare and the Voltaire of his own nation and time. Pushkin's narrative work, whether in prose or in verse, even if we neglect the too obvious example of such an "extravagant" piece as *Gavriliada,* remains incredibly close to the literary ideal of the French eighteenth-century *roman;* even his more romantic tales seem to be written in the dry and lucid style of Voltaire's *contes philosophiques.* This perhaps may explain why that work was able to attract such French masters as Mérimée and Gide, who even tried their hand at translating it. As for *Evgeni Onegin,* although it makes fun of Byron, it reminds us of the verse tales of that writer, which, despite their new and wild ideas, are couched in the witty and dry diction of Pope and his school. It is not so much as a belated classicist, but rather as a romantic of the moderate wing, still in love with eighteenth-century *esprit* and *clarté,* that Pushkin criticizes in his masterpiece "that obscure and weak style — which we call romanticism." It is from the same standpoint that, in another passage of the same work, he protests against "the garbage of the Flemish school" — in brief, against the vulgar realistic whims of that trend which the French call *bas romantisme.* This is the kind of Pushkinian ideal that remained alive in Russian literature, especially among those writers whom, after all, it is proper and right to designate, for this very reason, as "classical realists."

In other words, the Pushkinian tradition failed to influence the Russian writers of the following generations exactly through the most important component of that tradition, which was its romantic element. The same can be said in the case of Gogol, a master whom Russian criticism has always treated unhistorically, and who, owing to the falsity of such a perspective, has not yet been placed where he properly belongs. It is only recently that Russian scholarship has rightly evaluated the relevance of the traditional elements in Gogol's work — for instance, the picaresque trend of his imagination, his kinship with such authors as Lesage, Smollett, Fielding, and Sterne, and the very eighteenth-century quality of his conception of Cervantes' masterpiece, as shown by the attempt to give a modern equivalent of *Don Quixote* in *Dead Souls.*

It is this failure to understand Gogol's connection not only with pre-romantic, but also with romantic literature (for instance, his debt to Hoffmann), which has created a series of misunderstandings about Gogol as a realist. Up to the end of the last century, critics believed in the absolute modernity and authenticity of Gogol's realism, and nobody would have argued Chernyshevski's characterization as "the Gogolian age in Russian literature" of what was merely its post-Gogolian period. This view was bound to provoke a chain reaction in the opposite direction. Starting with the end of the century, a host of critics, led by Rozanov and Bryusov, later followed by others, up to the straggler Andrey Bely, discovered the presence of an extreme romantic strain in Gogol's work; they failed, however, to recognize the historical roots of that strain. Unable as they were to admit that a romantic realism could be possible, they postulated the existence of a Gogolian "idealism" or "supernaturalism," which they anachronistically appraised as an anticipation of the esthetic and mystical revival of their time, the age of Russian symbolism. But, in spite of their errors, they were quite right in concluding that Russian classical realism had been to a great extent a denial of Gogol's work rather than a continuation of it.

If this is true, then one can say that the famous statement by Dostoevski — "We are all pieces from Gogol's 'Overcoat' " — applies, and only in part, solely to Dostoevski himself. What the Russian classical realists refused to accept from Gogol's heritage was what was romantic in it, a fact which Dostoevski ought to have understood, since no Russian was a harsher critic of romanticism than he. One must admit that the passage in the *Notes From Underground* where he depicts the Russian romantics amounts to a moral and psychological, rather than to a cultural or literary, portrait. That mordant satire must perhaps be ascribed to the hero of his tale, rather than to Dostoevski himself. Yet when all this is said, the passage may be read, and is still worth quoting, even as a critical statement in literary terms:

> We Russians, speaking generally, have never had those foolish transcendental "romantics" — German, and still more French — on whom nothing produces any effect. . . . The characteristics of our "romantics" are absolutely and directly opposed to the transcendental European type, and no European standards can be applied to them. . . . The characteristics of our romantics are to understand everything, *to see everything and to see it often incomparably more clearly than our most realistic minds see it.* . . .[5]

What Dostoevski means to say in this ambiguous statement is that Russian romantic psychology is not idealistic but realistic, in the practical and negative sense of this word; yet one cannot help feeling that his condemnation could be validly extended to include cultural and literary romanticism also. The satirical character of this portrait does not detract from its truth, and perhaps it is not too far-fetched to suggest that the model for this caricature might have been Gogol himself, either the man or the writer or both.[6]

It was of course to another Gogol that Dostoevski referred when he spoke of the debt of gratitude which he and the Russian writers of his generation felt they owed to the author of "The Overcoat." There he spoke, literally, of the author of that piece, and that piece alone. In a certain sense even Belinski, who is more responsible than anybody else for the dubious theory that Gogol is the father of Russian realism, based his own opinion mainly on "The Overcoat," and on a few generalizations by Gogol himself, such as the famous pages in *Dead Souls* where the poet apologizes for evoking, rather than noble heroes and lofty ideals, the vulgarity of life and the meanness of man. Belinski believed that Russian life was the real object of the contemplation of Gogol, and that Gogol represented the ugliness of that life not only to exalt it to the beauty of art, but also to help his readers change it. Belinski assigned the same task to all those writers who were part of what he called the "natural school." Yet Gogol cannot be made responsible for Belinski's program. Nor can the program be attributed to those later masters of Russian classical realism who, although fully aware of the social mission of art, refused to interpret it with the narrow-minded dogmatism and the fanatic zeal of the radical critics of the following decades, who were Belinski's degenerate offspring. That program attracted most some of the more recent authors, especially such neorealistic writers as Chekhov and Gorki. No better restatement of Belinski's ideal can be found than in Chekhov's words: "My goal is to kill two birds with one stone: to paint life in its true aspects, and to show how far life falls short of the ideal life. . . ." [7]

It is from views like this that the so-called "tendentiousness" of Russian literature was to derive: a tendentiousness different in quality from, but of no less intensity than, romantic or esthetic tendentiousness, which causes the work of the artist to be all too often an *apologia pro vita sua*. It is the latter kind that the classical realists refused to serve, thus failing to follow Gogol's example, as they failed to imitate him in his attempt to humiliate life to the advantage of art — an attempt which produced some of Gogol's idiosyncrasies, such as his fondness for "ornamental style" and "purple passages."

Such differentiation between their respective conceptions of art may also help to distinguish the Russian classical realists from the late realists and the naturalists. Practically all the great Russian masters were unfriendly, not only toward these trends which later developed in Zolaesque naturalism, but also toward the aims and methods of Flaubert, the Goncourts, and the writers of the second generation of French realism. They reacted against the latter primarily for literary reasons, through their own inability to accept the theory and practice of *écriture artiste*. This does not mean that they were indifferent to problems of craftsmanship; nothing could be further from the truth. But they were less conscious and articulate in this regard than their French contemporaries. The vague and not too intense quality of the Russian concern with style may be assessed by referring to the connotation of the adjective "artistic" in the language of prerevolutionary Russia. A suggestive definition of that meaning is given by Prince Mirsky. After having stated that the word, at least as then used, was indicative of the mild "esthetic" tendencies of the eighties, Mirsky proceeds by saying of the writers of that decade:

They reverted to the examples of Turgenev and Tolstoy, and tried to be what is called in Russian *khudozhestvenny*. This word really means "artistic," but owing to the use to which it was put by the idealist critics of the forties. . . , it has a very different emotional "overtone" from its English equivalent. Among other things, it conveyed to the late nineteenth-century Russian *intelligent* a certain mellowness and lack of crudeness, an absence of too apparent "purpose," and also an absence of intellectual elements — of logic and "reflection." It was also colored by Belinski's doctrine that the essence of "art" was thinking in images, not in concepts. This idea is partly responsible for the great honor in which descriptions of visible things were held — especially emotionally colored descriptions of nature in the style of Turgenev.[8]

This peculiar interpretation of what is "artistic" resulted in a vague conception of style as well as in a loose conception of form. The Russian writer of fiction is far less concerned than his Western counterpart with the demands of diction and structure. This is true even of Dostoevski and Tolstoy, although their lack of concern for form had differing causes and effects. Thus Dostoevski was often led to unbalance both by his hectic method of composition and by the excessive tension of the "idea," while Tolstoy became classically perfect almost against his will, and created, unconsciously and effortlessly, works giving the impression not of artifacts but of natural organisms. The Russians' relative indifference toward the pre-established harmony of a structural design is revealed, almost symbolically, by the frequence of narrative works containing in their titles the word *zapiski,* which has perhaps no Western equivalent except the German *Aufzeichnungen,* and which has been indifferently rendered into English as "notes," "sketches," and even "memoirs." [9] *Zapiski* evidently suggests that the written work aims only at conveying a series of *impressions vécues,* and that the writer's task is to reproduce those impressions in their freshness and immediacy, with neither finish nor plan. This hints at the presence within Russian realism of an impressionistic trend, antedating the conscious impressionism of such later European realists as Daudet and Maupassant, and explains the appearance within that tradition of such an artist as Chekhov, whom Tolstoy himself defined as an "impressionist." Such a relative indifference toward narrative interest and plot structure anticipates, according to Mirsky, some of the methods of modern fiction in the West, as exemplified in the works of James, Proust, and Joyce.[10]

This neglect of the claims of order and form was more than a mere matter of taste, and was due to other reasons than purely literary ones. The great Russian masters felt that an excessive emphasis on style and shape could lead to estheticism, or to an attitude of moral neutrality toward the content of literature, to the *impassibilité* of the "art for art's sake" movement and the Parnassian school. Some of them realized that the same tendency could also lead to naturalism, or to a cynical curiosity for what is morbid and sordid in life, which may be redeemed esthetically through the perfection or fidelity of the representation, but which remains ethically unredeemed. They felt that the cult of style and form, which, like any idolatry, exalts the means at the expense of the ends, could lead even to decadence, or to a perverse predilection for all that is sickly and unhealthy in the texture of life and in the condition of man. We find frequent warnings against such dangers in the writings of the masters of the Russian golden age, but the warnings are almost always qualified by the assurance that, while these dangers are threatening the fabric of Western realism, they have not yet sensibly affected its Russian counterpart. Such is the position taken by Goncharov, in a page which remained unpublished up to a few years ago, where he claims that extreme realism is not realism at all. After having declared that for him realism means an esthetic quality universally and permanently valid, equally shared by all the masters of ancient and modern art, the author of *Oblomov* denies the presence of that quality in the movement which takes realism for its realm: "Realism is one of the main bases of art, but not that realism which the latest school abroad and even in this country is preaching. . . ." [11]

Goncharov is rightly considered the most typical representative of the right wing of Russian classical realism, and such a statement is not surprising from him. It is therefore highly significant that the same position was taken by Saltykov-Shchedrin, the "Menippean satirist" of Russian realism. What is even more significant is that the author of *The Family Golovlev,* a novel generally considered the extreme manifestation of the naturalistic trend in classical Russian literature, protested vigorously against that curiosity for the morbid and the sordid which he finds typical of the French realists of his own time:

The extent of our realism is different from that of the modern school of French realists. We include under this heading the whole man, in all the variety of his definitions and actuality; the French for the most part interest themselves in the torso, and of the whole variety of his definitions dwell with greater enjoyment in his physical abilities, and amorous feats.[12]

The closing words of this statement remind us of one of the best-known qualities of Russian fiction, at least up to the end of the nineteenth century. That quality may be defined by such words as purity, chastity, even prudery. In this respect, the great Russian novelists and storytellers seem closer to their English than to their French colleagues. This trait explains their lack of interest in the work of Zola, although, at least as a pamphleteer and an essayist, he was granted such a generous reception by the Russian press.

The relative sexual innocence of the great Russian masters differentiates them not only from the naturalists and the late realists, but also from Stendhal and Balzac. Stendhal and Balzac, however, were interested in "the amorous animal" because they were interested, to use Saltykov's phrase, "in the whole man," and in this regard Dostoevski and Tolstoy were at least equally "adult." Yet it is for the wholeness of their vision of man that the classics of Russian realism are perhaps more entitled than their French contemporaries to be considered the progeny of Stendhal and Balzac. This was clearly seen and forcefully stated by Georg Lukács, for whom naturalism and even late realism are not the development or continuation, but rather the corruption or degradation, of early realism. For this very reason, Lukács is led to affirm that "the true heirs of the French novel, so gloriously begun early in the last century, were not Flaubert and even less Zola, but the Russian and Scandinavian writers of the second half of the century. . . ." [13]

Russian realism was prevented from degenerating into biological naturalism, which contemplates only part of "the whole man," not only by its acceptance of a social mission or content, as Lukács claims, but even more by its willingness to set definite moral restraints upon the artist, upon art, upon realism itself. Goncharov, for instance, used his Oblomov as a mouthpiece to record his protest against "the realistic trend in literature," which had supposedly replaced that invisible "laughter through tears" recommended by Gogol, with the "all too visible sneer" of a new grudge. Probably what Goncharov had in mind was the *odium theologicum* preached by the critical realists [14] and practiced by their literary followers, yet the validity of the statement transcends its immediate polemical purpose. His words reveal fully that Russian realism aimed at exercising a power of moral discrimination in the field of psychology, considered both as the object and the subject of art — on man as both the model for and the author of man's portrait.

As Goncharov's protest against the naturalistic "grudge" clearly shows, Russian realism limited its scope not only in the sphere of sex but also in the area of cruelty. If the former is always covered by the veil of chastity, the latter is always covered by the veil of pity. With the partial exception of Dostoevski, all the scenes of cruelty which we find in Russian fiction are contemplated from the viewpoint of the victim, without complacency or ambiguity. Nothing proves this point better than the famous episode in *War and Peace* when Rostopchin, the governor of Moscow, delivers the poor wretch Vereshchagin to the rioting mob, as a scapegoat or a sacrificial lamb. Despite the epic detachment of the narration, no reader can fail to notice that the writer aims at suggesting a parallel between Rostopchin and Pontius

Pilatus, Vereshchagin and Jesus Christ. *Ecce homo:* such are the very words that would be a fitting epigraph for that tragic scene.

As a matter of fact, Tolstoy a few years later had the opportunity to define clearly his position in regard to that kind of realism which claims the absolute right of the artist to observe and paint reality, while denying any value to the human reality observed and painted by him. This was when he protested publicly at the report that the famous painter Vereshchagin (what a strange coincidence of names!) had requested the military authorities to schedule the execution of two men condemned to death so as to enable the artist to make a study of their agony.[15] How Tolstoy's position differs from the conception of Ortega y Gasset, who defines the artistic faculty as the ability to draw the portrait of a man on his death bed! No Russian writer, not even the tortured and torturing Dostoevski, could ever accept such a view of art, even of realistic art, as an esthetic or scientific *experientia in corpore vili!* Not even Vereshchagin himself would have accepted that view. He was held, and certainly held himself, to be the master of realistic painting in Russia, and, during a series of exhibitions of his works which took place in the United States, he published in English translation a pamphlet entitled *Realism.* There we can read the following passage, proving that even for him there is no true art, no true realism, when the work fails to carry a meaning, or to convey a sense of value:

I . . . assert that in cases where there exists but a bare representation of a fact or of an event without idea, without generalization, there can possibly be found some qualities of realistic execution, but of realism there could be none: of that intelligent realism, I mean, which is built on observation and on facts — in opposition to idealism, which is founded on impressions and affirmations, established a priori.[16]

"Idealism" and "cruelty" are, of course, part of Dostoevski's province. This truth has been proved in the first place by many of his mystical and metaphysical critics, and in the second by the definition of Dostoevski's genius which the radical critic Mikhailovski gave in the very title of his famous critique "A Cruel Talent." But Dostoevski the "idealist" remains a "realist," and his "cruel talent" is often mitigated by that compassion which is part of its make-up. What prevented Dostoevski from falling into the pitfalls of naturalistic cruelty was not only his distaste for the French representatives of that school, which he so clearly manifested when he made fun, through Dmitri Karamazov, of Claude Bernard, the scientific positivist of whom Zola considered himself the disciple in the literary field. What saved Dostoevski from becoming a genuine naturalist was his sensational and melodramatic taste, his predilection for situations and tensions that remind us not so much of Balzac and Zola as of Eugène Sue. All his masterpieces are transcendental sublimations of the early nineteenth-century "thriller" or *roman feuilleton.* Yet it is for this very reason that Dostoevski's realism, unlike Turgenev's, is never middle-of-the-road realism.

Even Tolstoy did not always limit himself to the evocation of what is common and average, habitual and daily, in the existence of man. Nor did his realism often keep to the middle of the road. This is especially true of those works of his middle and late period, which were all tragedies of sex, or, as he would have said, "tragedies of the bedroom": *The Power of Darkness* and *The Kreutzer Sonata,* "The Devil" and "Father Sergius." The first of these works was considered in its day the masterpiece of naturalistic drama, and was performed for the first time on the stage of Antoine's *Théâtre Libre* under Zola's sponsorship. And yet, how it differs, as do all Tolstoy's works of its kind, from such a piece as *Thérèse Raquin!* The gulf separating them is the difference between the ethical realism of the Russian and the biological naturalism of the French master.

For historical and psychological reasons, only such a belated writer as Chekhov could be affected by the strain of naturalism. It will suffice to cite as an example such a story as "Mire," which Chekhov defended against a lady's disapproval in this fashion: "To a chemist nothing on earth is unclean. A writer must be as objective as a chemist; he must abandon the subjective line; he must know that dunghills play a very respectable part in a landscape, and that evil passions are as inherent in life as good ones."[17]

The Zolaesque flavor of this passage is unmistakable, as we may see from the parallel between the tasks of the artist and the scientist and from the metaphor of the dunghill. Such words would be inconceivable from the pen of Dostoevski, Tolstoy, or any one of the classical realists, though we could very easily imagine Gorki's having written them. Yet, even in Chekhov's art, there is no resolute attempt to represent human existence in terms of inarticulate and objective "still life," or to reduce all man's experiences to the level of *tranches de vie.* On the contrary, one could say of Chekhov what Baudelaire said of himself in an unfinished poem, where, after having stated, with the same image as Chekhov's, that he had done his duty *comme un parfait chimiste,* he concluded with this line:

On m'a donné la boue et j'en ai fait de l'or.

Whether or not there is the impure mud of life in the works of the masters of Russian realism, we find almost always the pure gold of art. Yet these writers would never have dared to exalt beauty as highly as Baudelaire, or even as Flaubert, so frequently did. With very few exceptions, exemplified by Pushkin and his Pleiad and by the decadents and the symbolists, the literary artists of Russia in the main were inclined to treat the beautiful as iconoclasts rather than idolaters. The very word "beauty" is rarely found in the prose of imaginative writers during the classical age, and when it appears, as in Tolstoy's *What is Art?* it is no less mistreated than in the utilitarian philippics of the "critical realists." Perhaps the only two great Russian masters who meditated deeply upon the idea of beauty were Pushkin and Dostoevski. The object of their meditation, however, was beauty not as an esthetic and artificial product but as a physical and natural phenomenon, as a grace and a wonder in life and man. Both of them tried to penetrate its miracle, only to conclude that beauty was too great a mystery for the human mind. There is a famous poem by Pushkin in which the poet recalls a vision haunting him as a school child: "Two wonderful beings fascinated me with their beauty: they were two demon's faces. One, a Delphic idol, was a youthful countenance: severe, full of awful pride, he breathed the sense of an unearthly power. The other, an ideal of feminine semblance, passionate and deceptive, was a charming genius, deceitful, but lovely. . . ." [18]

It was perhaps from these lines that Dostoevski derived his own idea of the duality and duplicity of beauty, which he stated at least twice in his novels. When General Epanchin shows the portrait of Nastasya Filipovna to the protagonist of *The Idiot,* that sudden revelation of feminine beauty leads Prince Myshkin to declare that beauty is an ambiguous value, containing in itself the opposites of good and evil. And in *The Brothers Karamazov* Dmitri thus confesses to Alyosha the true nature of his passion for Grushenka: "Beauty is a terrible and awful thing! It is terrible because it has not been fathomed and never can be fathomed, for God sets us nothing but riddles. Here the boundaries meet and all contradictions exist side by side. . . ." [19]

It was perhaps because he shared this view of beauty as something "beyond good and evil" that Tolstoy ended by blaspheming its very name. Yet in his youth he held that beauty was sacred, as a vessel is sacred because it contains a holy thing. There is a passage in one of his early works where he considers beauty as a value derived from the higher value of truth, which, in its turn, he treats as a synonym of goodness. It occurs in *The Sevastopol Sketches,* and it reads thus: "The hero of my tale, whom I love with all the power of my soul, whom I have tried to portray in all its beauty, who has been, is, and will be beautiful, is truth." [20] Nothing could be more conventional than this identification of the true, the good, and the beautiful, which is both a *locus communis* and a *locus classicus* of traditional esthetic thought; yet the commonplace is made fresh and green by the new ground wherefrom it springs. That new ground is Tolstoy's realism, which could be defined as the "realism of the heart."

Dostoevski's esthetic generalizations contain more and newer insights. In a youthful article on the art of painting, he unfolds his theory of realism, revealing also his own method as a realist, and what he recommends and conveys could be defined as the "realism of the spirit." Dostoevski states that the artist should look at nature realistically but not photographically, with the human eye rather than with a camera lens. Since man looks at the world also with the vision of his mind, he will ultimately discover in reality more than meets the eye. The article ends with these words: "In antiquity one would have said that man must look not only with his physical sight, but also with the eye of the soul, with the sight of the spirit." [21]

Of course, there is no great art without "second sight": a principle which is equally valid for all the masters of Russian realism. Yet, that "second sight" is generally of a not too mystical kind, and this applies especially to an artist like Tolstoy. This quality of Tolstoy's vision of reality may be suggested by a real life anecdote he retells in *Childhood*. The childish hero re-evokes one of the pastimes of his family circle:

We children brought papers, pencils, and paints, and arranged ourselves at the round table in order to draw. I had only blue paint; but for all that I took into my head to draw the hunt. Having very vividly depicted a blue boy on a blue horse, and blue dogs, I was in doubt whether one could paint a blue hare, and ran into papa's study to consult him. Papa was reading something, and in answer to my question whether there were blue hares, replied: "Yes, my dear, there are," without raising his head.[22]

The "second sight" of Tolstoyan realism may be simply stated as the faculty of perceiving hares that are both blue and true. Of course, not all artists see and paint in that hue. Gogol, for instance, shades everything in gray, especially the human figure. All his characters, as he says of those people living in a forgotten section of Moscow, whom he describes in "The Portrait," could be defined "ashen-colored." In the Rembrandtian chiaroscuro of Dostoevski, men are clothed in black, and the world is dominated by the color symbolic of death. As we well know from the protagonist of "The Overcoat," from so many Dostoevskian and Tolstoyan figures, from all the humble heroes of Russian fiction, "the whole of Russian literature" seems to consist of the attempt to perceive and to express, as D. H. Lawrence once said, "the phenomenal corruscation of the soul of quite commonplace people." [23] This is why even gray and black people end by radiating all the colors of the rainbow. There are indeed more than blue hares in the splendid gallery of Russian realism.

NOTES

1. Aleksander Brückner, *Historija literatury rosyiskiej* (Lwów-Warszawa-Kraków, 1922), vol. II, pp. 15–16.

2. D. S. Mirsky, *A History of Russian Literature* (New York, 1949).

3. Georg Lukács, *Studies in European Realism* (transl. by Edith Bone; London, 1950).

4. In the essay "Problemy poetiki Pushkina" (The Problems of Pushkin's Poetics).

5. *Notes From Underground,* II (quoted as translated by Constance Garnett). The italics are Dostoevski's.

6. The guess is not as wild as it may seem, in view of the claim by the Russian critic, Yuri Tynyanov, that Gogol was the model for the hypocrite Foma Fomich (the protagonist of *The Manor of Stepanchikovo,* translated into English as "The Friend of the Family"). This is supported by passages from the text of that tale and by the speeches of Foma Fomich, both reminiscent of Gogol's statements in the *Excerpts from the Correspondence with his Friends.*

7. From the letter of A. N. Pleshcheev, written on April 9, 1889. Quoted as translated by S. S. Koteliansky and Leonard Woolf in *The Personal Papers of Anton Chekhov* (New York, 1948), p. 150.

8. Mirsky, p. 334.

9. Practically all the narrative works by Sergey Aksakov are entitled *Zapiski.* More famous in the West are Gogol's *Zapiski sumasshedshchego* (Memoirs of a Madman), Turgenev's *Zapiski okhotnika* (A Sportsman's Sketches), and Dostoevski's *Zapiski iz mertvago doma* (Notes From a Dead House) and *Zapiski iz podpolya* (Notes From Underground).

10. Mirsky, p. 171.

11. From the piece entitled "Better Late Than Never," in Goncharov's *Literaturno-kriticheskie stati i pisma* (Essays and Letters, Literary and Critical), edited by A. P. Rybasov (Leningrad, 1938), p. 187.

12. Quoted as translated by Ivy Litvinov in Mikhail Alpatov's *The Russian Impact on Art* (New York, 1950), pp. 228–229.

13. Lukács, Preface, p. 5.

14. By this term I mean the radical critics, some of whom chose to call themselves "realists." In this usage, I differ from the terminology of Marxist and Soviet literary criticism, according to which the "critical realists" are the classics of Russian and European realism, who criticized prerevolutionary reality, while the practitioners of post-revolutionary "socialist realism" are supposed to glorify it.

15. The episode is thus summed up in the most famous biography of Tolstoy in English: "The passage of Vereshchagin's *Memoirs,* where that artist mentions persuading General Strukov to hasten the hanging of two Turks that he might sketch the execution, aroused Tolstoy's profound indignation" (Aylmer Maude, *The Life of Tolstoy — Later Years,* in "Tolstoy Centenary Edition," London, 1930, 2, II, p. 20). This incident occurred in 1879, in the aftermath of the Russian-Turkish War. Shortly after, Tolstoy expressed his protest in the preface he wrote for Ershov's *Recollections of*

Sevastopol, which in the same centenary edition has been used as a kind of introduction to Tolstoy's far earlier *Sevastopol Sketches.*

16. *Realism,* by Vassili Verestchagin (sic) (Philadelphia, 1899), p. 5.

17. From the letter to Madame Kiseleva, of January 14, 1887; translated by Kotelian-sky and Woolf, p. 130.

18. Closing lines of the poem "V nachale zhizni shkolu pomnyu ya," which deals with the poet's schoolboy reminiscences.

19. *The Brothers Karamazov,* part I, book III, ch. 1. Quoted as translated by Constance Garnett.

20. "Sevastopol in May 1855" (Aylmer Maude's translation).

21. From an 1861 article on "The Exhibition at the Academy of Fine Arts."

22. *Childhood,* XI ("What Went On in the Study and the Drawing Room"). Quoted as translated by Constance Garnett.

23. D. H. Lawrence made this statement in an unpublished preface for one of his translations from the Italian novelist Giovanni Verga, printed for the first time in *Phoenix: The Collected Papers of D. H. Lawrence* (London, 1936).

Dostoevski, or Reality and Myth

I N the January 1861 issue of *Vremya* (The Times), a Petersburg periodical of which Dostoevski was in effect the publisher and editor, as well as chief contributor, there appeared an unsigned article, which we know without any doubt to have been written by him. It can still be found in his collected works, where the curious reader of today will be certainly struck by this significant opening: "If there is a country in the world that seems destined to remain unexplored and unknown by any other nation, either nearby or faraway, that country is certainly Russia, at least as far as her Western neighbors are concerned. Not even China or Japan could ever hide from the curiosity of Europe as successfully as Russia has been doing in the past and in the present, and will probably continue to do even in the distant future. . . ."

We may feel sure that Dostoevski held this opinion before writing this piece, and we know that he continued to hold it to the very end of his life. At the same time he remained equally convinced of an opposite truth: namely, that while Europe was unable to understand Russia, Russia was quite able to understand Europe. One year before his death, in the famous speech he delivered for the inauguration of the Pushkin monument in Moscow, he stated that the greatness of that poet consisted in a power peculiar to the Russian spirit and mind — a power of concrete universality, by which Pushkin could feel and represent foreign themes and characters as well as any native genius.

There is no need to argue whether Dostoevski's claim, that to be a Russian means to understand equally well what is not Russian, should be taken for a valid psychological generalization, or merely for a mystical nationalistic belief. It will suffice to say that the statement is valid for Pushkin, who in the cultural sense was in fact a "good European" in the Goethean meaning of the term. As far as his literary culture is concerned, the same can be said of Dostoevski himself, although with some limitations: he was certainly unable to grasp the idea of a *Weltliteratur* in the way that Goethe and Pushkin had done. Yet, after Pushkin, no Russian writer was as perceptive as Dostoevski of the literary traditions and ideals of the West.

Dostoevski's own universality certainly surpasses even that of Turgenev, the most typical Russian literary "Westerner." Turgenev, to be sure, was certainly able to appreciate far better than Dostoevski the attempt, peculiarly French, to reconcile the ugliness of reality with the beauty of art. Yet Turgenev's literary culture had far less breadth and depth than Dostoevski's. As for Tolstoy, far more "Western" than Dostoevski in his stylistic approach, he was far less "catholic" in his taste and far more arbitrary in his judgments, based, as they were, on the critical idiosyncrasies of a sectarian mind, which could understand only the "grammar of dissent."

This is true not only of the fanatical author of *What is Art?* and the iconoclastic essay on Shakespeare, but of the entire Tolstoy. Merezhkovski was the first to notice this essential feature of Tolstoy's temperament, and to remark that, at least in this regard, Dostoevski was nearer than Tolstoy to the Western conception of the "man of letters." How false and rhetorical must therefore sound to our ears the exclamation by which Melchior de Vogüé warned and prepared the readers of his book, *Le Roman Russe,* for the apparition of Dostoevski: "Here is the true Scythian!" (*Voilà le vrai Scythe!*)

We must realize that by reason of his allegiance to the cultural values of the European heritage, Dostoevski was something better than another "barbarian of genius." We must recognize that his mind was well trained and highly cultivated in literary matters. This can be easily proved by the youthful letters he exchanged with his brother Mikhail while he was still at college. They are full of keen critical analyses, of new interpretations, of original evaluations. Dostoevski shows there an intelligent appraisal, rare in a man of his age, nation, and time, of the French classical tragedy of Corneille and Racine. His understanding of the blend of poetic and artificial elements in the creative imagination of the latter is vividly shown in his definition of Racine's characters as splendid statues, even if made of plaster. His ability to feel "the shock of recognition," the sudden revelation of a new talent, is already apparent in the decision that led him to his first literary undertaking, a translation of Balzac's *Eugénie Grandet.*

Literary inspiration played an important role in his most significant and original creations. Thus, the idea of *The Idiot* is based on literary models and sources, chiefly Pushkin's poem "The Poor Knight" and Cervantes' *Don Quixote,* a figure in which, with an original interpretation, he saw the type of the good man. In his late years he toyed with the idea of writing a Russian *Candide,* thus proving his ability to appreciate that famous tale by Voltaire, whom he was bound to detest, both as man and as writer.

Even Dostoevski's errors of judgment, if any, were due to the positive quality of an infectious enthusiasm. Such is the case with his exaggerated opinion of George Sand, who remained his life-long idol, or with his youthful infatuation for the poetry of Victor Hugo, whom he considered superior to the Shakespeare of the sonnets. (At least he showed thereby that at an early age he had already read Shakespeare's sonnets, even if only in a French translation.) His admiration for Hugo lasted into his later years, and extended also to his prose works, where he singled out for special praise the characterization of Jean Valjean.

If we follow the recent fashions of taste, we could find equally uncritical Dostoevski's adoration for Schiller, which also lasted a lifetime, and, like his idolization of George Sand, was addressed more to the human being than to the poet, to the ardent preacher of noble feelings and exalted ideals. This admiration for Schiller, as a matter of fact, will help us to see another trait of Dostoevski's genius, which generally escapes the attention of his Western critics and readers. Yet this trait is essentially Western in character, and Dostoevski shares it with Pushkin, the most European of all Russian masters.

As every reader of *Evgeni Onegin* knows, each character of that "novel in verse" represents in his own make-up a human ideal that is at the same time literary in character: Rousseauism in Tatiana, German romanticism in Lenski, Byronism in Onegin. This process or device enables Pushkin to portray his characters through the perspective of their "sentimental education." In the case of Dostoevski, as in the case of Pushkin's *Evgeni Onegin,* it is literary culture which determines, structurally and symbolically, the "sentimental education" of his fictional heroes.

In his own psychological constructions, Dostoevski makes frequent use of Russian literary materials, taken either from Pushkin or Gogol. Devushkin, the humble hero of *Poor Folk,* Dostoevski's first creative effort, is not only a piece of Gogol's "Overcoat," the cloth of which, according to Dostoevski himself, is the stuff his own writing and Russian writing of his time are made of. But Devushkin is also described as a reader of that famous Gogolian masterpiece; and, in a whim of poetic fancy, Dostoevski makes him reject Gogol's tale as both evil and untrue, for the very reason that in the mirror of Gogol's fiction Devushkin has recognized himself. Thus Dostoevski seemingly implies, if not that nature imitates art, at least that life imitates literature.

This literary quality of Dostoevski's imagination and his adoration for Schiller combine to produce a unique effect in *The Brothers Karamazov,* his last and supreme masterpiece. Here the Schillerism of the author objectivizes itself in the Schillerism of his characters, symbolizing at the same time their inner and outer conflicts. The dramatic situation of *The Robbers* seems almost to repeat itself: and this parallelism is revealed and emphasized by the allusions of Dostoevski's protagonists and antagonists.[1] As for the famous confession of Dmitri to Alyosha ("a confession by an ardent heart, in verse"), it is a literary medley of Schilleresque quotations and reminiscences, "contaminated" with other sources. This example may suffice to show that Dostoevski treats literary materials as if they were living matter; and from this standpoint, Europe and her culture were always for him something more than they ever were for Ivan Karamazov, who saw in Europe merely a "beloved graveyard."

It is one of the many paradoxes of Dostoevski that this man, endowed with a rich literary culture, and born to become one of the classical masters of his craft, was at the same time a practitioner of "lowbrow" fiction, as it was manufactured by the most popular writers of the West. One of his early stories, "The Landlady," is essentially a gothic tale. Even his more mature creation is affected by the sensational novel, as in the case of *The Insulted and the Injured;* or, as in the case of *Crime and Punishment,* by the murder story or detective story. This facet of his talent and taste may also be seen in his high regard not only for *Les Misérables* of Victor Hugo, but even for *Les Mystères de Paris* of Eugène Sue. Without this taste for the "thriller" he would not have brought the pathos of his characters to the emotional pitch it attains in those exhibitions of self-pity and self-torture, to which he gives the name of "laceration" of one's heart, or *nadryv.*

Popular fiction, which during romanticism had taken in France the strange name of *mélodrame,* took later the name and shape of *roman feuilleton,* literally, a sensational narrative published serially in a newspaper. We know that in Russia serial publication came to be adopted even by the literary journals, and that Dostoevski was bound to avail himself of this method of publication far more often than his great literary rivals. It is well known that his hard financial conditions forced him to sell a novel before writing it. He would compose the current installment while the preceding one was at the printer's, and the sequel existed only in his brain.

For this reason, he used to consider himself a "proletarian of literature," and would protest, not without a feeling of envy, against the invidious

comparisons of his critics: "They demand from me artistic finish, the purity
of poetry, without stain, without waste, and they point to Turgenev and
to Goncharov. Let them take a look at the conditions under which I
work!" [2] Yet this compulsion was also his natural creative element; and for
this very reason, the Western novelists he resembles most are Dickens and
Balzac, who, like him, paid for the privilege of their fecundity and popularity
by the uneven quality of their work. Yet, like them, Dostoevski thereby
learned an insight into life of which a more academic craftsman could not
even dream.

In other words, Dostoevski the writer was more liable to commit faults of
taste than Dostoevski the critic. Yet this liking for the sensational, the melodramatic, and the thrilling affected not only his literary practice, but also
his literary theory. It determined his very conception of realism, and with
it, a creative method which differed from, and even opposed, the methods of
both the Russian and the Western realists of his time.

In one of his letters we find this significant text: "I have my own special
view of reality in art; what the majority consider to be almost fantastic and
exceptional is sometimes for me the very essence of reality. In my opinion,
the commonness of a happening and the public view of it are not realism
at all, but quite the contrary. In every issue of a newspaper you find accounts
of the most real, and yet amazing facts. For our writers they are fantastic;
they pay no attention to such things; nevertheless, such things are reality,
because they are *facts!*" [3]

The first thing to notice in this statement are its qualifications ("almost
fantastic," "sometimes"). Yet the statement implies that exceptional events
are the predominant material of Dostoevski's fiction, that his imagination
thrives on what is ordinary and extraordinary at the same time. In matters
of action and plot, this may be stated by saying that Dostoevski is interested
in real, but extreme, situations. This may be proved by that famous page
in *The Diary of a Writer* where he discusses an episode in Tolstoy's *Childhood, Boyhood and Youth*. It is the story of a resentful child, who dreams
of avenging himself on his parents by committing suicide. The project fails
to materialize, and remains merely a wishful thought. Dostoevski triumphantly quotes the newspaper account of how a real child, in a similar
situation, ended by taking the fatal step. The implication is that as a writer
he would have followed not the path taken by Tolstoy, but the one indicated
by that extreme case, by the cruelty of reality itself. In this parallel, Dostoevski rightly judged Tolstoy's method as antithetic to his own. He felt
that Tolstoy simplified reality and criticized him for it. The criticism itself

was directed not only at Tolstoy but at the very foundation underlying realistic fiction, as it was at that time conceived not only in Russia, but also in the West.

In choosing his fictional situations, the nineteenth-century realist was always bound by the conventional restraint of what in the theory of classicism took the name of verisimilitude. Verisimilitude implies the probable rather than the merely possible: what is more likely to happen. And the judge of this likelihood was reason, or at least common sense. Verisimilitude could thus be defined as what is qualitatively true. But the realists, children of a scientific age, conceived of verisimilitude as what is likely to happen more frequently, as what is quantitatively true. To be sure, the criterion was never reduced to bare statistics, but rather was held to be observation and experience.

This reduction of verisimilitude from the universal to the general, and from the rational to the empirical, was brought to its extreme consequences by the very rival of Dostoevski, by Tolstoy. That master identified reality with the static and the permanent, with the recurring and the habitual. In *War and Peace* even the historical, that is, the peculiar and the exceptional par excellence, is submitted to the unalterable laws of natural history. Dostoevski, on the other hand, was interested in what is strange, dramatic, and dynamic, in other words, in what is real and unlikely at the same time.

This preference for the improbable is not merely a whim of Dostoevski's. As a writer, he chose to describe the human condition in those circumstances that can be objectively expressed only in tense and extreme manifestations. In other words, the sociological background of Dostoevski's fiction is quite different from the social milieu portrayed by his great Russian colleagues. In Gogol, Turgenev, Goncharov, and Tolstoy we see almost exclusively the world of the landed gentry, of the provincial bureaucracy, of the petty nobility; occasionally, but at a great distance, the aristocracy of the capital. At the opposite pole, we see only the peasant and the domestic servant. Merchants and artisans are very rare, while bourgeois in the Western sense of the word are nowhere to be seen. This gives the background of Russian fiction a quite different atmosphere from that of the Victorian novel, or the French *roman,* where there dwell predominantly representatives of the upper bourgeoisie and of the middle class.

The bourgeois is almost absent also from the world of Dostoevski, who saw him only abroad, among those respectable citizens of London and Paris whom he detested so much. Perhaps he represented "this strange creature, the bourgeois," only once, in the figure of a money lender who is at the same time both a loving and a cruel husband, in one of his last stories, "Krotkaya" (The Meek), which the English translator entitled "A Gentle Spirit."

Equally absent from his work are the landowner and the peasant. Perhaps his heroes are only social outcasts and uprooted intellectuals: in brief, those two groups which in Marxist terminology are called the *Lumpenproletariat* and the "intellectual proletariat." Mikhailovski had this fact in mind when he defined Dostoevski as "the *raznochinets* of literature," that is to say, the spiritual offspring of that classless intelligentsia against which Dostoevski led such a hard fight in his books.

For this very reason, Dostoevski is the only classical master of Russian fiction who portrays the life of the cities, the existence of the modern cave-dwellers, the urban prisoners in their tragic jail of brick and stone. As such, he even anticipates artistically, if not ideologically, the urban and proletarian spirit of Zola's naturalism. Like Zola, he knew that city life may mean living in slums, a fact he did not discover from the outside, with an organized expedition into the poor section of Moscow, as Tolstoy did; like his hero Raskolnikov, Dostoevski had breathed and suffered in them.

In the passages quoted above, we have seen Dostoevski proving his point by referring to newspaper accounts of real events. Even more often, newspaper accounts of real facts were used by him as a starting point for his creative inspiration. Dostoevski was not the only nineteenth-century novelist who used journalistic sources in a work of fiction: it will suffice to recall the example of Stendhal's *Le Rouge et le Noir,* or the case of Tolstoy's *Resurrection,* which was inspired by a similar document, even if related to Tolstoy through an oral report.

Yet no writer introduced in his work as many criminal cases and public trials as Dostoevski did in the web of his plots. This may be shown by *The Idiot* and *The Brothers Karamazov,* and above all, by *The Possessed.* The latter novel was inspired by the notorious affair of the young revolutionary Nechaev, who forced his fellow conspirators to kill the student Ivanov, under the pretense that he was an informer, but with the purpose of binding his own followers by the tie of murder and blood.

Nothing, however, is more distant than *The Possessed* from a *pièce d'occasion* on a *cause célèbre.* In a famous letter, Dostoevski described in this way his own method of reconciling poetry with truth within this novel: "Except from the newspapers, I did not know at all either Nechaev or Ivanov or the circumstances of the murder. And if I did know, then I would not copy. My fantasy may differ completely from the factual reality, my Petr Verkhovenski may not in the least resemble Nechaev; but it seems to me that in my astonished mind there has been created a figure, a type that fits that crime. . . ." [4] In other words, Dostoevski claimed to have discovered intuitively, yet objectively, the real nature and meaning of the factual crime, in spite of the scarcity of his own information about it, and to have invented a fictional murderer more authentic than the real one.

At this stage, it is perhaps necessary to remark that Dostoevski was not only a consumer, but also a producer of such journalistic copy. He was himself a publicist, a commentator on current events, often even an interpretative reporter of public trials and criminal cases. This makes his ability to raise those facts to the level of a higher poetic reality an even greater achievement; yet only a journalist who was at the same time a great satirist and a great dramatist could have created such a piece as the trial of Dmitri in *The Brothers Karamazov*.

In spite of the metamorphic power of his imagination, the topical remained one of the mainsprings of Dostoevski's literary production. This is shown by *The Diary of a Writer,* and by his ideological and polemical writings, which brought him nearer than he realized to the conception of literature held by that radical intelligentsia which he despised. Yet he rejected consistently their utilitarian view of the work of the artist, and attacked Dobrolyubov and his fellow "realists" by maintaining that art must be free, and by seeing in this very freedom its highest social utility. But the role that topical subjects and questions played in his work cannot be denied. The first seed of *Crime and Punishment,* the story of Marmeladov, was a projected novel to be entitled *The Drunkards,* and dealing, as Dostoevski states in a letter, with "the problem of alcoholism." Even his most metaphysical work, *Notes From Underground,* was partly conceived as a historical and psychological document, or, as Dostoevski states in a note too easily overlooked by his philosophical critics, as the portrayal of a certain type of modern man.

On the other hand, even as a historian of Russian society, Dostoevski felt that he could approach truth better by looking at reality from the perspective of the exceptional and the extraordinary: "I have an understanding of reality and realism entirely different from that of our realists and critics. Lord! To relate seriously all that we Russians have experienced in our last ten years of growth — indeed, do not our realists cry out that this is phantasy! Nevertheless, this is primordial, real realism!" [5]

Once in a while, Dostoevski seemed to conceive of the task of the writer as the traditional one of representing faithfully a psychological situation or a social milieu. This is how he spoke, while he was writing it, of his novel *The Gambler:* "If *Notes From a Dead House* won for itself the attention of the public as a depiction of criminals whom no one had depicted graphically before, then this story will win attention for itself as a *graphic* and most detailed depiction of roulette gambling. . . ." Yet, almost in the same breath, he claimed to have made of his gambler something higher and more complex than the embodiment of his own vice: "He is a gambler, and not a simple gambler, as the miserly knight of Pushkin is not a mere miser. . . . He is a poet in his own way. . . ." [6] The root of the matter, of course, is that Dostoevski was a poet too.

Thus, for a "realist" like Dostoevski, reality is primarily apprehended through the perspective of a personal, almost mystical intuition. Dostoevski's realism is therefore projection and introspection at the same time. If this is true, it is perhaps timely and proper to discuss now what is the relationship between his imagination and his inner experience, between his creation and his life.

In spite of the personal pathos of his inspiration, Dostoevski never indulged in self-contemplation and narcissism. The ego of the author never intruded in his work, and from this viewpoint he followed the standards of impersonality and objectivity, as understood by Western realism. It is worth remarking that, in spite of the fact that introspection was perhaps the source of his own psychological insight, and that his interest in the morbid side of psychic life was perhaps a projection of his inner conflicts, he was always unable or unwilling to report directly his extraordinary autobiographical experiences. He preferred to relate them in the third person, objectivizing them in the creatures of his imagination.

It is perhaps true that it was the fear of censorship that led him to adopt the literary device of pretending to be the editor, rather than the author, of *Notes From a Dead House,* perhaps his most "documentary" work. Yet that device creates an effect of esthetic distance, transforming the writer from a witness and a victim into a judge and a contemplator, and raising to the level of the dramatic an experience which otherwise would have been merely pathetic.

There is no doubt that Dostoevski always felt a sense of awe for the ordeal he had undergone on the scaffold, waiting for his own execution, without knowing he would be granted a last minute reprieve. He often re-evoked that ordeal in his writings, but at a double remove, as when Myshkin relates his own impressions about an execution witnessed by him. Even the doubtful hypothesis, so eagerly embraced by André Gide,[7] that "The Confession of Stavrogin" is an autobiographical document, would be a further proof that Dostoevski, unlike Tolstoy and Rousseau, was unwilling to exhibit without veils the pathology of the self. It was with a sense of poetic justice that he distributed impartially the bliss or curse of his own epilepsy both to his positive and negative, even to his equivocal, heroes, like Myshkin, Smerdyakov, or Kirillov.

This study of the role played by self-analysis in Dostoevski's creation will make easier the task of defining the nature and scope of his fictional psychology. Once he made, in this regard, a paradoxical statement which is worth quoting: "They call me a psychologist: it is not true. I am merely a realist in the higher sense of the word, that is, I depict all the depths of the human soul." [8] Dostoevski was here alluding again to his conception of the significant reality of extreme psychological situations. Yet, logically, the statement would not stand on its feet without supposing that by "psychologist" Dostoevski meant a conventional realist, using traditional psychology merely as a representational and characterizing tool, or, as the investigating attorney Porfiri of *Crime and Punishment* says, as a tool that "cuts both ways," but never too deep. In other words, by higher realism Dostoevski meant a deeper psychology.

In his *Ideas about the Novel,* Ortega y Gasset sees in Dostoevski the first modern novelist interested in constructing hypothetical, private, and arbitrary psychologies. But Dostoevski thought rather in terms of reconstructing the exceptional and the extraordinary from the raw materials of everyday reality. This is why he was able to foresee some of the psychological discoveries of the scientific school of Freud and his disciples, and to precede them in the field which later, almost in his own words, they would call "depth psychology." Before Freud, he knew how many "indecent thoughts" can be found in the minds of "decent people." [9] Before the modern adepts of the "stream of consciousness" technique, he knew that the subconscious expresses itself in inarticulate, yet meaningful, signs: "It is well known that whole trains of thought pass through our brains instantaneously, without being translated into human speech, still less into literary language." Finally, as we shall see, he presented the dreams of his characters in such a way that they can be interpreted symbolically according to the theories of either Freud or Jung, that is, both as symptoms of psychic conflicts, and as universal archetypes.

Dostoevski's liking for the unverisimilar in action, and the abnormal in psychology, must not lead us to believe that he favored the characterization, against a realistic background, of romantic heroes, of Titans and Supermen. He was equally interested in ordinary lives, and in the psychology of Everyman. He was well aware that the common or average man was becoming the protagonist of both Russian and Western fiction. Yet he felt that that human type must be made worthy not only of our sympathy, but also of our curiosity and interest. This was stated in a famous page of *The Idiot,* from which we must quote too briefly:

There are people whom it is difficult to describe completely in their typical and characteristic aspect. These are the people who are usually called "ordinary," "the majority," and who do actually make up the vast majority of mankind. Authors for the most part attempt in their tales and novels to select and represent vividly and artistically types rarely met with in actual life in their entirety, though they are nevertheless almost more real than real life itself. . . .

What is an author to do with ordinary people, absolutely "ordinary," and how can he put them before his readers so as to make them at all interesting? It is impossible to leave them out of fiction altogether, for commonplace people are at every moment the chief and essential links in the chain of human affairs; if we leave them out, we lose all semblance of truth. To fill a novel completely with types or, more simply, to make it interesting with strange and incredible characters, would be to make it unreal and even uninteresting. To our thinking a writer ought to seek out interesting and instructive features even among commonplace people. When, for instance, the very nature of some commonplace persons lies just in their perpetual and invariable commonplaceness, or better still, when in spite of the most strenuous efforts to escape from the daily round of commonplaceness and routine, they end by being left invariably for ever chained to the same routine, such people acquire a typical character of their own — the character of a commonplaceness desirous above all things of being independent and original without the faintest possibility of becoming so.[10]

This page reminds us of a passage in Gogol's tale "The Portrait," where the writer also spoke of the difficulty of portraying those characters whom he defined by the term of "ashen-colored," and whom Gogol used to paint in shades as gray as possible. But Dostoevski's statement implies that even they must be painted in both the brightest and the darkest colors; that even ordinary psychology must become extraordinary psychology. From this viewpoint, he followed the method of Balzac, in whose works, according to Baudelaire, "even janitors are endowed with genius."

This is why, in spite of what Mikhailovski called his "cruel talent," Dostoevski was never willing to see merely the "human beast" even in the most degraded human beings. Yet there are naturalistic elements in his work, as may be seen by the use in *The Brothers Karamazov* of the doctrine of "heredity," which, to be sure, is treated as a kind of ethical nemesis.

His naturalism, again, differed very much from the kind that appeared in the works of the late Tolstoy, where it was limited to the evocation, with strong moralistic overtones, of what Tolstoy himself called "the tragedy of the bedroom." Dostoevski's imagination, however, operated in different directions from those indicated by Degas's definition of naturalism as "life seen through a keyhole." Sex, even if described naturalistically, preserves some glamor after all, while Dostoevski's naturalism is below glamor, or beyond it. While his interest in the trivial and vulgar side of life led him to commit breaches of the code of manners and taste, which even a Zola would hesitate to commit, those very violations, on the other hand, opened for him the gates of the metaphysical and the transcendental.

No other writer would have dared to surprise his hero Dmitri, during the dramatic scene of his arrest, in the process of undressing himself and of showing to everybody, including the reader, his filthy socks. Yet these naturalistic details symbolize the tragic nakedness of human existence, the sense that man lives in the mud. Dostoevski used in the same way the animal and elemental reality of the human need for food. Generally, fictional heroes never eat: either they "dine," as in fashionable novels, or, as in proletarian fiction, they merely starve, yet without ever starving to death. Few writers would have thought of interrupting the hectic action of *The Possessed* to follow Petr Verkhovenski into those cheap restaurants where he suddenly orders, and coarsely devours, a rare, almost raw, beefsteak.

This is not the only case where a meaningless detail becomes a revealing symbol, or at least a significant fact. Sometimes the same effect is produced by the presence of odd, and yet common, things. Dostoevski treats them merely as such, yet, in the mind of the reader, they become also signs. This is due to a vision so penetrating and lucid that it impresses the reader as a revelation, or, as Joyce would say, as an "epiphany." There is a famous episode of *The Idiot* where such an "epiphany" is produced by two incongruous objects.

In the tragic scene where the murderer Rogozhin and the witness Myshkin keep watch near the bed on which the dead body of Nastasya Filipovna still lies, Dostoevski introduces two strange pieces of stage property in the room of the crime: a jar of disinfectant and a piece of American leather. Dostoevski had taken these two objects bodily from the newspaper accounts of a real murder, the famous Mazurin case. They are, so to speak, the interpolation of a real "slice of life" in the text of fiction: the detail, more than naturalistic, is factual. But the painstaking scholars who discovered the origin of this detail were wrong in making fun of their less learned colleagues who maintained that the presence of those objects had a hidden meaning. The latter's interpretations may have been false; still, the former's assumption is wrong: an object does not cease being symbolic merely because it was found by the poet ready-made, rather than invented anew.

That in Dostoevski's works there is a symbolism only half hidden under the appearance of reality is shown by the very name of the family Karamazov. *Kara* is a Tatar word which means "black," while the Russian corresponding adjective is *cherny*. To be sure that the symbolic allusion contained in the etymological meaning of the name Karamazov is not lost on his readers, Dostoevski reveals it in a slip of the tongue, made by the half-witted wife of Captain Snegirev, when she addresses Alyosha as Mr. Chernomazov.

In other words, the naturalistic and the symbolic are interchangeable in the world of Dostoevski. This may be seen in the treatment of those "vile tales" [11] which are so frequent in his fiction. They seem to transcend their coarseness and brutality by becoming "scandals" in the religious sense, while still remaining "scandalous scenes" in the everyday meaning of the term. In the same way, Dostoevski was able to transform an insignificant fact into a tremendous emotional experience, full not only of tragic meaning, but also of poetic awe. Such is the case with that "faint tinkling of the bell" rung by an unexpected visitor, which re-echoes in the room of the crime, and in the soul of Raskolnikov, like the thunder of doom. This detail produces in the reader the same effect so well described by De Quincey in his analysis of "the knocking at the gate of Macbeth," and here Dostoevski becomes indeed Shakespeare's peer. That Dostoevski was aware of being endowed with a Shakespearean gift may be seen in the flight of poetic irony that led him to put in the mouth of Dmitri's prosecutor, whom he satirizes as a progressive and a "Westerner," the famous words: "They have their Hamlets, and we have our Karamazovs!"

Dostoevski has been praised not only as a poet, but also as a philosopher, or, as Merezhkovski would say, as a "seer." There is no doubt that he worked with ideas, and with ideas of his own, yet we must never forget that those ideas were not superimposed, but embodied in the flesh of his heroes, and intimately connected with the living substance of his plots. For him, ideas are not only springs of action, but also modes of being: Dostoevski's is not an ideal, but an ideational universe. This is why his ideas become myths, while these myths spring from real life and from a prosaic world. Even his myth-making faculty accepts the conventions of realism, and operates within a naturalistic framework.

The complex myth of the "underground," according to which modern man is cornered between the disorder of a vitalistic consciousness and the order of a devitalized social design, is developed by Dostoevski in the homely metaphors of the mouse and the cellar, of the henhouse and the ant heap. As for the social utopia he rejects, it is symbolized in that very Crystal Palace which he had seen in his previous visit to London, several years after the World Exhibition of 1851.

Dostoevski always presents his own myths and ideas not as subjective revelations, but as objective visions: as spiritual realities taking place in the minds of his heroes. Very often, these visions take the shape of dreams. The idea of the end of our social order manifests itself in Raskolnikov's apocalyptic and prophetic dream of a future plague destroying the fabric of life and the house of man. Even more frequently, Dostoevski projects his myths and ideas into his fictions as conscious and active productions of his characters' minds, revealing them in the give-and-take of conversation, or in the very process of thought.

Thus the myth of the blind force of nature, which submits even the Son of God to the indignity of death, is developed in *The Idiot* by Ippolit, in the shape of a commentary about Holbein's *Deposition from the Cross.* Another painting, Claude Lorrain's *Acis and Galatea,* becomes the very myth of a future Golden Age, as longed for by Stavrogin in that "Confession" which Dostoevski failed to publish, and by Versilov in *A Raw Youth.* The same device, nay, the same painting, combines with the dream device to suggest the same myth, this time in a tragic version, in "The Dream of a Ridiculous Man." As for the most complex allegory in Dostoevski's works, "The Legend of the Grand Inquisitor," it is presented as a literary production of Ivan Karamazov, even if composed only mentally, and as related by him in a dialogue with his younger brother Alyosha. In brief, all these myths appear as figments of the characters' fancies, rather than as creations of the author's imagination.

In other words, Dostoevski's method aims at suggesting the ambivalence of the real and the symbolic, of the naturalistic and the mythical. Sometimes he aims even at creating an atmosphere of ambiguity, veiling his own intentions and clouding his view of things. There is no doubt that Raskolnikov's crime is, in Dostoevski's interpretation, the monstrous child of intellectual pride and of radical thought. Yet he persistently insinuates through various characters that Raskolnikov's frame of mind and his criminal act have been determined by external factors and material circumstances. Raskolnikov's mother, his friend Razumikhin, the investigating attorney Porfiri, even the mysterious Svidrigaylov, point their accusing fingers not to Raskolnikov, but to his surroundings. The mother sees the dominating factor in that sickening garret where her son has been living, and which she likens to a tomb; others, apparently including both Raskolnikov and his creator, seem to share this opinion. Svidrigaylov blames the crime upon the eerie influence of Petersburg, "a town of crazy people," while in other cases the blame is placed on Raskolnikov's bodily illness. Porfiri, who knows better, accepts for a while the idea that "environment accounts for a great deal in crime": a hypothesis which initially had been advanced by Razumikhin himself, who realized that Raskolnikov's design "had started with the socialist doctrine," a doctrine which Razumikhin rejects, while at the same time he seems to accept the contention that crime is both a product of, and a protest against, the social order.

This singular ambiguity seems to dominate Dostoevski's imagination whenever the supernatural makes its entrance into the material universe. How this effect of ambiguity is obtained may be seen in a conversation held by Raskolnikov and Svidrigaylov. Svidrigaylov confesses to seeing often the ghost of his deceased wife, to which Raskolnikov replies with the objection that ghosts appear only to diseased minds. Svidrigaylov, while admitting as much, denies however that from this fact we can logically deduce that ghosts do not exist.

The problematic mind of Dostoevski seems to accept both hypotheses at the same time. This can be seen in one of his highest creations, the conversation between Ivan Karamazov and the Devil. There is no doubt that Ivan is mentally sick, and that the Devil is a hallucination. Yet this imaginary devil plays in this realistic novel a role almost as important as Mephistopheles' in Goethe's *Faust*. Dostoevski's devil is, of course, not a romantic figure but a prosaic creature, a petty bourgeois in modern dress and shabby clothing. On the literal plane, he is described as a social parasite, which, on the symbolical level, implies that he is a parasite of Ivan's mind. Yet this vulgar figment of a delirious fancy becomes a kind of *deus ex machina,* transforming Ivan's nightmare into a powerful metaphysical drama.

The method used by Dostoevski in presenting the myth of the Devil might be likened to the method followed by Flaubert in *La Tentation de Saint Antoine,* but the parallel would not be exact. In Flaubert's representation of the obsessive visions of the saint, the approach is realistic in the scientific and esthetic sense: for him, supernatural appearances have no objective reality except literary. Both the poet and the reader know that the monsters seen by the saint are only chimeras. But in the case of Ivan's hallucinations, neither the poet nor the reader is quite sure. As a matter of fact, in the world of Dostoevski, the very existence of the Devil is based not so much on faith as on doubt. As claimed by the Devil himself, only a microscopic amount of belief is needed to create his reality.

It was on the foundation of this same ambiguity that Dostoevski built another magnificent episode of *The Brothers Karamazov,* an episode which is based on the problem of belief and disbelief in the matter of miracles. Every reader remembers the events attending the death of the saintly "elder," Father Zosima. His disciples are naïvely hoping that their master will give a sign of his saintliness by performing again a miracle reported in the pious legends of old. In brief, they expect that the body of the "elder" will be spared the degrading indignity of physical death, the breath of corruption and the decay of the flesh.

Against their expectations, and to the satisfaction both of the unbelievers and of those believers who were enemies of the "elder," what takes place instead of the miracle is a scandal, or, in material terms, a manifestation of the physical process of decay which seems almost unnaturally rapid and intense. Dostoevski does not stop here, but lists all the external factors to which the rapidity and the intensity of the process are due: the age and the frailty of the deceased, the heat, the pressing of the crowd, the closed windows and locked doors. Since Dostoevski, besides being a believer, was also an admirer of the religious type and of the ecclesiastical discipline which Father Zosima represents, there is no doubt that he conceived this episode in a spirit of poetic irony, transcending the narrow view of any positivism and skepticism.

In other words, in this episode Dostoevski aims not at a "suspension," but rather at a tension, of "belief" and "disbelief." That such is the case is shown by the fact that the opposite phenomenon unexpectedly happens, in an equally natural and unnatural way, at the death of the child Ilyusha. While the "scandal" attending the death of Father Zosima is developed in a long chapter, the "miracle" attending the death of Ilyusha, which takes place at the end of the book, occupies only two lines: "His thin face was hardly changed at all, and strange to say there was no smell of decay from the corpse." This detail suffices to prove that in Dostoevski's work the path of the distasteful may lead up to the sublime.

Yet, even in this case, the miracle may be explained by purely natural causes. Dostoevski is never more realistic than in his moments of mystical insight. After all, he was a man of the nineteenth century, endowed, like Ivan Karamazov, with a "Euclidian mind." His "second sight" allowed him to contemplate also a non-Euclidian cosmic order, and in the desperate attempt to reconcile immanent and transcendental reality, his imagination achieved a paradoxical feat, by performing, so to speak, a "squaring of the circle." Dostoevski may have been a great seer, but he was primarily a great artist. In his work, the "spirit" lives because the "letter" is never dead: the "spirit" is not breathed into the "letter," but emanates from it. The metaphysical and the supernatural are the fourth dimension of his universe, yet they remain a projection of our three-dimensional world. Even the ideal and the symbolic spring in him from the Western sense of reality, and this is why all his work is a "prologue on earth." Dostoevski understood, like the Devil of Ivan, that only if it is given to him in "homeopathic doses" will modern man accept a reality beyond his reason and senses.

NOTES

1. The problem of the influence of Schiller on Dostoevski, and especially on his last masterpiece, has been studied by Dmitrij Čiževsky in "Schiller und die Brüder Karamazov," *Zeitschrift für slavische Philologie,* 1929, vol. VI.

2. *Pisma* (Letters), ed. by A. S. Dolinin (Moscow–Leningrad, 1928–1934), vol. II, letter 333. This and other passages from Dostoevski's correspondence are given as translated by Ernest J. Simmons, in his important book *Dostoevski: The Making of a Novelist* (New York: Oxford University Press, 1940), which I found quite useful while writing the present essay.

3. *Pisma,* vol. II, letter 323.

4. *Pisma,* vol. II, letter 356.

5. *Pisma,* vol. II, letter 318.

6. *Pisma,* vol. I, letter 178.

7. In his *Dostoïevsky* (Paris, 1923).

8. This statement was reported by N. N. Strakhov in a collection of biographical materials which he published shortly after Dostoevski's death.

9. This is one of the many ideas of his own that Dostoevski attributes to the protagonist of the *Notes From Underground.*

10. Given as translated by Constance Garnett.

11. The formula derives from a title which literally means "an obscene anecdote," but which Miss Garnett bowdlerized into "An Unpleasant Predicament" in her translation of that story.

On Goncharov and His Oblomov

I

Ivan Alexandrovich Goncharov was born in 1812, in Simbirsk, a city in the remote Volga region. His parents belonged to a family of prosperous grain merchants, recently raised to the nobility. His memory and imagination were to be forever affected by his early experiences, by the recurring vision of the torpid and yet charming way of life of the provincial backwater where he spent his youth. At the proper time he went to study at the University of Moscow, where, however, he failed to meet those brilliant and restless representatives of the new generation who were destined to agitate the still waters of Russian culture. Unlike them, Goncharov settled down immediately after graduation; rather, he moved to the capital, where he entered the Civil Service, at first in the Ministry of Finance, thus beginning a thirty-year bureaucratic career. Disappointed in love, he remained a bachelor, leading a life of endless solitude and unbroken quiet. In later years he became a hypochondriac, and found gratification only in self-indulgence, especially in the pleasures of the table. Death overtook him in 1892, after a long retirement and many years of oblivion and neglect, during which he had changed into a bitter caricature of his main creation, into a cantankerous and misanthropic Oblomov.

In his relatively long life, there are only three events standing out against a background of habit and routine. The first of these events is perhaps the most exceptional of all three. In 1852 the Russian government decided to follow in the footsteps of Commodore Perry, and to send a warship to Japan, in order to open to Russian trade the still half-closed doors of that realm. Goncharov was appointed secretary to the admiral charged with that mission, and sailed on his flagship. The Suez route was yet to be opened, and the ship had to circumnavigate half of the globe before reaching the Pacific Ocean. The political complications of the European situation forced Goncharov to cut short his stay in Japan, and to return home by land, almost half a century before the construction of the Trans-Siberian Railroad. The adventure seems preposterous in such a sedentary life as his, and one feels like asking, with the proverbial phrase of a Molièrian farce, "Mais que diable allait-il faire à cette galère?" The answer may perhaps be found in a true-to-life anecdote, according to which Goncharov had casually and thoughtlessly stated his willingness to go on that trip, and had to comply when his words were taken at their face value.

At any rate, while aboard that "galley," he kept a diary and wrote letters home, which he reworked and published in 1857 in the form of a logbook, entitled *The Frigate Pallas,* after the name of the warship. This work, wholly unknown beyond Russia, is full of charm, and could be defined as a travel book written exclusively from an Oblomovian viewpoint. Landscapes and seascapes are neglected in favor of genre painting: even the most exalted spectacles of a wild and exotic nature are reduced to the proportions of the homely and the picturesque. The entire book is filled with the writer's intense nostalgia for his distant homeland, or merely for his fireside chair. At the slightest sign of an impending storm, the traveler retires to his cabin; and what interests him most is the little world aboard ship, centering around his orderly, and the sailor's cat. Of the wide world abroad, what attracts him most are the oddities and delicacies of foreign cooking, and it is not exaggerated to say that Goncharov reduced his *periplos* to another *voyage autour de ma chambre.*

The second most important event in Goncharov's life was what in the career of a more commonplace bureaucrat would have been a normal shift to a different job. In 1856 he left the Ministry of Finance for the Ministry of Education, where for about ten years he was in charge of censorship. It is difficult to decide whether Goncharov considered writing as his calling, or merely as an avocation; perhaps he felt that bureaucracy was his wife, and literature his mistress. Still it seems quite strange that a writer who was at the same time a civil servant should accept the censor's office, of all the positions available to him. Perhaps he considered that office less burdensome than others; at any rate, it appears that he performed his odious and tedious task to the best of his abilities, displaying discretion and common sense, and making decisions not too illiberal for the temper of the times.

The last, and the most saddening, of the main incidents of his life shows that Goncharov failed to remain amiably indifferent when, rightly or wrongly, he felt wounded in his artistic ambitions or in his literary susceptibility. What we have in mind is his feud with Turgenev. Of this feud

Goncharov wrote a very biased and personal version, which he called "An Uncommon Story," thus parodying his first novel's title. The manuscript remained unpublished up to 1924, when Soviet scholarship recovered it from the archives where it was buried. In that document Goncharov claims to have once read to Turgenev some sections from his work then in progress, the novel *The Precipice,* and accuses the listener of plagiarizing some of his ideas, and of passing others to such foreign masters as the German story-teller Auerbach and the French novelist Flaubert. This strange report is obviously the morbid product of a warped mind, obsessed with a persecution mania and an inferiority complex. It is evident that in the last period of his life Goncharov must have suffered "a million torments," to use the title of one of his last writings, a brilliant critique of Chatski, the main character of *Woe from Wit.* One could observe in passing that the protagonist of Griboedov's comedy is one of the most un-Oblomov-like figures in Russian literature, and we may wonder why Goncharov chose him as the subject of this critical profile, which is perhaps the best among his minor works.

II

Before discussing at length Goncharov's unique and lonely masterpiece (after all, we still remember him as the author of a single book), we must say something of the two novels preceding and following *Oblomov.* Goncharov broke into print relatively late, with the usual poems, sketches, and translations. All these, however, were mere *juvenilia,* and the writer revealed his genuine gift only when he had reached the threshold of middle age. He was already thirty years old when, in 1847, he published in the review "The Contemporary" the novel *A Common Story,*[1] which won public acclaim, and earned him the even higher prize of Belinski's approval. The narrative deals with the usual theme of the changing over, within an individual life, from the enthusiasm and exaltation of youth to the sedateness and practi-cality of maturity. Alexander Aduev, a jejune idealist raised in the provinces, comes to the metropolis with no other capital than his naïve dreams. The harsh realities of life disenchant and disappoint the young dreamer, and an unlucky love affair almost wrecks his life. What saves him from ruin and despair is the worldly wisdom of Peter Aduev, his paternal uncle, who is a successful bureaucrat and business man. The old man teaches him the lesson of experience, of a skeptical, rather than cynical, opportunism. The young man shows himself to be an apt pupil, and learns all too well the values of social advancement and of material advantage. Thus the dreamer is converted into a go-getter and a careerist, and ends by becoming a replica of the man who taught him the facts of life. The novel closes quite properly with a marriage of interest, presumably implying that at least the groom, if not the bride, will live happily thereafter.

Goncharov's stated intent was to show the fallacy of romantic idealism, and to prove that their national mores made Russians unable to deal with hard facts. Thus *A Common Story* may be considered a negative or paradoxical version of the "pedagogical novel," as it was conceived in its original model, which is Goethe's *Wilhelm Meister*. Belinski welcomed Goncharov's novel as a wholesome denial of all romantic nonsense, but was wrong in maintaining that it ends with an actual victory of the real over the ideal. The claim is dubious at best, since such a victory is more a matter of appearance than of fact. Yet this suffices to make *A Common Story* a quite different work from the two novels to which it is constantly compared, Balzac's *Illusions Perdues* and Flaubert's *Education Sentimentale*. Externally these two French stories end in failure, while the Russian ends in success. Yet Lucien de Rubempré's and Frédéric Moreau's failures are more significant and convincing than Alexander Aduev's success. There is something more positive in their inability to adjust to bourgeois society, than in his sudden conformity to a way of life based on security and profit. What we witness here is not so much the practical education, as the sentimental diseducation, of the hero. At the closing of this ambiguous novel we feel that Alexander Aduev is bound to become a more respectable, and less likable, Oblomov, or even an alter ego of the older Goncharov, ending like him a *gourmet,* a *rentier,* and a *rond de cuir.*

If *A Common Story* is limited in scope, restrained in temper, and classical in structure, Goncharov's last novel, *The Precipice,*[2] is topical, pretentious, and diffuse. The protagonist, Boris Raiski, was defined by the writer as "an awakened Oblomov." In reality Raiski is a man who, after having courted in vain art and poetry, decides to play with other people's lives, as well as with his own. He retires to the forgotten corner of a distant province, the most important landmark of which is a cliff overlooking the Volga, which provides the novel with both a title and a central symbol. There Raiski tries to stir the sleepy souls of two cousins of his, the sisters Marfinka and Vera, who, as their names indicate, play respectively the roles of the practical Martha and of the contemplative Mary.[3] Soon enough, Raiski falls in love with Vera, who, however, does not like the dilettantes of life, and gives herself to Mark Volokhov, a radical who has been banished there. Volokhov, who is described as "a force of the future," is in effect only a destroyer, trying

to attract Vera into the "precipice" of an existence devoid of all social and
moral restraints. Volokhov is a brutal parody of the "nihilist" Bazarov, the
hero of Turgenev's *Fathers and Sons,* and therefore a far less human and
convincing character than his model. When the story closes, both protagonist
and antagonist disappear, and Vera marries an older man, the merchant
Tushin, a conventional personification of all the virtues of simplicity and
common sense. The only successful creation of *The Precipice* is the two
sisters' grandmother, a concrete and powerful embodiment of the instinctive
conservatism of life, of "the dear old truths" of tradition and custom. The
novel, which appeared in 1869, after many years of toil, was a complete
critical failure, although it remained very popular with the Russian public.
Its condemnation was certainly justified, even though it was based on ideological, rather than on esthetic, grounds. Goncharov always considered
The Precipice as his own supreme achievement, and this fiasco embittered
him for the rest of his life.

III

Goncharov's masterpiece, like *The Precipice,* took many years to be written, or rather, to ripen: the verb is quite proper, since *Oblomov*[4] grew slowly
and steadily into a perfect fruit, which now, nearly a century later, looks
almost as fresh and juicy as when it appeared. The book was brought out
in 1859, and its seed was "Oblomov's Dream," a fragment published in 1849.
The organic wholeness of this work is suggested even by the most trivial
of all criticisms leveled against it: that it is devoid of any plot worth the
name. The stricture must be taken as praise, since, after all, *Oblomov*'s subject matter is a condition or state, not a series of happenings or events. This
absence of plot does not mean a lack of structure, and a brief résumé of the
slim narrative sequence around which the novel is centered may help us to
understand better its matter and form.

The first of the four parts into which the novel is divided is but a long
re-evocation of one of the typical days of Oblomov's life in what one might
call its metropolitan phase, when he lives in an apartment in the center of
Petersburg, with no steady company except that of his valet Zakhar. Oblomov
is a wealthy landowner, who has settled down after realizing that he was
not born for that life of hustle and bustle that is required by any quest,
career, or pursuit. With the passing of time he has become so lazy as to let
himself be dressed and undressed by his valet. Incapable of reading a book,
or of writing a letter, he spends his time in dressing gown and in slippers,

lying on a divan, dozing and daydreaming. The main object of his waking dreams is his remote family property, Oblomovka, to which he expects to return as soon as he has completed a plan of reorganization and renovation, which he never succeeds in putting down on paper. During a long afternoon sleep, he sees again his native place, this time in a real dream, as it was at the happy time of his childhood ("Oblomov's Dream"). His musings, yawnings, and naps, or his vain projects and wistful resolves, are interrupted by a constant flow of casual visitors, appearing in the apartment as the shadows reflected by outside reality on the walls of Plato's cave, as figments or fragments of the external world. All these guests look like active people, while their host is a passive being: yet they act like parasites, intruding and feeding on him. Oblomov's only gesture of self-defense is to keep them from coming too near him, in order not to catch cold. And his day ends with the unexpected visit of a childhood friend of German origin, Andrey Stolz, who leads an energetic life, and has already made a place for himself in the world.

Stolz rouses Oblomov from his idleness, brings him into society, and introduces him to a young woman friend, Olga Ilinskaya. The second and third part of the novel are devoted to the sudden love of Olga and Oblomov. Olga, both practical and romantic in spirit, falls in love with "an Oblomov of the future," restored to activity and work. But the torpid routine of daily life reconquers Oblomov, who is unable to overcome even the slightest of the obstacles he finds on his new path. He sinks again into the old groove, and the marriage plan, along with Olga's love, dissolves into thin air. In the meantime Oblomov has moved to another house in the city's outskirts, and begins what one might call the suburban phase of his life. There, deprived of his friends' support, he indifferently yields to the influence of his new environment; and the good landlady's cousin, who is a crook, soon puts him into an ugly mess from which he is rescued only through the providential intervention of Stolz, who has meanwhile become engaged to Olga. After having admirably prepared the reader for what is the foregone conclusion of such a life and such a story, Goncharov in the fourth and last part shows Oblomov gradually and inertly surrendering to the naïve and easy love of his mature landlady, the widow Agafa Matveevna Pshenytsina. Reduced to a purely vegetative being, Oblomov drags out his days, while the woman becomes his cook, his nurse, and his maid. Only at the end of the book, on the occasion of one of Stolz's recurring visits, do we come to know, almost by chance, that our hero has married the woman. After several years of the same monotonous existence, enlivened only by all too many meals, Oblomov has a stroke and dies of apoplexy. The novel ends when Stolz and

Olga, now married, assume the guardianship of Oblomov's son and of his servant, the old and forlorn Zakhar.

Oblomov is certainly a character worthy of a place in the gallery of immortal figures shaped by the imagination of man. Goncharov beholds his creature with a strange mixture of indulgence and irony. He begins by pointing out, with a discreet insistence, all the good qualities of his hero. Although Goncharov fails to dwell on the physical side of Oblomov's portrait, the reader is led to suppose that nature has favored him with good looks; and this guess is confirmed by the writer's fond description of his hero's natural poise, of the graceful charm of his languid indolence. Almost effortlessly the writer makes him attractive and lovable. At least at first, he never depicts his idleness as lack of vitality, as blunt lifelessness. Oblomov's soul and mind may be slumbering, but they are not yet lethargic, and they are easily filled with wishes and feelings, with visions and thoughts. The impression of all this is conveyed by Goncharov in a wonderful passage evoking Oblomov's lively psychological activity through the concrete image of a swarm of ideas, that hover and flutter over his face rather than inside his head: "The thoughts flew like birds across his face, they sprang up to his eyes, they paused on his half-closed lips, they hid in the furrows of his brows; later, they disappeared altogether, and then the whole face beamed with the light of unconcern."

Oblomov's serenity is that of a purely contemplative mind, blissfully lost in a nirvana of his own making. Nothing can really shake his quietude and equanimity: "Neither fatigue nor boredom could even for an instant erase the dominant, fundamental expression, not only of the face, but of the entire soul; and the soul glowed so openly and clearly in his eyes, in his smile, in every gesture of his head and hand." Being contemplative, Oblomov's wisdom is skeptical and passive; despite his native intelligence, the sphere of speculation is even more alien to him than the sphere of action: "To him, science went one way and life another. . . ." Fully aware of the shortcomings of his temperament, Oblomov still accepts them as an inflexible law of nature. Thus he bases his personality squarely on a sense of autonomy and self-sufficiency: "He discovered that the horizon of his existence and his activity lay within him. . . ." When lying on his sofa, he feels that he is sheltered from all the restlessness and coarseness, from all the agitation and confusion that go with human intercourse: "He lay there preserving his dignity and quiet. . . ." His aloofness may estrange him from the real world, but not from the ideal one, since he is endowed with an imagination that is both objective and detached: "The dream was so clear, vivid, and poetic. . . ." In brief, Oblomov has the "nature," if not the "nurture," of a poet, and is gifted with what Keats called "negative capability," the ability to make fruitful the passivity of one's being.

Despite all appearances to the contrary, Oblomov is a man of strong convictions, indifferent to the opinion of the majority. In life and man he appreciates only what is straight and simple and hates cant and humbug. It is not merely in self-justification that he heaps scorn on all those who believe they are leading a better and more productive life than his: "Do they not, too, sleep away their own lives at their working desks and gaming tables?" For him they are not real, and nothing offends him more than Zakhar's casual comparison of his master with people like those. Making Zakhar's way of alluding to all outsiders his own, Oblomov calls those people "the others," with a concise and proud formula of contempt. Their existence, which even Stolz finds normal and natural enough, seems to Oblomov "a factory, not a life," and it is in reaction to their mode of living that Oblomov considers himself "a poet of life."

Whether he considers Oblomov's life poetic or not, Goncharov, who is a born prose writer, avoids conveying its sense through the easy suggestions of an ornate or musical speech. His art is classical and visual, and one could say that in the main he represents his hero plastically, now in full, now in partial, relief. At the beginning of the narrative Oblomov stands out in high relief against a flat, two-dimensional world: he dominates the scene, and, without lifting a finger, shapes into his own image all people and objects surrounding him. Everything lying within his orbit and circle becomes Oblomov-like: "From his face, unconcern passed into the posture of the whole body, and even into the folds of his dressing gown. . . ." But in the course of the action, or rather in the process of time, his figure loses, if not stature, at least weight and volume, receding gradually into the background, as if it were represented only in bas-relief. By the end, he scarcely emerges from the shallow world that will finally submerge him: "Oblomov was the natural reflection and full expression of that quiet contentment and very tranquil calm. . . ."

What can love and friendship do to a man like this, or rather, what will such a man do with them? Love and friendship are often able to stir even the most sluggard souls, and for a while they seem to awaken Oblomov, and to overwhelm him. But Oblomov finally succeeds in mastering them, and does so by reducing those feelings to the status of dreams. He will of course remain forever loyal to friendship because it is a dream of the past, requiring only the passive loyalty of his heart. But he will betray love because it is a dream of the future, and man must respond with his will to its demands. The dream of love carries with itself the fever of life, what the author later calls, with a suggestive formula, "the music of the nerves." That dream may bring joy and happiness but it will also bring trouble and turmoil. All Oblomov's nature unconsciously and spontaneously rebels against this; with the tactics of temporization and passive resistance he finally breaks through the ring of love at the very time it seems to encircle him. After this experience, the dangerous game of passion will no longer seduce his heart. Unlike friendship, love is a dream which refuses to be dreamed away, or anew; and Oblomov will remember it only as a whimsical fancy, as a midsummer night's dream.

Not only Oblomov, but also Goncharov treats these two emotions and their objects as unsubstantial realities. This is why there is no real justification for the critical commonplace accusing Goncharov for having failed in his characterization of Stolz and Olga, and for having made them shadow-like and lifeless. After all, they are supporting characters in the literal sense of the term. This is particularly true of Stolz, who plays his role with incredible diligence, with the mechanical efficiency of an automaton or of a jack-in-the-box. Always worried and businesslike, Stolz enters the stage as soon as a new crisis has arisen, whether great or small: like a monitor or a pedant, he teaches Oblomov his lesson, puts his affairs in order, and leaves, only to reappear again, at long intervals, to perform anew, with the same perfection, the same tasks. Olga is more lively and human, a little less obvious and predictable; there is something of the eternal feminine in her. Yet she remains superficial and conventional, and appears to be hardly more than the perennial romantic heroine, searching not so much for love as for exaltation and sacrifice.

In conclusion, while friendship is an inborn and permanent trait of Oblomov's psychology, equally incapable of alteration and development, love is for him an "affection" in the pathological sense, as natural as a sunstroke or a brain fever. While avowing that "passion is only imagination," Oblomov still realizes that it changes man, and subverts his life. Upon the sudden appearance of that unexpected feeling within the soul of the protagonist as well as within the world of the novel, both author and character betray their views about love in this significant utterance on Oblomov's part: "I feel in my heart something superfluous, that was not there before." This seems to suggest that, while acknowledging that love has added something new to his life, Oblomov still refuses to recognize the addition as either necessary or useful, as something good in itself.

In view of the unbounded vitality of the protagonist, Oblomov's passivity is a tremendous force, far more powerful than Olga's emotional restlessness or Stolz's physical dynamism. How wrong were both the patriotic and the radical critics who either blamed or praised Goncharov for exemplifying all the negative values in the Russian protagonist, and all the positive ones in his foreign-born antagonist! Whatever Goncharov's intentions might have been, the actual results are that the active hero does nothing, and the passive one does everything. Oblomov, although motionless, is the prime mover of this fictional universe, and everything and everybody revolves around him. If there is in the novel a character almost as central as Oblomov, that is Zakhar, his valet and alter ego, and his moral twin.

Goethe once used, in the title of a famous novel, the formula of "elective affinities," used by the then youthful science of chemistry, to suggest the reciprocal attraction that may finally join together two separate souls. One could say of Oblomov that at first he believes himself to be bound to Stolz and Olga by the "elective affinities" of friendship and love, but that as soon as the expected chemical reactions fail to materialize, he gradually turns, or returns, his affections toward two creatures of a lower order, in whom he finds his twin souls. Those two creatures are his valet and his landlady, who occupy in his heart the places left empty by his old friend and his former fiancée. Oblomov is bound to Zakhar and Agafa Matveevna by far stronger, even if nonelective, affinities: by almost a physiological tie, by something like an umbilical cord. Perhaps the biological term "symbiosis" may convey better than any other the quality of this tie between master and servant, as well as of the bond between landlady and tenant.

Precisely because he is the only character in the novel worthy of Oblomov, Zakhar is studied, so to speak, from his very beginnings, in regard to his social origins and ancestral inheritance, or, more simply, to the destiny that made him such a servant, and gave him such a master. The characterization of Zakhar is comic, but it belongs to the sphere of high comedy; he is a person, not merely a type. As for literal comedy, in the form of dramatic dialogue, it appears in the novel when servant and master talk and argue with each other. Through a series of complex parallels, the writer presents Zakhar as if he were both an original and a copy, or rather, a highly personal replica, of Oblomov. While Don Quixote and Sancho symbolize two opposite world views, Oblomov and Zakhar represent the same philosophy of life. Zakhar is an Oblomov on a smaller, or rather, on a lower scale, thus acting as his caricature. He has few of his master's good traits, but all of his weaknesses, only exaggerated. Thus the unconcern of Oblomov becomes in him carelessness; the indolence, sloth; the inertia, ineptitude; the absorption, torpidity. But even in Zakhar the nobler faculties are never fully asleep, and he becomes wide awake when his master is in trouble or in need, or merely when he is spoken ill of by any other than Zakhar himself.

Zakhar's affection for Oblomov is doglike: but rather like that of an old dog looking with superciliousness at the antics of the human race. Master and servant look at each other with a different outlook, and this changes each one of their conversations into a sort of comical agon. Their wrangles and arguments are almost always followed by Zakhar's monologues, which are silent continuations of the daily feud with his master. Both dialogues and soliloquies are among the highlights of this masterpiece, and it is through them that Goncharov reveals more fully his two main characters. The artist frequently takes the point of view of one of the two parties in order better to portray the other. One could even say that he is more effective when he describes Oblomov through Zakhar's perspective, than when he does the opposite; this may hint that he takes more seriously the more comic of the two characters.

While Zakhar coexists with Oblomov from the novel's very beginnings, Agafa Matveevna appears there only after the failure of that romance of a summer which was Oblomov's love dream. The slow, constant attraction he feels for his housekeeper, who sees and understands nothing beyond her housework, is described as a gradual surrender to the warmth of a fireplace, to the soft embrace of any easy armchair. In conveying this attraction, Goncharov reveals an understanding of the "facts of life" which may be particularly appreciated by the modern reader, so well acquainted with the concepts of depth psychology, and thus able to recognize in this phase of Oblomov's life the ever-childish urge to return to the womb. Agafa herself is represented as an almost faceless, inarticulate being, with no other will than her blind motherly instinct. Through Oblomov's eyes, we see only her large back and fat neck, her round, white elbow, and her large bosom, vast and soft like a bed. A creature equally devoid of selfishness and selfhood, a passive soul in a strong body, she becomes the Martha of Oblomov's paradise. Her kingdom, where she is authoritarian and majestic as a queen, is the kitchen, the only thing in the entire novel which Goncharov describes with mocking solemnity: "The kitchen was the real Palladium of the magnificent mistress and her worthy damsel."

Living with Agafa, Oblomov realizes his own ideal of life, and finally fulfills his aspiration of lying on cotton, like a baby on the cushions of his crib. Everything runs smoothly in the household, without that attrition which is normal even in the happiest ménage, and which so much troubled Oblomov when living with Zakhar alone. The only events affecting Oblomov now are the changes of cosmic time, such as the revolutions of the stars and the phases of the moon: "Ilya Ilich lived within life's golden frame; as in a diorama, only the periods of day and night, and of the seasons, changed." If childhood at Oblomovka had been the golden age of his life, the stay at Agafa's home is his Land of Cockaigne; and the only real metamorphosis taking place in this life without biography, empty of all pursuit, even of the pursuit of happiness, is the transformation of the country idyll of youth into the cozy Arcadia of the nest, with the comforts of middle age. At this stage even the adventure with Olga has so faded as to appear to Oblomov the lesson that has taught him to appreciate the animal love of the woman who is both his landlady and his handmaid: a love which ignores the frenzy of passion, and produces too much heat and too little light. Finally Oblomov's inertia degenerates into atrophy; his unconcern, into apathy. The grown-up man ends his life as he began it, a spoiled child. And through the final paralysis he enters forever, almost without realizing it, the world of eternal rest, where "the angel of silence protects his sleep."

The obvious, if not the conscious, aim of a novel like this is to evoke a mode of living based on being, rather than on doing: an existence that refuses to move in the sphere of actions and things, and that chooses to stand still, against the tide of events, within the cycle of time. For this very reason the ideal tense of this narrative would be the imperfect (which, strictly speaking, does not exist in the Russian tongue), the tense of habit, of that power that rules Oblomov's existence and triumphs unchallenged and supreme in the three main stages of his life. As already stated, those three stages are represented in three typical days, taken from different periods of the protagonist's life. These three days, along with the love episode, supply by themselves all the living matter needed to give the novel its substance and form. The rest, which is made of all the gaps or interruptions in the narrative sequence, is filled with the direct or indirect account of what has happened before, or in the intervals. The novel is thus built, so to say, on a series of "eternal returns": the most vivid and poetic of which is "Oblomov's Dream." The chapter or section so entitled is the re-evocation not only of a summer day in the hero's childhood, but also of his family and ancestral home, of the moral and physical world of Oblomovka. In describing his hero's, and his own, native province, Goncharov emphasizes the commonplace character of its landscape, devoid of any outstanding landmark, with the usual flora and fauna, and thus fully attuned to and commensurate with the simple and traditional customs of its inhabitants. Yet the slow and splendid flow of the images, the florid magnificence of all colors and forms, the huge and solemn proportions of every object, change this homely picture into an immense canvas, and expand Oblomovka into a land as vast as the whole of the Russian empire.

This vision of Oblomovka and of Oblomov's childhood is devoid of that complacent and benevolent irony that prevails at the novel's beginning, especially in the description of a typical day of the protagonist's adult life. This section is in a sense the heart of the work, and this is why it has taken in this summary and comment more space than all the rest. Here the rare power of Goncharov's art flows into every line, every image, every word. Our personage should be studied primarily as he appears in these pages, where he rests in a sort of ideal center, equidistant from the blossoming of his childhood and the withering of his decline. It is here that Oblomov fully reveals himself for what he is: the only one of all the Russian literary characters representing the idea of passivity who seemingly enjoys his inertia as a *dolce far niente*. Thus Oblomov, who treats his curse as a blessing in disguise, could be defined as the only Belacqua in the tragicomedy of Russian life. Belacqua is a friend of Dante, whom the poet meets while waiting with other shades to climb the mountain where they will purify their souls. Embracing his own knees and reclining his head, Belacqua breaks his immobility only to utter a few mocking words against all those who are all too eager and hasty.[5] If Dante is to be forgiven, and even praised, for allowing laziness and negligence in the realm beyond life and death, then Goncharov must be equally forgiven and praised for portraying so lovingly the laziness and negligence of a poor sinner still dwelling in the purgatory of the world.

The laziness of his creature seems to infect even Goncharov's art. The writer examines the smallest details with unhurried attention and unharassed calm, projecting them in vast images on the screen of his vision, which he unfolds at the slowest tempo possible. Through such a process of enlargement and retardment, he expands the dimensions of both space and time, and transforms the main figures of his creation, especially Oblomov and Zakhar, into portraits larger than life. The secret of Goncharov's art lies in this expansive nonchalance, in what one might call the summerlike quality of his genius. The author must have been aware of this, as shown by this statement he made later in life: "I saw or beheld only what had grown and matured within myself." Summers, however, are shortlived, and his own practically coincided with the writing of this book. Yet, in consonance with this, he was the poet of noontime and of the siesta of life, when the sun is at its zenith and all things and beings stand still, in the consummation of their fulness, in the illusion of their eternity.

It is in such a sense of plenitude, even if it is ephemeral, that Goncharov's most marked originality lies, in contrast with his great rivals. Goncharov knew that his position within the Russian tradition was almost unique, and this is why he felt aloof from the other realists of his time and place. In *Oblomov* he made fun of "the real trend in literature," and used a famous Gogolian formula to condemn all the writers in whose work "one feels no invisible weeping but only a very visible and clumsy sneer and grudge." And if he meant to caricature himself in the man of letters who appears at the end of Oblomov — "fat, with expressionless and rapt, almost sleepy eyes," — he did so with tongue in cheek, or he was unfair to himself, since his artist's eyesight was extraordinarily keen and alert. Knowing that he was unable to write "little things," he gave us, instead of a series of easel paintings, a single, great fresco, which occupied alone the four walls of his mind. Thus he raised autobiography to the level of a peerless objectivity, and created a cosmos out of his own hesitations and doubts.

The traditional Russian interpretation of *Oblomov* follows, with slight variations, the stand which the radical critic Alexander Dobrolyubov took once and for all, immediately after the appearance of this classical work. Dobrolyubov caught at a word coined by the author, which occurs at the novel's end and seals it with a smile that perhaps is not guileless. That word, which Goncharov attributes to Stolz, is "oblomovism." Dobrolyubov took it upon himself to define the term, and wrote a famous essay entitled "What is Oblomovism?," where he answered that question himself. The point of the essay is that the novel is not so much a psychological portrait as a diagnosis of the moral and social disease of serfdom. Marxist criticism developed this view thoroughly. Yet, about thirty years ago, shortly before being shot, the old Bolshevik Nikolay Bukharin dared to assert that "oblomovism" was not an ailment exclusively of the landowning class and of the tsarist regime, but an affection still surviving under the dictatorship of the proletariat. The assertion was taken as a libel against the revolution and the Communist Party, and the Russian nation as well; and yet it could be construed as praise, as a belated acknowledgment that there is some virtue in "oblomovism." And it is perhaps through that very virtue that the Russian people have preserved, in this iron age, for so many years of blood, sweat, and tears, the mythical vision of a golden age, of a land of milk and honey, where the soul lives blissfully, at peace with itself and the world.

If this is true, then *Oblomov* must be understood as the concrete and personal symbol not of the inertia of old Russia, but of what Karamzin used to call her everlasting "historical patience." At any rate, even if we are willing to admit as valid the dominant hypothesis that the novel intends to convey the unnerving influence of serfdom on the masters, even more than on the serfs, that very intention would not necessarily imply that Goncharov treated his hero as a clinical case. As a matter of fact he failed to do so even in the closing part of the novel, where we witness the slow, annihilating process of Oblomov's decline. The curve of decay is as fatal as the curve of growth, and it is an equally natural part of the parabola of his life. If there is anything extraordinary in this work, it must lie in the enormous size of the characterization itself. Oblomov is indeed a Gargantuan figure: a real giant, even if a passive one. The novel itself is Rabelaisian even in a more literal sense: what is Oblomovka, if not a childish and earthy Abbaye de Thélème? Goncharov's greatest feat was to create such a giantlike character out of a man devoid of any power, even of the power of will. This amounts to saying that Oblomov is an epic creation, a hero in the more than purely literary sense of the term. It is worth remarking that his Christian name is the same as that of the highest of all the heroes of the ancient Russian folk-epos, Ilya Muromets, who reconquers his immense strength after having sat for thirty-three years, unable to move his limbs.

The heroic proportions of Oblomov's portrayal contrast with the unheroic quality of his temper and way of life, without ever producing mock-heroic effects. The artist achieves this result by the simple device of portraying his character in the round, in the whole. It is worth recalling that passage of the first part where Oblomov discusses contemporary writing with the scribbler Penkin, and reproaches him for drawing conventional vignettes, in which human beings are reduced to the typical traits of their condition, profession, or class. "Give me the whole man!" exclaims Oblomov, thus anticipating and denying the critical view that will reduce him to a caricatural or satirical portrait. Oblomov is neither a satire nor a caricature, but a monumental figure; and, as such, he reminds us of Rodin's Balzac. That celebrated statue portrays its famous subject standing heavily on its pedestal, ruffled and ungroomed, with his leonine head emerging from an open nightshirt, and his short and rotund body wrapped only in a bathrobe. It is true that that sculpture, so shocking that the Parisian bourgeoisie prevented it for a long time from being placed in a public square, represents not an eternal idler, but a night-time worker, who produced a galaxy of characters and books from his feverish brain, while drinking numberless cups of coffee and emptying numberless ink bottles. Oblomov did not drink coffee or wine, but only *kvas;* as for writing, he could not pen even a letter. Yet his creator reshaped him into a statue of no less heroic proportions than Rodin's Balzac, and it matters little that the personage so represented wears no other armor than his morning garments. Oblomov is indeed the towering hero of a great cyclic poem, of a vast epos in prose, even if it is only an *Odyssey* of the slippers, or an *Iliad* of the dressing gown.

NOTES

1. Translated by Constance Garnett (London, 1890).
2. Translated by M. Bryant (New York, 1916).
3. Marfinka is a diminutive of Martha, and Vera means "Faith."
4. Translated by Natalie Duddington (London, 1929).
5. *Purgatorio,* Canto IV, 103–139.

A Portrait of Tolstoy as Alceste

I

IT IS well known that George Orwell drew a parallel between Tolstoy in his old age and King Lear. He did so in a brilliant essay, where he tried to explain the motives that led the Russian writer to single out *King Lear* in his indiscriminate indictment of the Bard.[1] According to Orwell, Tolstoy's extreme dislike for the story of King Lear was due to its strange similarity to the history of his own life:

There is a general resemblance which one can hardly avoid seeing, because the most impressive event in Tolstoy's life, as in Lear's, was a huge and gratuitous act of renunciation. . . . But the deeper resemblance lies in the fact that Tolstoy, like Lear, acted on mistaken motives and failed to get the results he had hoped for. . . . Tolstoy renounced the world under the expectation that this would make him happier. But if there is one thing certain about his later years, it is that he was *not* happy. On the contrary, he was driven almost to the edge of madness by the behavior of the people about him, who persecuted him precisely *because* of his renunciation . . . he even had two children whom he had believed in and who ultimately turned against him though, of course, in a less sensational manner than Regan and Goneril. . . . And though Tolstoy would not foresee it when he wrote his essay on Shakespeare, even the ending of his life — the sudden unplanned flight across country, accompanied only by a faithful daughter, the death in a cottage in a strange village — seems to have in it a sort of phantom reminiscence of *Lear*.

Orwell's parallel is conceived in a spirit of poetic justice, and of tragic irony; and this makes it convincing and paradoxical at the same time. The comparison acts like a flash of lightning, instantly illuminating the tragic finale of Tolstoy's biography. Orwell's analogy finds confirmation in similar suggestions by other witnesses or critics. For instance, another English writer, Isaiah Berlin, closed a recent and penetrating study by likening Tolstoy to Sophocles' Oedipus:

At once insanely proud and filled with self-hatred, omniscient and doubting everything, cold and violently passionate, contemptuous and self-abasing, tormented and detached, surrounded by an adoring family, by devoted followers, by the admiration of the entire civilized world, and yet almost wholly isolated, he is the most tragic of great writers, a desperate old man, beyond human aid, wandering self-blinded at Colonus.[2]

Both comparisons are touching and striking, and yet they fail equally to throw an even and steady light on the perplexing complexity of Tolstoy's figure. They are not life portraits, but death masks, molded on Tolstoy's face while it still held the traces of his agony. The great man died before men's eyes, making of his death both a denial and a confirmation of his life. After all, he had lived for a long time on the stage of the world as a lord and a king, as a leader and a master, as a banner of truth and a beacon of light. Thus the closing episode of his life was both a sacrifice and an ordeal; he died not only like a martyr or a saint, but also like a demigod or a hero.

Tolstoy's more than human greatness had been noticed long before his departure from this world. Only a few years before Tolstoy's end, Gorki had seen him as the reincarnation of a legendary figure from Russia's mythical past, as a new *bogatyr* rousing wonder and awe: "His disproportionately overgrown individuality is a monstrous phenomenon, almost ugly, and there is in him something of Svyatogor, the *bogatyr,* whom the earth can't hold. Yes, he is great." [3] Even Anton Chekhov, who came to dislike increasingly some aspects of Tolstoy's personality, was forced again and again to acknowledge the supernatural proportions of his stature. Thus, after reading a minor piece of writing by his former idol, Chekhov felt compelled to proclaim, with a sudden cry from his heart: "Oh, that Tolstoy, that Tolstoy! He, at the present time, is not a human being, but a superman, a Jupiter." [4] It is hardly surprising to see Tolstoy treated like an almost godlike figure; yet the interpretation of his life in heroic terms is as misleading, or at least as one-sided, as the interpretation of his ultimate destiny in tragic terms.

Rainer Maria Rilke, who, by the way, loved Tolstoy very deeply, used to say that every man is granted the kind of death he lived for. But in the case of Tolstoy the realization of how he died hardly helps us to recognize what he had lived by. His final apotheosis is no less wrong than was his canonization while he was still alive. It was against that canonization that Gorki once raised a voice of protest: "I do not want to see Tolstoy as a saint: let him remain a sinner close to the heart of the all-sinful world, even close to the heart of each of us." The danger of interpreting a historical personality in a legendary vein or in a hagiographic key can be avoided only by measuring it with the yardsticks of psychology and biography, and by correcting the tragic or epic outlook with the comical insight. An all too well known saying claims that no great man is such to his valet; yet what is needed in Tolstoy's case is not the viewpoint of low comedy, the only one which can adopt a lackey's perspective. Tolstoy cannot be looked at from below, by reducing him to the level of farce. We may view him far better by choosing the ground of high comedy, thus placing ourselves on the same plane as our subject. We shall understand him only if we remember that he was as human as we are, without forgetting, however, that he was incommensurably greater than even the best of us. Such a critical inquiry, if lucid and honest, will ultimately lead to a fairer evaluation of his greatness, since, as Gorki said, "he is great and holy because he is a man, a madly and tormentingly beautiful man, a man of the whole of mankind."

It is in this spirit that the following pages will unfold a comic parallel, to illuminate some lasting trends of Tolstoy's personality, some recurring aspects of his life. The character chosen for this purpose, although genuinely comic, was originally conceived in a mood of high seriousness. This character is Alceste, the protagonist of *The Misanthrope,* and perhaps the supreme creation of Molière: of an author, needless to say, on a par with Tolstoy, and not too inferior to the tragic creators of Oedipus and Lear. It may be worth remarking that the Russian master felt constant sympathy for Molière, while he always felt only distaste and contempt toward Shakespeare. There is no better proof of Tolstoy's high regard for the greatest of all comedy writers that that famous page in *What is Art?* where he contrasts the universality of the Joseph story in the Bible with the limited appeal of a few classical and modern writers, all of them great masters. Yet, while doing so, he still finds it fitting to qualify his invidious comparison to the almost exclusive benefit of the author of *The Misanthrope:* "though Molière is perhaps the most universal, and therefore the most excellent artist of modern times." [5]

II

The most typical trait of Molière's Alceste is not a mere concern for truth, but an outright obsession with sincerity per se. We learn this from the very beginning of the play, when the protagonist indignantly accuses Philinte of hypocrisy for having treated a third party as if he were a bosom friend, while hardly remembering his name. At the climax of his tirade, Alceste proudly and earnestly proclaims:

> *Je veux qu'on soit sincère, et qu'en homme d'honneur*
> *On ne lâche aucun mot qui ne parte du coeur.*

I'd have them be sincere, and never part
With any word that isn't from the heart.

Tolstoy shares with Alceste this mania for sincerity, as his letters and diaries, as well as many other testimonials, so abundantly prove. Such a mania was in him not an acquired, but an inborn trait. This is fully apparent in *Childhood,* Tolstoy's earliest literary product, as well as in its sequels, *Boyhood* and *Youth.* To appraise the documentary value of the whole cycle, one should recall that the author represented there not his own family, but several members of the friendly Islenev clan, whom he adumbrated under the name of Irtenev. Thus the writer depicted himself, as he had been at the early stages of his life, in the child Nikolenka Irtenev, who becomes more and more the single protagonist of the series. Nikolenka is the first of Tolstoy's many self-portraits, and it hardly matters that he is painted against the background of another family group. Here, as in other cases, the reader will do well to distrust the disclaimer of the old Tolstoy, who unjustly disliked this early exercise and denied that it was an autobiography at all, and to rely instead on what he had originally stated in his preface to *Childhood.* There the writer had justified the absence from his book of "all the mannerisms of authorship" on the very ground that "he was writing in autobiographical form." [6] The statement, however, must not be taken too literally: "autobiographical form" must be understood as a fusion of "poetry" and "truth," of imagination and memory, of unrelated experiences and events. The author extends some of his biographical and psychological traits to characters other than the one representing himself, especially to Dmitri Neklyudov, Nikolenka's best friend.[7]

The fact that both youngsters reflect some important facets of Tolstoy's personality makes quite significant the first intimate conversation taking place between them. It occurs in the closing chapter of *Boyhood,* entitled "The Beginning of Friendship." It is Neklyudov who speaks first:

"Do you know why . . . I care more for you than for people with whom I am better acquainted and with whom I have more in common? I have just discovered it. You have a wonderful and rare quality — frankness."

"Yes, I always say the very things I am ashamed to confess," I assented, "but only to those in whom I have confidence."

Nikolenka's qualification intimates a difference in temperament between these moral twins. One could say that in this composite self-portrait Tolstoy unconsciously gives us a double, youthful version of the Alceste prototype. Nothing proves this point better than the naïve, reciprocal commitment made by the two youths. Nikolenka and Dmitri resolve to exact from each other what Molière's hero could never obtain from his own bosom friend: a total, reciprocal forthrightness, with an absolute disregard for any consideration but truth. This time too Neklyudov speaks first:

"Do you know what has occurred to me, Nicholas?" he added. . . . "Let us promise to confess everything to one another. We shall know one another. We shall know one another and not be ashamed, and not be afraid of other people; let us promise never to tell anything to *any one* about each other! Let us do that!"
"Let us!" I said.

In this double self-reflection the young Tolstoy reveals an all too intransigent temper, seemingly alien to the Tolstoy of maturity, who, very often, out of prudence or indifference, kept his truth to himself, and cared little for friendship. The two youngsters, like the far older Alceste, consider friendship an exclusive bond, a privilege to be granted to a limited number of chosen beings, to the happy few. One of the reproaches Alceste addresses to Philinte is that the latter does exactly the opposite: that, apparently at least, he extends the privilege of friendship to any undeserving creature he may chance to meet. Alceste maintains that:

c'est n'estimer rien qu'estimer tout le monde;

to honor all men is to honor none;

and concludes his protest with the famous words:

Je veux qu'on me distingue, et, pour le trancher net,
L'ami du genre humain n'est point du tout mon fait.

I choose, sir, to be chosen; and in fine
The friend of mankind is no friend of mine.

"The friend of mankind": the formula is quite striking, and seems but a paraphrase of the Greek "philanthrope." By his ironic use of such a term, Alceste reveals himself, at least in this passage, as a "misanthrope" of a peculiar sort. The "philanthropy" he rejects is that which consists in being nice to everybody, or in liking mankind in the abstract, rather than in earnestly loving a given person, a concrete, individual being. Alceste hates the habitual or professional lover of the human kind, who treats all men with equal benevolence or indifference. It is well known that Tolstoy felt like Alceste in this matter. He projected that feeling through Konstantin Levin, the most autobiographical of all his fictitious characters, and, besides the protagonist, the most important figure in *Anna Karenina*. That feeling itself is well exemplified in Levin's strong reaction against his brother Sergey's tendency to exalt an entire class of men, treated in mass. The object of Sergey's exaltation is the Russian peasantry. Levin cannot accept that exaltation, since, as Tolstoy says, "he liked and did not like peasants, just as he liked and did not like men in general. . . ." [8]

The words just quoted become quite important in view of the fact that Tolstoy himself later became a fanatic asserter of the moral superiority of the *muzhik* over all other human types and groups. Such an evolution is already hinted at in the characterization of Levin, who will ultimately find in simple peasants' hearts that meaning of life he had vainly sought for so long. This is but one of the many Tolstoyan contradictions, and it would be unwise and improper to reproach him with the words: "Physician, heal thyself." Yet it is only fair to recall that after his so-called conversion, which took place immediately after the publication of *Anna Karenina,* Tolstoy became the most famous "philanthrope" of his time, while remaining a "misanthrope" like Alceste, perhaps even more so. Failure to understand this radical contradiction in Tolstoy's psyche will make incomprehensible and senseless all the moral conflicts which embittered the last period of his life, and which at the end of his days changed him from an Alceste into a Lear. In Tolstoy the lover of mankind is inextricably bound up with the scorner and despiser of man; like Levin, he both likes and dislikes the human species in general. This is another of the many paradoxes of his Alcestian make-up. Yet, unlike Alceste, Tolstoy could realize that the fatal outcome of an intransigent sincerity might be the opposite of truth. This is what happens in *Youth* when Nikolenka and Dmitri try to put into effect their reciprocal commitment to absolute sincerity: "Carried away by frankness, we had sometimes gone so far as to make quite shameless comparisons, describing (to our shame) suppositions and fancies as wishes and feelings. . . ."

This episode reveals Tolstoy's precocious insight, and suggests that he well knew that one may run the risk of becoming like Rousseau while behaving like Alceste. Even the latter seems to be vaguely aware of that danger when he tells Oronte:

Mais l'amitié demande un peu plus de mystère.

But friendship requires a little more mystery.

Tolstoy, however, would go further than this, up to the point of admitting the wisdom of Philinte's retort:

Il est bon de cacher ce qu'on a dans le coeur.

It's often best to veil one's true emotions.

The conclusion to be reached, then, is that Tolstoy frequently acted and felt like an Alceste saddened by experience, and thus willing to heed the lesson of the Philintes. Despite this, sincerity remained forever his idol, and from maturity on it shaped his literary works, dictated his esthetic theories, conditioned his moral preachings, in short, made him the man he was born to be. Above all, this yearning after sincerity led him to confess himself in writing to the entire world as perhaps only Rousseau had done before him. True enough, after seeing how the world took his confession, he must have often thought that it would have been better if he had listened to the counsel of discretion given him by the Philinte within himself. Tolstoy frequently made Alceste's mistake, and weakened his case by taking, even in small matters, too rigid a stand. Thus he often did disservice to his own cause, which was indeed the cause of truth. He was blamed for this even by his best friends, who were no Philintes. Of all too many of his pronouncements one could repeat what Chekhov said about *The Kreutzer Sonata:* "On reading it one could hardly refrain from exclaiming: 'This is true!' or 'This is preposterous!' " [9] While realizing that sincerity may not be enough, and that sometimes it is too much, Tolstoy could never refrain from yielding anew to sincerity's urge, from obeying truth's command. This is why, like Alceste, he failed to learn in full the cynical, and yet wise, lesson of the world.

Strength of character may be made of weakness too. La Rochefoucauld maintains that "vices enter into the composition of virtues, as poisons enter into the composition of drugs." [10] The maxim applies to Alceste, since there is some disguised vice behind his evident virtue. His soul is made of a noble alloy, which contains, however, a small quantity of base metals, such as a touch of *amour propre* and a shade of pride. In brief, the righteous man is self-righteous as well, and there is some poetic justice in the fact that the censorious Alceste is bound to be not too unfairly censured by people who are ethically inferior to him. Célimène, while being perhaps too harsh, is objectively, if not subjectively, right when she claims that what rules Alceste is not truthfulness but a spirit of contradiction and dissent:

> *Le sentiment d'autrui n'est jamais pour lui plaire:*
> *Il prend toujours en main l'opinion contraire,*
> *Et penserait paraître un homme du commun,*
> *Si l'on voyait qu'il fût de l'avis de quelqu'un.*
> *L'honneur de contre dire a pour lui tant de charmes,*
> *Qu'il prend contre lui-même assez souvent les armes;*
> *Et ses vrais sentiments sont combattus par lui,*
> *Aussitôt qu'il les voit dans la bouche d'autrui.*

> What other people think, he can't abide;
> Whatever they say, he's on the other side;

He lives in deadly fear of agreeing;
'Twould make him seem an ordinary being.
Indeed, he's so in love with contradiction,
He'll turn against his most profound conviction
And with a furious eloquence deplore it,
If only someone else is speaking for it.

Alceste is present while Célimène refers thus to him in the third person;
and he feels so deeply the bitter truth of her remarks, that he fails to make any
retort. The only thing he can do is to complain acidly:

Les rieurs sont pour vous, Madame, c'est tout dire;
Et vous pouvez pousser contre moi la satire.

Go on, dear lady, mock me as you please;
You have your audience in ecstasies.

Célimène's remarks could be suitably extended to Tolstoy, as the latter
would have been the first to admit. Tolstoy was aware that his longing for
sincerity was a genuine trait of his character; yet he was equally aware that
the longing derived at least in part from a yearning for distinction, from a
desire to be different, or even unique, to stand out against the gray background of the average norm. He confessed as much, for instance, in a letter
to Peter Biryukov, a friendly disciple: "A trait of my character, which, either
good or bad, was certainly always peculiar to me, is that despite myself I
would always react against all external or superficial influences. . . . I felt a
repulsion for the general current."

Tolstoy's struggle against public morality and the established church, his
rebellion against any official authority in the cultural and esthetic field, his
universal scorn for ready-made concepts and *idées reçues,* his hatred for cant
and respectability, in brief, all the things he stood for or against, were deeply
rooted not only in the demands of his conscience, but also in his compulsion
to act, feel, and think unlike anybody else. His first and second nature, made
respectively of sincerity and vanity, joined together spontaneously, with the
effect of enhancing even more the exceptional, almost exasperating singularity
of his being. Originality is rather uncomfortable, and men often feel uneasy
in its presence. Gorki understood this very well, as shown in the page where
he described the great old man in one of those moments when he was un-
conquerably himself. In such moments, Tolstoy's strangeness would become
estrangement, and the consciousness of his own uniqueness would change into
a sense of alienation from his fellow men: "At times he gives one the impression of having just arrived from some distant country, where people think
and feel differently and their relations and language are different." Tolstoy

had, of course, to pay very dearly for his dual nature, for his repulsions and compulsions, for his estrangement and alienation from other human beings. The very complexity of his character led him not only to contradict others, and even himself, but to deny the values for which he stood, and to do violence to his soul. Hypocrisy rules the world, and men never forgave him for many of the things he did. Yet it was the nemesis of his own character, rather than the revenge of society, that at times made him the laughing stock of the world. And it was reality itself that retaliated against this supreme realist by making him the butt, not always unjustly, of the harshest of all satires, the satire of fact.

III

Alceste's spirit of contradiction is not so universal that it rejects or protests at everything. His pessimism is often only relative, being directed not against man in general, but against the type of man fashioning the society of his time, and being shaped by it. Molière felt that this side of Alceste's mind was highly important, and this is why he took pains to emphasize it with the utmost frequency and intensity. Thus both Alceste and Philinte repeatedly affirm that the object of the protagonist's wrath is primarily the moral standards of his own age and milieu. Philinte does so in the first of his many warnings to his friend:

> *Je vous dirai tout franc que cette maladie,*
> *Partout où vous allez, donne la comédie;*
> *Et qu'un si grand courroux contre les moeurs du temps*
> *Vous tourne en ridicule auprès de bien des gens.*

> I'll tell you plainly that by being frank
> You've earned the reputation of a crank,
> And that you're thought ridiculous when you rage
> And rant against the manners of the age.

Philinte expresses the same view a little later, when, vexed with his friend's intolerance, he exclaims:

> *Mon Dieu, des moeurs du temps mettons-nous*
> *[moins en peine. . . .*

> Come, let's forget the follies of the times. . . .

It is true that at least once Philinte reproaches Alceste for hating all mankind:

> *Vous voulez un grand mal à la nature humaine,*

> Your hatred's very sweeping, is it not?

and that Alceste himself claims elsewhere that his misanthropy is universal
in character, transcending the boundaries of place and time:

> *Non: elle est générale, et je hais tous les hommes:*
> *Les uns, parce qu'ils sont méchants et malfaisants,*
> *Et les autres, pour être aux méchants complaisants. . . .*

> No, I include all men in one dim view:
> Some men I hate for being rogues; the others
> I hate because they treat the rogues like brothers. . . .

Yet, in the end, even Alceste feels that in practice the object of his moral
hatred is his own generation, rather than the generality of mankind; and says
as much when he seems to welcome the eventual loss of his legal suit, and even
his impending ruin, as an eloquent proof of the wickedness of his contemporaries:

> *Comme une marque insigne, un fameux témoignage*
> *De la méchanceté des hommes de cet âge.*

> As a great proof and signal demonstration
> Of the black wickedness of this generation.

The same view is explicitly stated by Alceste when, for the first time in the
play, he announces his decision to withdraw from a world made wicked not
so much by the generic perfidy of man, as by the specific corruption of the
times:

> *Trop de perversité règne au siècle ou nous sommes,*
> *Et je veux me tirer du commerce des hommes.*

> This age is evil, and I've made up my mind
> To have no further commerce with mankind.

Tolstoy exhibits all too often the same tendency to attack evil from the
perspective of time, rather than from that of eternity. This tendency is one
of his chief psychological fixations, of his main ideological prejudices. His
writings are full of numberless variations of the old-fashioned cry of complaint, *O tempora, O mores!* and in this he is more consistent and extreme
than Alceste, who is a hater of the present without being a lover of the past.
Logically, however, the man who rejects the manners and the morals of his
age is bound to be at the same time a *laudator temporis acti.* Such a truth,
half-hidden in Alceste's case, is all too apparent in Tolstoy's. It may seem
paradoxical that the man who wrote *War and Peace,* a historical novel which
denies the value of history, and who claimed to preach and teach only what is

permanent and universal in human nature, was often inclined to see too much evil in the present and too much good in the times gone by. This is especially true of the earlier part of Tolstoy's life. Nothing could better prove this point than *An Infected Family*, a comedy written in 1864, which remained unknown in Tolstoy's lifetime, to be made public only in the centenary edition of his writings (1928). Conceived in the shade of such novels as Turgenev's *Father and Sons* and of Chernishevski's *What is to Be Done?* this earliest of all Tolstoy's plays is a violent tract against the times, against that new generation which was trying to shape Russian life into its own ideal image. If Chernishevski treats the "new men" as the harbingers of a bright future, Tolstoy instead considers them as uprooted and shallow destroyers of all traditional values. Tolstoy's attitude differs even more sharply from the stand of Turgenev, who saw both sides of the issue, and treated with equal fairness the upholders of the old system and the announcers of the new order.

Tolstoy's nostalgic admiration for an idealized past is fully apparent in "Two Hussars," the most subtly tendentious of his earliest tales. The author betrays his bias in the very structure of the story, which is made like a diptych. Its two parts contrast the behavior of two hussars, who chance to stop briefly in the same provincial place, at an interval of more than twenty years. The first hussar, a warm-blooded daredevil, intoxicated with life, who represents the exuberant vitality of the men of the beginning of the past century, obeys only his spontaneous impulses, showing in all his actions a strange and yet captivating mixture of generosity and violence. The second hussar, who represents the calculating and mean mind of the new generation, the selfish opportunism of the men of the mid-century, betrays the trust of the family which has welcomed him as a friend and a guest. The oldest members of that family still preserve in their hearts the glorious memory of the hussar who had visited their place twenty years before. In their feeling of shame for the behavior of their visitor, they try to forget the second hussar as soon as he leaves. From an objective moral viewpoint, neither of the two hussars is much better than the other; there is after all no great moral difference between a rake and a cad. Yet Tolstoy stacks all the cards in favor of the bold and romantic representative of the old generation, and manages to make a villain out of the more vulgar or prosaic man of the new times. The lesson is brought home even more forcefully by the hardly coincidental fact that the second hussar is the son of the first. The obvious moral of this simple fable is that even among nobles the sons are but the degenerate offspring of their fathers. The belief that men were far better in the days just gone by is stated with great assurance in the tale's introduction, which is worth quoting, at least in part:

> Early in the nineteenth century, when there were as yet no railways or macadamized roads, no gaslight, no stearine candles . . . no disillusioned youth with eye-glasses, no liberalizing women philosophers, nor any charming *dames aux camélias* of whom there are so many in our times, in those naïve days, . . . when our fathers were still young and proved it not only by the absence of wrinkles and grey hair but by fighting duels for the sake of women. . . .[11]

The entire passage should be placed at the head of any biography of the young Tolstoy, where it could serve as a kind of reminder of the way of life into which he was born and raised, and also as a telling document of the backward-looking nostalgia which inspired not only this mediocre composition, but also a masterwork like *War and Peace*. This longing after a nobler past survived forever, even if repressed and hidden, in the depths of Tolstoy's personality, and was the cause, rather than the effect, of his Alcestian scorn for the values, the standards, and the men of his time.

This nostalgia is a characteristic aristocratic trait. Yet it comes to the fore only when aristocratic values are on the wane, or put in doubt. Alceste does not need to project his ideals into the past, since he sees them universally accepted in the present, if not in practice, at least in theory. His chief protest is merely that his peers honor them more in the breach than in the observance. The peculiarity of Tolstoy's situation lies, rather, in the conflicting demands of his aristocratic upbringing and breeding, and of the democratic spirit of the new times. Unlike Alceste, Tolstoy could not take his status as a nobleman for granted, and was bound to consider it a problem as well as a fact. Even before his conversion, as shown by his repeated attempts to improve the lot of his peasants and to educate their children, he followed, like his hero Levin, the commandment implied in the motto *noblesse oblige,* by which a nobility no longer sure of itself tries to justify its very existence. Alceste does not need to restate that norm, since he has no reason to fear that the aristocratic way of life will ever be doubted or challenged. After all, Molière wrote *The Misanthrope* for a *parterre de rois,* or at least, for a public of courtiers, and even now the spectator or reader who wishes to understand the play must assume, at least provisionally, an upper-class point of view. This does not exempt Alceste from being treated comically, although Molière never makes him as ludicrous as the commoners he portrayed in other plays, as for instance Tartuffe, Georges Dandin, or Monsieur Jourdain. *The Misanthrope,* like all Molière's comedies, is addressed to the social élite; its main point is that the ungovernable temper of his noble protagonist prevents him from behaving as sensibly as a gentleman should.

Tolstoy, however, did not live in seventeenth-century France, but in nineteenth-century Russia, not in the capital or the court, but in the country and in the provinces, as a member of the landed gentry, a class and a society which could still be considered feudal on many counts. Despite this, the spirit of the age was already so democratic that even then many of his admirers failed to put the title of nobility before his family name. Yet it may be wrong to forget that Leo Tolstoy was born a count, and that he remained one to the end of his days. After all, Tolstoy's plight was similar to Alceste's also in the sense that his fellow noblemen strongly resented his obstinate refusal to act like one of them, to live in the settled nobleman's ways. Yet, looking more deeply, one may see that his deviations from the aristocratic pattern were only relative. Even now the aristocrat seems to retain the privilege of being different, exceptional, eccentric. A nobleman is still entitled to behave in an ungentlemanly way, while a bourgeois cannot afford to do so. In brief, Tolstoy acted like a nobleman even when he denied the *raison d'être* of his class. All his moral crises unfolded within the framework of the aristocratic way of life, which at first he understood in a shallow and narrow sense, as the mode of being of the privileged upper crust. In *Youth* there is a passage where the writer confesses with charming irony his youthful snobbishness:

My favorite and chief division of people at the time of which I am writing, was into the *comme il faut* and the *comme il ne faut pas*. The latter I subdivided into those inherently not *comme il faut,* and the common people. The *comme il faut* people I respected and considered worthy of being on terms of equality with me; the *comme il ne faut pas* I pretended to despise but in reality hated, nourishing a feeling of personal offence against them; the lower classes did not exist for me — I despised them completely.

For a long time, even when he was no longer a child, Tolstoy felt allegiance only to the class of the well born and the chosen few, and that allegiance was so exclusive as to imply an absolute contempt for all those who were beyond the pale of the élite of which he was part. Tolstoy attested as much in a famous page of *A Confession:* "It seemed to me that that narrow circle of rich, learned, and leisured people to which I belonged formed the whole of humanity, and that those billions of others who have lived and are living were cattle of some sort — not real people." [12] It is true that in the end he withdrew from high society, not so much to embrace mankind as to live less falsely, and be more like himself. Or, as he says in *A Confession:* "I turned from the life of our circle, acknowledging that ours is not life, but a simulation of life." It is equally true that he had gradually started leaving *le monde* a long time before his final break, precisely because he had learned his lesson earlier and more easily than Alceste. Yet, in the innermost recesses of his being, Tolstoy remained a Russian aristocrat even after his so-called conversion, when he preached the brotherhood of man and exalted the *muzhik* as the purest and noblest representative of humankind. Nobody recognized this as shrewdly as Maxim Gorki, whose life as an outcast had taught him to see through all pretense, beyond the mask of humility as well as of pride:

And suddenly, under the peasant's beard, under his democratic crumpled blouse, there would rise the old Russian *barin,* the grand aristocrat; then the noses of the simple-hearted victims, educated and all the rest, instantly became blue with intolerable cold. It was pleasant to see this creature of the purest blood, to watch the noble grace of his gestures, the proud reserve of his speech, to hear the exquisite pointedness of his marvelous words. He showed just as much of the *barin* as was needed for those serfs, and when they called out the *barin* in Tolstoy, it appeared naturally and easily, and crushed them so that they shriveled up and whined.

The persuasive voice which uttered those words still seems to sound a warning to all those who are too willing to forget that Tolstoy was born in "a nest of gentlefolk."

IV

The indestructibility of the aristocratic strain in Tolstoy's personality does not cast any doubt on the sincerity of his rebellion not only against society in general, but also against society in the narrow sense of the term. There is no doubt that the man who was born Count Tolstoy rebelled against the class from which he had sprung. His revolt was moral, rather than social or political, in temper. Perhaps his peculiar brand of universal anarchism derived, at least in part, from his psychological inability to find a valid alternative to the ancient regime, although he condemned it with all his mind and heart. He found that order wanting, yet he found equally wanting all other possible orders. Aristocratic liberalism, no less than bourgeois democracy, was anathema to him. Yet he rejected with equal scorn the Marxist belief in industrial progress, with its implied faith in the redemption of and by the urban masses. As for his cult of the peasantry, he saw in that class an example of ethical perfection, but not the active agent of a transformation for the better of the social system. He hated revolution as much as reaction, and refused to justify the excesses of terrorism by the provocations and repressions of tsardom, while indicting the latter with harsh and powerful words. His single social or political imperative took a passive and negative form, and he directed his followers not to resist organized evil, except by martyrdom.

In brief, Tolstoy was a dissenter from the old social order, rather than the builder of a new one. In this too, strangely enough, he reveals psychological traits akin to Alceste's. Molière's misanthrope does not question the social structure of which he is part; he is not a critic of society, but of man. The criticism itself is passive rather than active, and this makes Alceste a "protestant," not a "reformer." In brief, Alceste plays the role of a conscientious objector, upholding his ethical principles against society, and accusing the latter of not measuring up even to its own standards. His stiff-necked intransigence sharply contrasts with the easygoing tolerance of practically everybody else, yet he fails to do anything more than to preach sermons, or to set an example. He hardly tries to win over converts to his cause, realizing perhaps that converts are not gained by upbraiding alone. Nor does he strive to bring about even the slightest change of heart in those whom he censors or judges. Philinte is quite right when he warns his friend:

> Le monde par vos soins ne se changera pas;
>
> The world won't change, whatever you say or do;

Yet even he fails to realize that Alceste is more interested in uttering his solemn jeremiads than in helping to correct the shortcomings or to improve the behavior of his fellow men. Philinte is nearer to the truth when he exclaims:

> Mon Dieu, des moeurs du temps mettons-nous
> [moins en peine,
>
> Come, let's forget the follies of the times,

since now he seems to guess that the only thing that Alceste wants to do is to worry, and to get angry, at the ways of the world. One of the intentions of the play could be defined as the attempt to portray in Alceste the opposite of Tartuffe. The two types are opposites not only through the moral contrast between the sincerity of the one and the hypocrisy of the other, but also through their being made equally grotesque, Tartuffe by the extreme vileness, and Alceste by the excessive nobility, of his character. Molière makes Alceste ridiculous by endowing him not only with a noble soul, but also with an unruly temper, with a temperament largely made of intemperance.

It may be worth recalling that at first Molière intended to entitle his comedy *L'Atrabiliaire*. This clue, and the other clues left in the text, may prove that the play was originally conceived in the key of a "comedy of humors," which later became a "comedy of character," and a "comedy of manners," as well. Yet the author's original intent is still evident in the attention he pays to all the idiosyncracies of Alceste's temperament. With great dramatic insight, Molière reveals such idiosyncrasies through the peculiar mannerisms of the hero's speech. Any time he utters a general principle, Alceste states it in subjective, imperative terms, and opens his utterance with a proud and childish *je veux:* "Je veux me fâcher" (I choose to be rude); "Je veux qu'on soit sincère" (I'd have them be sincere); "Je veux qu'on me distingue" (I choose, sir, to be chosen); "Je veux que l'on soit homme" (Let men behave like men).

When he loses his patience or nerve, Alceste bursts out with a flood of bitter words. He announces such outbursts by using, in the first person and in the present tense, one of the many synonyms of the verb *s'enrager*. Even righteous wrath may derive from a psychological flaw, rather than from an earnest and severe conscience; it may be the symptom of a mental disorder, a *maladie,* as Philinte calls it, rather than the by-product of a lofty concern for moral truth. At least on one occasion Alceste himself describes his *saeva indignatio* in psychopathological terms. The key words of Alceste's self-diagnosis, "melancholy" and "gall," are directly related to the old medical belief that the structure of the psyche is determined by the prevalence within the body of a given set of "humors":

> Mes yeux sont trop blessés, et la cour et la ville
> Ne m'offrent rien qu'objets à m'échauffer la bile.
> J'entre en une humeur noire, en un chagrin profond,
> Quand je vois vivre entre eux les hommes comme ils font.

> All are corrupt; there's nothing to be seen
> In court or town but aggravates my spleen.
> I fall into deep gloom and melancholy
> When I survey the scene of human folly.

This does not mean that Alceste should be reduced to a mere hypochondriac. He is not only a generic "humor," but also a specific character, made peculiar by the excessive delicacy of his moral sense. Alceste's "misanthropy" is but the outcome of his delusion that all men should be naturally provided with a conscience as delicate and sensitive as his own. Like most pessimists, Alceste is a former optimist, who has seen his expectations disappointed by experience. This singular mixture of idealism and susceptibility makes him ridiculously vulnerable to even the slightest blows. Yet the idealist in him remains visible even when he utters his harshest pronouncements against the human race, which fall short of the merciless lucidity of Philinte. If the latter refuses to condemn men for being what they are, it is only because he knows that evil is part of nature. We must take human malice for granted, he says, as we take for granted the cruelty of wild beasts:

> Oui, je vois ces défauts dont votre âme murmure
> Comme vices unis à l'humaine nature,
> Et mon esprit enfin n'est pas plus offensé
> De voir un homme fourbe, injuste, intéressé,
> Que de voir des vautours affamés de carnage,
> Des singes malfaisants et des loups pleins de rage.

> Why, no. These faults of which you so complain
> Are part of human nature, I maintain,
> And it's no more a matter for disgust
> That men are knavish, selfish, and unjust,
> Than that the vulture dines upon the dead,
> And wolves are furious, and apes ill-bred.

One may find it surprising that Molière attributes such hard thinking and plain speaking to the skeptical but hardly cynical Philinte. After all, the author conceived him not only as the wise man, or the sensible character of the piece, but also as another "humor," as a phlegmatic temperament to be contrasted with Alceste's bilious one. Alceste implies as much when he tells his friend:

> Mon flegme est philosophe autant que votre bile.

> My phlegm's as philosophic as your spleen.

Philinte exhibits such a constant equanimity in the course of the play that it is not hard to surmise that it is Molière's passionate voice that speaks in the passage where men are compared to rapacious animals. Yet Philinte's assertion of man's indignity is but a corollary of the pessimistic view of human nature characteristic of traditional Christianity. It is true that Philinte dresses that view in worldly wisdom, and that he treats with unruffled indulgence the weaknesses of all the children of Adam:

> Je prends tout doucement les hommes comme ils sont.

> I take men as they are, or let them be.

A man speaking thus, and behaving accordingly, may be defined an enlightened conformist. As for Alceste, everything he says and does shows that

he belongs instead to the type of man whom we call, in either a religious or a
psychological sense, a nonconformist. The nonconformist is both a fanatic and
an enthusiast, yet his fanaticism and enthusiasm do not necessarily lead him to
any kind of public action, unless merely negative in character. The nonconformist is often in theory a sectarian, or the member of a partisan faction, but in
practice he is a lone wolf, a rugged individualist. His real allegiance is to the
way of life he has chosen to follow, which means that ultimately he is loyal
only to himself. It is by obeying his "inner voice" that he tests the validity
of his moral choice, or contests the choices of his fellow men. He hardly cares
for doing more, and scarcely bothers to force on the public the pattern of
his private conduct. The most famous of Tolstoy's declarations of faith,
which may be read in *A Confession,* proves that he was a nonconformist
of this kind: "The arbiter of what is good and evil is not what people say
and do, nor is it progress, but it is my heart and I."

These words, which Alceste could have uttered without change, represent the perfect antithesis of all Philinte thinks and feels. Experience teaches
us that the world needs the conformist as well as the nonconformist; the
social order would break down without Philintes, while it would stagnate
without Alcestes. We may learn this lesson from Tolstoy's novels as well as
from *The Misanthrope.* If this is true, then it hardly matters that Tolstoy
preferred the Alcestes over the Philintes, or that he chose to portray himself
in the type of the nonconformist. The important point is that he considered
each of these two social and psychological archetypes as necessary as the
other. *War and Peace* presents many Philintes among its minor figures,
while treating its three main heroes as variations of the Alcestian character.
Pierre Bezukhov is an Alceste who remains forever young, preserving his
naïve idealism unscathed through the ordeals of life. Andrey Bolkonski is
an Alceste without illusions, although passion and ambition force him for
some time to act and behave like a Philinte. Nikolay Rostov is a boorish and
provincial Alceste, steadfastly refusing to be seduced by society, living quietly
in his corner, with the proud assurance of being both right and upright.
Dmitri Neklyudov, the protagonist of Tolstoy's last novel, *Resurrection,*
after having led for too many years the life of a Philinte, finally succeeds in
becoming an Alceste. The contrast between these psychological prototypes
appears even in *Anna Karenina.* The masculine world of that novel is based
not only on the conflict between Vronski and Karenin, but also on the contrast between them and Levin, and even on the antithetical characters of
Levin and his friend Stiva Oblonski. The last of these contrasts, which is
very similar to the one between Alceste and Philinte, was shrewdly observed

and commented on by a brilliant American sociologist, David Riesman. After having formulated the concepts of "inner-direction" and "other-direction," by which he defines psychological attitudes not too different from those designated here by the terms of conformism and nonconformism, David Riesman picks Stiva Oblonski as an almost perfect specimen of the other-directed type: "Stepan Arkadyevich Oblonski in *Anna Karenina* is one of the more likable and less opportunistic examples, especially striking because of the way Tolstoy contrasts him with Levin, a moralising inner-directed person." [13]

While David Riesman is more directly concerned with Stiva Oblonski, with the "other-" rather than with the "inner-directed" man, we are far more interested in Konstantin Levin, in the Tolstoyan variant of the Alceste, rather than of the Philinte, type. Yet we must follow for a while in Mr. Riesman's footsteps, and study Tolstoy's version of the "other-directed" man, of the conformist *à la* Philinte. The passage where Tolstoy describes the mental make-up of Stiva Oblonski is of great sociological interest. He first sketches Stiva's moral portrait through the perspective of his political opinions:

> Stepan Arkadyevich had not chosen his political opinions and his views: these political opinions and views had come to him of themselves, just as he did not choose the shape of his coat, but simply took those that were being worn. And for him, living in a certain society — owing to the need, ordinarily developed at years of direction, for some degrees of mental activity — to have views was just as indispensable as to have a hat. If there was a reason for his preferring to conservative liberal views, which were held also by many of his circle, it arose not from his considering liberalism more rational, but from its being in closer accordance with his manner of life. . . . And so liberalism had become a habit of Stepan Arkadyevich. . . .

Tolstoy points out that the political ideology of Stiva Oblonski is but a consequence of that open-mindedness which is a characteristic trait of the most worldly and least traditional members of a social élite. Stiva Oblonski embodies in modern terms the ideal of the *honnête homme*. He is a perfect gentleman, since his "perfect liberalism," as Tolstoy says, "was not the liberalism he read of in the papers, but the liberalism that was in his blood, in virtue of which he treated all men perfectly equally, exactly the same, whatever their future or calling might be." Stiva's liberality of mind consists in his willingness to extend the policy of *laissez-faire, laissez-passer* from the domain of political economy to all the spheres of social endeavor and of human intercourse. It sounds strange to call liberal a type of man previously labeled as conformistic and "other-directed," and it sounds even stranger to

define conservative or reactionary the type already described as noncon-
formistic and "inner-directed." This paradox may be solved with the help of
Mr. Riesman, who claims that the nonconformist is not only "inner-," but
also "tradition-directed." This is certainly true of Konstantin Levin, whom
his friends consider a conservative and a reactionary, as he is himself willing
to admit. After all, the reactionary and the revolutionary minds are both
"radical," although in a different sense, while the liberal mind is always
"moderate" in all the meanings of that term. In Levin's radical conservatism
Tolstoy portrays not only a specific tendency of his character, but also a
general social attitude, no less typical of aristocratic mentality than its opposite, which is Oblonski's liberalism. It is to Stiva that Levin confesses his
allegiance to the traditional way of life of the landed gentry, now being
threatened by the forces of historical change, by what the liberals call progress: "You'll say again that I'm a reactionist, or some other terrible word;
but all the same it does annoy and anger me to see on all sides the impoverish-
ing of the nobility to which I belong, and, in spite of the amalgamation of
classes, I'm glad to belong."

These words by Levin sound like a belated echo of the youthful Tolstoy's
decision "to reject the temptation of liberalism." This motto fully reveals how
innately conservative was the mind of the man who was fated to become
the foremost of all modern "levelers," the most radical of all the moral rebels
of his time. Yet this contradiction between Tolstoy's character and his destiny
is not so great as it may seem, since there is no irreconcilable conflict between
the two psychological tendencies which we have respectively named "traditionalism" and "protestantism." Romain Rolland acknowledged this truth in
terms of both biography and ideology, when he described the doctrines of
the Russian master as "those free theories of a revolutionary conservative, as
he always was."

All the notions we have used up to now to understand the contradictions
and the complications of Tolstoy's personality may be suitably shifted from
him to the character of Alceste. The latter, like the former, looks at life *sub
specie aeternitatis,* thus failing to understand its irrationality, its complexity,
and its absurdity. He refuses to bend his body, or to lower his eyes, to better
follow the uneven flow of reality, all the divergent streams of experience.
Philinte often blames Alceste for this fault, as Stiva also blames his friend:
"You're very much all of a piece. That's your strong point and your failing.
You have a character that's all of a piece, and you want the whole life to
be of a piece too — but that's not how it is." Stiva reproaches Kostya not only

for this, but also for his particular scorn toward any kind of public employ-
ment and service. Such scorn is typical of the landed gentry or provincial
nobility, proud of its economic self-sufficiency as well as of its freedom and
independence. The individual member of that social group may often translate such class feeling into a personal sense of pride at his own inability to
breathe in the moral climate of the centers of authority and power. Alceste
does the same thing when he describes his maladjustment to courtly life as
a moral virtue rather than as a psychological defect:

> *Le Ciel ne m'a point fait, en me donnant le jour,*
> *Une âme compatible avec l'air de la cour.*

> The soul God gave me isn't of the sort
> That prospers in the weather of a court.

When trying to convince Kostya that the civil servant's task is not so
hollow and false as the latter thinks, Stiva employs the same arguments as do
Alceste's friends, when they try to dispel his prejudices against serving at
court: "You despise public official work because you want the reality to be
invariably corresponding all the while with the aim — and that's not how
it is. . . . All the variety, all the charm, all the beauty of life is made up of
light and shadow. . . ." Despite Stiva's protestations, Levin goes on despising those who are more willing to serve the dubious cause of the public
good rather than the private, and higher, demands of the self. In this Tolstoy
fully identifies himself with Levin, to whom he attributes his own absolute
"disbelief in the sense of all public institutions." In the same novel Tolstoy
projects that disbelief in his negative characterization of Alexey Karenin,
the only figure portrayed with consistent antipathy, with all the author's
bitter hatred for the ambitious bureaucrat, for the opportunist and the time-
server, for the man equally able to yield and to coerce, equally willing to
obey and to command. It is against him that Tolstoy speaks with full Alcestian severity. As for Levin, he plays his Alcestian role with less intransigence than his prototype: and this is shown by the way he treats the Philinte
of the novel, Stiva Oblonski. In their reciprocal reactions, the two friends
seem equally able to discriminate between friendship and prejudice. By
doing so, Levin unwittingly proves that he is not all of one piece, as his
friend and everybody else think he is. One could say, paradoxically, that Stiva
is the more consistent of the two; it is he, rather than Kostya, who is all of
one piece, even if the stuff he is made of is not hard, but soft.

V

The Philinte within him taught the young Tolstoy the most useful and the most difficult of all wisdoms: wisdom in the affairs of the heart. Alceste learns this wisdom the hard way, and too late to profit by it. Love, the second of his ordeals, besides the ordeal of friendship, is the leading motive of the play's subplot. *The Misanthrope* is after all not a tragedy by Racine, but a comedy by Molière, and thus it contains but a moderate amount of love interest. Yet the love angle contributes to both the characterization of the hero and the dénouement of the intrigue. Alceste's foolish infatuation for frivolous Célimène enhances the play's comic effect, since it proves that even the most solid masculine character may be highly vulnerable to passion's blows. It is his disappointment in love, more than anything else, which seems to determine his decision to abandon forever the world.

Through his inborn wisdom in the affairs of the heart, Tolstoy limited the scope of love within his life even more than Molière did within *The Misanthrope*. Unlike Alceste, he was almost always able to keep that passion in check. Eros, as distinguished from sex, played a small role in his biography, and even less in his works. The man who wrote *War and Peace* and the second part of *Domestic Happiness, Anna Karenina* and *The Kreutzer Sonata*, "The Devil" and "Father Sergius," stands almost alone among modern authors in his inward and outward rejection of romantic love.[14] Tolstoy condemned romantic love both in words and deeds, and he was hardly able to make himself as ridiculous as Alceste by losing his head over a bluestocking or a flirt. As a matter of fact, what would have made Tolstoy look funny in the moral climate of Molièrian comedy is his outright denial of sentiment in matters of love. It would be hard to find anything more alien to the French literary imagination than that family cult and marriage worship which dominated the life and works of Tolstoy's maturity; or, even more, than the theory or the practice of sexual abstention which ruled the latter part of his life. In contrast to the traditional French preoccupation with *le romanesque*, or with what Stendhal calls *l'amour-passion*, Tolstoy as a man was successively attracted by three different tendencies, promiscuity, uxoriousness, and asceticism, each one of which in its special way is a denial of romantic love. While *l'amour-passion* derives from a profane apotheosis of the Eternal Feminine, promiscuity, uxoriousness, and asceticism are but different forms of the same contempt for woman. In brief, Tolstoy was not only, like Alceste, a misanthrope: unlike him, he was a misogynist too. His work is full of eloquent proofs of this truth, which finds confirmation also in Gorki's significant testimony:

Woman, in my opinion, he regards with implacable hostility, and loves to punish her, unless she is a Kitty or a Natasha Rostova, i.e., a creature not too narrow. It is the hostility of the male who has not succeeded in getting all the pleasure he could, or it is the hostility of the spirit against "the degrading impulses of the flesh." But it is hostility, as cold as in *Anna Karenina*.

While almost always able to master *l'amour-passion,* Tolstoy was all too often incapable of mastering the sexual instinct. Yet this failure, only imperfectly corrected by his desperate attempt to deny and repress the force of *libido,* enabled him to see through the veils which imagination and sentiment, along with hypocrisy and self-deceit, throw on the sexual act, to cover and idealize it. Being himself a slave and victim of sex, he was lucidly and adultly aware of "the facts of life," as well as of the everlasting misery they may bring into our existence. "Man survives earthquakes, epidemics, the horrors of disease," he told Gorki, "but for all time his most tormenting tragedy has been and will be the tragedy of the bedroom."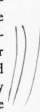

Tolstoy was not a courtly aristocrat, but a country squire, and in his love affairs or sexual experiences he was naturally led to choose the easy rather than the hard path. While avoiding, almost with no effort, all *liaisons dangereuses* with high-placed ladies of his class, he could hardly resist the temptation to pick up a harlot in a city street or a peasant woman in the fields. His diaries, as well as many of his most autobiographical stories, refer all too frequently to episodes of this kind, which Tolstoy records in a vein of confession and introspection, in a mood of repentance and remorse. This is why he early saw in marriage the only escape from corruption and sin. In his long quest for a bride, he almost always laid his eyes on that type of woman who is neither glamorous nor fashionable. Tolstoy was generally able to recognize the despicable Célimènes around him, and found it rather easy to escape from their nets. Although respecting, like Alceste, the experienced and mature Arsinoës, he did not care for them either, since he longed for purity but not for prudery. He was fascinated by the Eliantes, by fresh and innocent girlhood. Sonya Bers, the woman whom he married, was like this; and he represented her, as his feminine ideal, in the Kitty Shcherbatski of *Anna Karenina,* who becomes the bride of Levin. Life, however, is a continuous paradox; thus, despite this ability to recognize the feminine ideal best suited to him, for a while even Tolstoy felt the attraction of a girl whom he himself accused of being a bluestocking and a flirt, and with whom he finally broke, far earlier than Alceste ever did.

The story is worth retelling in detail. In 1856, Tolstoy fell in love with a girl far younger than himself, Valeria Arsenyeva, a rich orphan living not far from his estate. As a friend of the family, the writer had been legally appointed her tutor. Attracted by her unspoiled freshness, Tolstoy seriously contemplated marrying his ward; yet in the depth of his heart he never took the girl too seriously, or held her in great respect. He toyed with the idea of educating Valeria, of submitting her to that process of self-reform he was then imposing on himself. Besides documenting all this, Tolstoy's letters and diaries of that time prove that at first he conceived the hope that Valeria would improve under his moral guidance. At the beginning of the play, Alceste nourishes the same illusions in regard to Célimène:

> Sa grâce est la plus forte; et sans doute ma flamme
> De ces vices du temps pourra purger son âme.

> Her charm outweighs her faults; I can but aim
> To cleanse her spirit in my love's pure flame.

Despite those hopes, Tolstoy was, however, unable to dispel his inner doubts concerning the wisdom of his choice. Valeria's actions and words made him frequently wonder whether she was the woman for him. In brief, he often told himself the same things which in a similar situation Alceste is told by Philinte. The latter shows in this a frankness which normally we would hardly expect from him. Shocked by his friend's inclination, Philinte questions the wisdom of Alceste's choice:

> Et ce qui me surprend encore davantage
> C'est cet étrange choix où votre coeur s'engage.

> And what is more amazing, I'm afraid,
> Is the most curious choice your heart has made.

Philinte points out that Alceste could find a better partner in either the honest Eliante or the prude Arsinoë; and that his infatuation for Célimène,

> De qui l'humeur coquette et l'esprit médisant
> Semble si fort donner dans les moeurs d'à présent,

> Whose brittle malice and coquettish ways
> So typify the manners of our days,

runs against the demands of his nature. Alceste's mind admits the truth of Philinte's words, but his heart rejects it. His reply to Philinte's objections is as bitter and lucid as a maxim:

> Mais la raison n'est pas ce qui règle l'amour.

> But reason doesn't rule in love, you know.

Tolstoy, however, was able to listen to reason and to do violence to his heart. Thus he renounced the idea of marrying Valeria Arsenyeva. The crisis which precipitated his decision was a fit of jealousy, yet even before this Tolstoy had felt offended by the girl's worldliness. The young maid attended the coronation festivities of 1856, when Alexander II succeeded his father on the Russian throne, and Tolstoy felt repelled by a letter of hers, describing with glowing colors the glamor of the occasion and the splendor of the court. The letter was of the kind which Célimène herself, if invited to Versailles, would have written to a not yet disappointed Alceste; and Alceste, being congenitally unable to breathe in a courtly atmosphere, would have reacted precisely as Tolstoy did. Tolstoy finally broke with Valeria after he learned of her sentimental attachment for an obscure music teacher. He felt wounded not only in his love, but in his pride too; he could not stand the thought that for a passing moment the woman he loved had preferred the company of a man inferior to himself. Tolstoy vented his indignation in an insulting letter, yet even this was not enough for him. He could find solace for his discomfiture only by proving to his satisfaction that, had the marriage taken place, it would have resulted in failure, and not for faults of his own. He did so by writing in 1858 the long story *Domestic Happiness,* undoubtedly the most perfect of his early works. Here is not the place to discuss in detail this little masterpiece, which transcends the motivation that dictated it. Yet it must be pointed out that the story was originally written with the intention of teaching a lesson to a naughty girl. Tolstoy felt ashamed for having written this work, and vainly tried to withdraw the manuscript, which was published in 1859. It is easy to imagine the embittered Alceste writing a similarly nasty libel against women after his disappointment with Célimène. One could likewise envisage no better epigraph for *Domestic Happiness* than the words by which Alceste reproaches his fiancée for her behavior:

> *Madame, voulez-vous que je vous parle net?*
> *De vos façons d'agir je suis mal satisfait.*
>
> Shall I speak plainly, Madam? I confess
> Your conduct gives me infinite distress.

Tolstoy felt the same urge for plain speaking, if not for fair dealing, when he condemned Valeria through the written word. Objectively, Tolstoy's resentment was hardly justified, and this is why jealousy plays a far smaller role in the tale than in the real event. Alceste's jealousy is made ridiculous by its exaggeration, but it never becomes absurd or grotesque, because he finds some foundation in Célimène's manners, if not in her deeds. Yet Tolstoy was able elsewhere to describe the passion of jealousy even when it is grounded on neither appearance nor fact. Literature generally represents this kind of jealousy only in extreme tragic or comic terms. Tolstoy avoided doing so and chose instead a middle ground between the two. He was unwilling to represent either too pathetically or too farcically a masculine weakness of which he had been the victim himself. There is in *Anna Karenina* a minor episode, probably based on a real incident in Tolstoy's married life. Stiva Oblonski pays a visit to the Levins' country place and brings along a young acquaintance named Vasenka Veslovski. Veslovski is attracted by the charming beauty of Kitty, and begins courting her, perhaps with too flattering insistence, but still without violating the code of manners of their social milieu. Yet Levin loses his head: he makes a scene in public, and asks the unwelcome guest to leave. Stiva Oblonski reacts to this stupid little scandal with words which could have been uttered by Philinte, the more so since they are in French: "Well, this I didn't expect of you. *On peut être jaloux, mais à ce point, c'est du dernier ridicule.*" Tolstoy shares the feeling of Levin, rather than that of Stiva, and this is why he represents the incident as a shameful experience, with bitterness and sadness, rather than with irony and mirth. Probably Tolstoy wrote this little scene with a heavy heart, with the spirit of a gnomic writer or of a *moraliste.* His aim was perhaps to convey the same truth which Molière sums up in Alceste's words:

> Montrer que c'est à tort que sages on nous nomme,
> Et que dans tous les coeurs il est toujours de l'homme.

> And I shall prove to you before I'm done
> How strange the human heart is, and how far
> From rational we sorry creatures are.

VI

The parallel between Alceste and Tolstoy-Levin could be further expanded into a comparison between *The Misanthrope* and *Anna Karenina.* Like Molière's play, Tolstoy's novel deals with contemporary life, which it represents with the fidelity of a historical document. In this *Anna Karenina* differs greatly from *War and Peace,* which is but the exalted evocation of a way of life forever past, "gone with the wind." Turgenev, though admiring it as a supreme masterpiece, noticed that that historical novel was strangely lacking in historical sense, and that despite its nostalgia for the past, it failed to reproduce the color of the times gone by. Merezhkovski pushed further Turgenev's point:

Reading *War and Peace,* we cannot help feeling that all the events reported, despite their historical appearance, are taking place today: and that all the characters described, notwithstanding their quality as historical portraits, are our own contemporaries. . . . The air we breathe in *War and Peace* and *Anna Karenina* is the same; the historical flavor is in both epochs the same; in either work there is the same atmosphere, so well known to us, of the second half of the nineteenth century.[15]

One may acknowledge the truth of the statement, while rejecting the criticism it implies. Tolstoy's inability to perceive any historical hue but that of his time betrays his classical temper, his universal tendency to reduce all experience to the standards of an eternal present. *Anna Karenina,* a novel of "contemporary" life, looks more genuinely "historical" than *War and Peace,* because direct social observation plays a far greater role in the former than in the latter. While *War and Peace* is based on the everlasting conflict between the public world of history and the private world of family and personal life, the contrast at the bottom of *Anna Karenina* rests on the more limited and particular conflict between the social élite, leading a conventional and artificial existence in the big city, and the landed gentry, living a more human and humane life through their closeness to nature and the soil. Kostya is the single representative of the second of these two ways of life, while the first is represented by Anna and her brother, by Vronski and his friends, by Karenin and his circle. Tolstoy idealizes into a romantic idyll Levin's country life, while portraying the other characters' worldly existence in a spirit of realistic irony. This concentration of a lucid critical attention on the restricted milieu which the French call *le monde* changes *Anna Karenina,* at least in part, into a novel of manners. Thus some sections of *Anna Karenina* give the effect of a "drawing room comedy" written in satirical key against the main theme of the novel, which is obviously "the tragedy of the bedroom." In brief, Tolstoy depicts the social élite in a way not too different from Molière's portrayal of the *précieux* and the *précieuses,* or of all those among his characters who are too exclusively ruled by the *esprit de société.*

Tolstoy is not a dramatic writer, and yet sometimes he makes direct use of action and character to project more impersonally his social satire. So, for instance, it is through Karenin's perspective that he gives his own criticism of the *précieux* side of "high life." The effect of this is highly ironical, because Karenin worships the "high circles," if not as centers of elegance, at least as centers of power. And it is quite significant that in the mocking compliment he pays to Princess Betsy and her coterie, Karenin alludes to one of the chief cultural objects of Molièrian satire: " 'Your Rambouillet is in full conclave,' he said looking around at all the party: 'the graces and the muses.' " Generally, however, Tolstoy is a far less detached critic of the social élite. In this he failed to follow the example of Molière, who refused in *The Misanthrope* to make his own the extreme viewpoints of either Philinte or Alceste, and chose a middle ground between the two. Such a central stand is the ideal comic position. Tolstoy instead, even when he remains behind the scene, uses Levin as his own mouthpiece, and fills the novel with his own asides. This means that in *Anna Karenina* the role of Alceste is unconsciously played by the author, as well as by one of the main characters. This may be proved by comparing the handling of the same situation in *The Misanthrope* and in *Anna Karenina*. *The Misanthrope* treats this situation in the scene where Célimène and her guests indulge in a detailed discussion of the shortcomings of all their mutual acquaintances. Here the chief object of Molière's satire is not the high-minded misanthropy of the protagonist, but the actual malevolence of so many of the play's minor figures. Molière unfolds the scene with a crescendo of comical effects. At first, he contrasts the spiteful prattle of Célimène and her guests with Alceste's wordless pantomime, and then, with the flow of bitter words by which Alceste suddenly breaks his ominous silence:

> *Allons, ferme, poussez, mes bons amis de cour;*
> *Vous n'en épargnez point, et chacun a son tour.*

> How bravely, sirs, you cut and thrust at all
> These absent fools, till one by one they fall.

Molière knows that Alceste is morally right, yet he makes him ludicrous through this outburst of wrath. Even here, the misanthrope is intellectually wrong and psychologically naïve. He fails to realize that man is the social animal par excellence, and that gossip is the most natural of all his social impulses. It is the inability to understand this that makes Alceste ridiculous. The nemesis of moral idealism is social clumsiness. Social ease is a value that Tolstoy could hardly respect: and it is with his nasty temper, or with the boorish seriousness so characteristic of Levin and himself, that he dealt with the same situation. He gave us the same picture as Molière, but he spoiled it by judging the situation *du côté de chez* Alceste, and by replacing genial laughter with disenchanted bitterness:

> Round the samovar and the hostess the conversation had been meanwhile vacillating in just the same way between three inevitable topics: the latest piece

of public news, the theatre, and scandal. It, too, finally, came finally to rest on
the last topic; that is, ill-natured gossip.

VII

The examples just given prove that the comedy and the novel of manners
portray society from the viewpoint not only of its mores but also of its culture.
In brief, they deal with the intellectual foibles, as well as with the ethical
and psychological flaws, of the milieu they have chosen as the subject of their
picture. They may even represent their characters through the highly conscious perspective of literature. This is especially true in the case of Molière,
one of whose favorite themes is the inability of a certain human type to adjust
itself to the cultural demands of a higher social status. So, for instance, the
bourgeois gentilhomme becomes ludicrous because his ambition to climb
higher in the social scale contrasts not only with his lack of breeding, but
also with his ignorance of cultural values. The *précieuses* become likewise
ridicules because they confuse affectation with elegance, and mistake fashion
for style. Molière measures intellectual and social intercourse by the standards
of the *honnête homme,* who is ruled by tact in conversation, and by taste in
the appreciation of culture. If we now apply these standards to Alceste, we
realize that he is almost wholly devoid of tact, while being richly endowed
with taste. Alceste's esthetic judgment is so keen that Molière uses him as
his mouthpiece in literary matters. As the spokesman for his author's artistic
creed, Alceste expresses a frank dislike for the mannerisms of the *précieux,*
and an outright predilection for simplicity of diction and directness of style.
Alceste states dramatically these principles in the magnificent sonnet scene,
which reveals him at once as a good critic of poetry, and as a bad judge of
human nature. The scene deserves being studied in detail, if for no other
reason than that in a similar situation neither Kostya Levin nor Leo
Tolstoy would have acted otherwise.

Oronte, whom Philinte has just introduced to Alceste, expresses his wish
to read them a sonnet he has recently composed. His purpose, or pretense, is
to get their expert opinion whether the piece is worth publishing:

> *Je viens*
> *Vous montrer un sonnet que j'ai fait depuis peu,*
> *Et savoir s'il est bon qu'au public je l'expose.*

> I intend
> To please you, if I can, with a small sonnet
> I wrote not long ago. Please comment on it.
> And tell me whether I ought to publish it.

Alceste, with some lack of candor, begs to be excused from a task for which he claims to be unfit. Yet, when Oronte questions the motive of his hesitation, he throws all prudence to the wind, and answers bluntly:

> *J'ai le défaut*
> *D'être un peu plus sincère en cela qu'il ne faut.*

> I am, I fear,
> Inclined to be unfashionably sincere.

Oronte replies that he asks for nothing better than an honest judgment, and Alceste is left with no other alternative than to comply with Oronte's request. The latter prefaces his reading with an inept apology, full of *amour propre* and false modesty. But Alceste impatiently brushes all those inanities aside, and forces Oronte to proceed with his reading.

Oronte's sonnet is written in short lines: its brevity makes it look like an epigram; its frivolity, like a madrigal. Full as it is with *pointes,* or with puns and conceits, it exemplifies in extreme form the literary ideal of *préciosité,* or, in English terms, not so much of "metaphysical poetry" as of "euphuism." In the play's context, Oronte's sonnet produces an effect of conscious parody, although, being presumably composed by someone other than Molière himself, we can only surmise whether it had been originally penned in a spirit of malice or of naïveté.[16] Philinte intervenes in every pause of the reading to marvel aloud at the poet's virtuosity, at his well-wrought phrases, at his display of wit. Alceste is shocked by the sycophancy of his friend, and rebukes him in a series of indignant asides. At the end of the reading, Philinte pays again his dutiful tribute to the vanity of Oronte, while Alceste chooses at first the path of false prudence, and condemns the poet in devious, impersonal terms. He strikes at Oronte's literary pretensions by shooting at a more general target, and he tries to soften his blows by feigning to repeat what he had said once to another would-be-writer, who remains nameless:

> *Mais un jour, à quelqu'un dont je tairai le nom,*
> *Je disais, en voyant des vers de sa façon,*
> *Qu'il faut qu'un galant homme ait toujours grand empire*
> *Sur les démangeaisons qui nous prennent d'écrire.*

> But once, to one whose name I shall not mention,
> I said, regarding some verse of his invention,
> That gentlemen should rigorously control
> That itch to write which often afflicts the soul.

Alceste concludes his tirade by advising Oronte not to become a professional author, or rather what we would now call a hack:

Si l'on peut pardonner l'essor d'un mauvais livre,
Ce n'est qu'aux malheureux qui composent pour vivre.
Croyez-moi, résistez à vos tentations,
Dérobez au public ces occupations;
Et n'allez point quitter, de quoi que l'on vous somme,
Le nom que dans la cour vous avez d'honnête homme,
Pour prendre, de la main d'un avide imprimeur,
Celui de ridicule et misérable auteur.

There's no excuse for printing tedious rot
Unless one writes for bread, as you do not.
Resist temptation, then, I beg of you;
Conceal your pastimes from the public view;
And don't give up, on any provocation,
Your present high and courtly reputation,
To purchase at a greedy printer's shop
The name of silly author and scribbling fop.

Molière was both a commoner and a man of genius. What's more important in this context, he was also a man of the theater. Even in his time the theater was a career, and had professionals as its main practitioners. Yet here Molière chooses to express through one of his characters the aristocratic conception of the artist as a cultivated and enlightened *amateur*. According to that conception, no *honnête homme* is such unless he is endowed with the *goût* of a connoisseur; but he ceases being one if he tries to become an artist himself, without being graced by the faculty La Bruyère will soon call *esprit,* and later others will name *génie*. The *honnête homme* endowed with normal or mediocre gifts may write or compose for his own benefit, but must never exhibit, even privately, the fruits of his labors or leisure. And if he is a genuine artist, the *honnête homme* will make public the products of his talent without thought of material gain, lest he reduce the cultivation of the liberal arts to the exercise of a mechanical craft. This would change the well-born man into an artisan or a merchant. Alceste fully represents this system of values. He sees no disgrace in not being a poet; but he knows that the *honnête homme* must be a critic, and above all a self-critic. While greatly admiring literature, he feels an aristocratic scorn for the scribblers, for all those who treat writing not as a vocation or an avocation but as a trade.

Oronte listens with impatience to Alceste's lecture: and when the lecture is over, asks what is wrong with his sonnet. Without further hesitation, Alceste replies that its faults are nothing less than a deplorable artificiality of feeling, and conventionality of style:

Ce n'est que jeu de mots, qu'affectation pure,
Et ce n'est point ainsi que parle la nature.

It's nothing but a sort of wordy play,
And nature never spoke in such a way.

Like every true critic, Alceste is able to point out what is good, as well as
what is bad; and he shows this ability by opposing to Oronte's sonnet an old
folksong, the *Chanson du Roi Henri*:

Si le roi m'avait donné
Paris, sa grand' ville,
Et qu'il me fallût quitter
L'amour de ma mie,
Je dirais au roi Henri:
"Reprenez votre Paris,
J'aime mieux ma mie, au gué!
J'aime mieux ma mie."

If the King had given me for my own
Paris, his citadel,
And I for that must leave alone
Her whom I love as well,
I'd say then to the Crown,
"Take back your glittering town;
My darling is more fair, I swear,
My darling is more fair."

Alceste quotes this song by heart not once, but twice. Willing as he is to
admit that its technique is unrefined, and its diction is old-fashioned, he still
claims that the song redeems such defects by sincerity of inspiration, and
by naturalness of style. Don't you see, he asks rhetorically,

que la passion parle là toute pure?

that there's passion in its every word?

and concludes, with triumphant finality:

Voilà ce que peut dire un coeur vraiment épris.

There speaks a loving heart.

Here Alceste obviously speaks with the voice of Molière: of that Molière
who tested the quality of a new play through the approval of his maid. A
great poet either is a good critic, or knows where to find one. This is true
not only of Molière, but also of Tolstoy, who, although far better at creating
literature than at judging it, was also a better critic and self-critic than it is

generally supposed. Despite his feigned indifference toward esthetic values, he was, like Alceste, a connoisseur; like him, he took art and literature very seriously, while taking far less seriously their practitioners. He belonged to a proud and traditional nobility, and this is why he felt about literary people precisely as Alceste feels. All the students of his life and works, although with different emphasis, have pointed out Tolstoy's congenital disrespect for the corporation he had to join. This disrespect toward his fellow men of letters is one of the most crucial traits of his psychological make-up.

Tolstoy first met the Russian literary greats just after the publication of his *Sebastopol Sketches*. Posterity has preserved a memento of that occasion in a group photograph representing him among such bright stars as Turgenev, Goncharov, Ostrovski, and such minor planets as Druzhinin and Grigorovich. André Suarès, describing Tolstoy's attitude as fixed in that portrait (he is the youngest member of the group, and stands stiff and proud in the background, wearing his officer's uniform), aptly observes that "he seems to be watching those people, rather than being one of their company: one could say that he is ready to bring them back to jail." [17] Tolstoy had no literary friendships, with the one exception of the poet Afanasy Foeth, who was his neighbor, and who was, despite his poetic talent, a hardheaded and a hardfisted landowner, and rather a boor. Tolstoy's feud with Turgenev, based on the younger man's irrepressible dislike for the older one, is retold in detail in all Tolstoy's biographies, and hardly does honor to him. As for Tolstoy's attitude toward Dostoevski, whom he never met, it was either overbearing or condescending, and often ambiguous, to say the least. His letters and journals amply testify to his unrelieved antipathy toward his literary colleagues and their way of life; and in one of his diaries, after having spoken of Annenkov, Goncharov, and other men of letters, he confesses: "The literary atmosphere disgusts me more than anything else."

In later and more formal writings, Tolstoy generally refrained from condemning his rivals by name and chose to indict the whole *confrérie* as a band of outcasts. This is especially true of *What is Art?* and of *A Confession*. A famous passage in the latter refers to the writer's first acquaintance with his literary brethren, with a tone of casual contempt. Yet at that meeting his majors and elders had officially consecrated the young author of the *Sebastopol Sketches* as a master of the word, and welcomed him as their peer. Tolstoy recalls that occasion in these curt and cold words: "At twenty-six years of age I returned to Petersburg after the war, and met the writers. They received me as one of themselves and flattered me. . . ." But later, Tolstoy goes on to say, "having begun to doubt the truth of the author's creed itself, I began to observe its priests more attentively, and I became convinced that almost all priests of that religion, the writers, were immoral, and for the most part men of bad, worthless character, much inferior to those whom I had met in my former, dissipated and military, life. . . ." In brief, the scorn of Tolstoy for his equals is as unmitigated as Alceste's scorn for Oronte. Tolstoy goes further than Alceste, since he condemns all men of letters as bad men as well as bad writers. Yet even this is but a logical extension of the same aristocratic attitude. The nobleman considers the writer a despicable creature on ethical as well as on social grounds, since nothing contrasts more to his own ideal of gentlemanly behavior than the *vie de bohême*. It is in the same spirit that in *What is Art?* Tolstoy condemns *in toto* the morals, as well as the manners, of the writers of his time. But what makes that book even more important is its unrestrained attack against artistic and literary professionalism. That plague or curse is for Tolstoy the root of all the evils of modern culture: "Professionalism is the first condition of the diffusion of false, counterfeit art."

There is no doubt that Tolstoy made this statement in good faith: its sincerity is not nullified even by the embarrassing circumstance that the man who spoke those words was perhaps the best paid of all the great authors of his age. Molière has stated the same view through Alceste, thus avoiding preaching directly a theory in disagreement with his practice, but in agreement with the ideas of his audience. By preaching the same doctrine, Tolstoy both denies his practice and runs against the historical trends of his time, revealing also in this his anachronistic bent and aristocratic cast of mind. Truly enough, he did not base his condemnation of professionalism on the old-fashioned notion of the writer and the artist as a gentlemanly dilettante; he was as hostile as any modern writer to genteel amateurism. It is equally true that his dislike for art as a profession derived at least in part from his cult of self-expression, from his conception of the artistic faculty as a universal gift, which may be shared by the ignorant and the unlearned, by peasants and children. This was, of course, the positive side and the progressive aspect of his doctrine, and it coincided in part with the socialist ideal of an art for all and by all, which would become a reality only in a society of equals. Yet Tolstoy's doctrine remained predominantly reactionary in spirit, being deeply rooted in a traditional aristocratic attitude, in a lofty disdain for the commercialization and industrialization of literature. Tolstoy refused to consider art as a commodity to be bought and sold, and disliked the very idea of writing and creating for gain. Art was for him the fruit of leisure, and in this context it matters very little that he wanted to change that leisure and its fruit from a class privilege into a universal right. Whether or not we consider the Tolstoyan hope of an art for all and by all as liable of realization in a near or distant future, we must still admit that that hope is highly unrealistic within the historical and social framework of modern culture. Even in Tolstoy's time artistic and literary professionalism was accepted without qualms by such different writers as the bourgeois Dickens and Thackeray, and the antibourgeois Balzac and Flaubert. All of them treated their career as professional men of letters not as an unnatural calamity, but merely as a natural necessity. Even in Russia, where so many writers were born to rank and wealth, and could enjoy, like Turgenev and Tolstoy, the privilege of creating in freedom without the pressure of want, there was at least Dostoevski, who accepted with both sorrow and pride the destiny that forced him to become a slave of the pen, or, as he said, a "proletarian of literature."

Alceste and Tolstoy are joined by other features than the ideological and sociological link of their common hatred for the shopkeepers and handymen of literature. If they seem to belong to the same type of critic, it is because they are so temperamentally akin as to take the same psychological attitudes. They face a critical challenge with the same mental posture, and react to it with the same responses. Like Alceste, Tolstoy feels equal to any critical task; he accepts one either with defiance or with only feigned hesitation. There is no need to ask him twice for his opinion: he will immediately offer it in the shape of a sharp, categorical judgment. It matters very little whether the work in question is minor and obscure, or by such a master as Beethoven or Shakespeare. Tolstoy is always a self-assured, but not always a self-controlled, critic. Like Alceste, he may ostensibly admit that his fault is to be a more outspoken judge than is fashionable or required. Yet, in their minds, both Alceste and Tolstoy consider this a merit rather than a demerit. At any rate, even if that tendency is a virtue, it has, like all virtues, its vices. Thus Tolstoy is not only outspoken and opinionated, but also biased and prejudiced. His prejudice is often based on considerations so personal as to make questionable, if not his judgment, at least its motives. This is true also of Alceste, who is led to exaggerate his condemnation of Oronte the poet by his dislike of Oronte the man, in whom he sees a rival in love, and whose sonnet seems addressed to Célimène. Generally, however, Tolstoy's slant is less subjective and more general in character, deriving from his moralistic bent, rather than from passion or interest. Yet the similarity between their critical minds is so great that there is nothing Alceste does and says in the sonnet scene that Tolstoy did not do or say numberless times in his long life. Thus, for instance, Alceste ridicules "the bad taste of the age," *le méchant goût du siècle,* as well as the mediocrity of Oronte's sonnet, by quoting most of its lines in a single rhetorical question:

> Qu'est-ce que, *Nous berce un temps notre ennui?*
> Et que, *Rien ne marche après lui?*
> Que, *Ne vous pas mettre en dépense,*
> *Pour ne me donner que l'espoir?*
> Et que, *Philis, on désespère,*
> *Alors qu'on espère toujours?*

> *For example,* Your face smiled on me awhile,
> *Followed by,* 'Twould have been fairer to smile!
> *Or this:* Such joy is full of rue;
> *Or this:* For death is fairer than the fair;
> *Or,* Phyllis, to hope is to despair
> When one must hope eternally!

Tolstoy uses the same device, only more copiously and conspicuously, in that famous chapter of *What is Art?* where he condemns the bad verse writing of his own time (by which he means the poetry of the French decadents and symbolists), by quoting in succession several poems by Baudelaire, Verlaine, Mallarmé, and Maeterlinck. To those poems, which often look like better specimens than Tolstoy thinks, he adds without comment other and worse samples by younger poets of the same school (Régnier, Vielé Griffin, Moréas, and Montesquiou), which he scornfully confines to a special appendix, where they are indicted with the mute eloquence of an accusing finger.[18]

What is Art? gives proof of Tolstoy's unconscious tendency to imitate Alceste's critical method in its "reason," as well as in its "madness." We remember that Alceste, to make Oronte's discomfiture as evident as possible, contrasts his specious and pretentious sonnet with such a simple composition as the *Chanson du Roi Henri.* The mere recitation of that folksong makes pale and insignificant the false and contrived brilliancy of the sonnet Oronte has just read. Tolstoy makes a similar, devastating use of the comparative method at least three times in *What is Art?* The first object of Tolstoy's invidious comparison is Western fiction of the end of the century, to which he opposes a children's story he had just chanced to read. Tolstoy makes his blow more telling by failing to mention the title of the story, and its author's name:

For my work on art I have this winter read diligently, though with great effort, the celebrated novels and stories praised by all Europe, written by Zola,

Bourget, Huysmans and Kipling. At the same time I chanced on a story in a child's magazine, by a quite unknown writer, who told of the preparations for Easter holidays in a poor widow's family. . . . Well! the reading of the novels and stories by Zola, Bourget, Huysmans, Kipling, and others, handling the most harrowing subjects did not touch me for one moment. . . . On the other hand, I could not tear myself away from the unknown author's tale of the children and the chicken, because I was at once infected by the feeling the author had evidently experienced, re-evoked in himself, and transmitted.

In the second case Tolstoy takes a celebrated stage interpretation of the most famous play of Western drama, and contrasts it, to its disadvantage, with the performance of a drama never committed into writing, by a group of primitive and ignorant actors. The first term of the comparison is the *Hamlet* of Shakespeare as played by Rossi; the second, the folk play of a remote Siberian tribe. While Tolstoy had watched the former, he admits, as if it were a matter of no importance, that he had not personally witnessed the latter. He had merely read about it; yet he does not care to refer to the document, nor does he bother to quote from the testimonial on which he relies. In this incredible page, Tolstoy reveals to what extreme limits he could push his critical tendentiousness, as well as his artistic iconoclasm:

I remember seeing a performance of *Hamlet* by Rossi. . . . And yet, both from the subject matter of the drama and from the performance, I experienced all the time that peculiar suffering which is caused by false imitations of works of art. But I lately read of a theatrical performance among a savage tribe — the Voguls. A spectator describes the play. . . . And from the mere description I felt that this was a work of art.

Tolstoy is quite capable of applying the same methods to his own work, of turning the same arguments against himself. In a footnote to one of the most crucial passages of *What is Art?* he places on the same scale all his literary writings, balanced against two slight pieces which no critic would ever dream of including in the canon of his work. They are a religious and a moral tale, the one written for peasants and the other for children, representing respectively his own two categories of "Christian" and "universal" art. Tolstoy claims that that little parable and that simple apologue weigh more than the whole of his narrative output, including such vast masterpieces as *Anna Karenina* and *War and Peace:* "I must moreover mention that I consign my own artistic production to the category of bad art, excepting the story 'God Sees the Truth but Waits,' which seeks a place in the first class, and 'A Prisoner in the Caucasus,' which belongs to the second."

Here Tolstoy turns his own critical misanthropy against himself. Yet, even in his worst exaggerations, he serves up to a point a literary cause which was not alien to Molière himself. What Tolstoy defends is a kind of liberal classicism, free from the taint of any pedantry or academicism. His great esthetic ideal is the natural, which he conceives of in a modern spirit, in terms of spontaneity rather than decorum. Sometimes, as Molière does, he expresses that ideal indirectly, through his fictional characters, rather than through direct statement. He does so more than once through Levin, and it is quite significant that he chose as his literary spokesman a character who does not care for literature per se. In this connection it is perhaps worth recalling that all men of letters who appear in Tolstoy's fiction are shallow and hollow men, unpleasant and even disgusting figures. Yet Tolstoy enhanced the genuineness of Levin's nature by endowing him with a fine gift for artistic appreciation. Although far less articulate and alert than Alceste, Levin is often able to make equally keen and sharp judgments. He shows his mettle in his visit to Anna, an episode which plays in Tolstoy's novel a role similar to the sonnet scene in *The Misanthrope*. The hostess and her guests are chatting when the talk suddenly shifts to artistic matters. One of the visitors attacks a modern French illustrator of the Bible for the brutal realism of his drawings. Levin, who agrees, condemns modern French fiction on the same grounds. He does so by taking a paradoxical position: while indicting French realism for its excesses, he partly justifies the latter as a reaction against the artificiality of the French tradition. Here Levin voices Tolstoy's views: "Levin said that the French had carried conventionality further than anyone, and that consequently they see a great merit in the return to realism. In the fact of not lying they see poetry." As the closing epigram shows, Levin's utterance is oracular and cryptic. By developing his point of view, Anna pays him a most charming compliment, and clarifies the fact that Tolstoy's target is here not as much realism as naturalism:

"What you said so perfectly hits off French art now, painting and literature too, indeed — Zola, Daudet. But perhaps it is always so, that men form their conceptions from fictitious, conventional types, and then — all the *combinaisons* made — they are tired of the fictitious figures and begin to invent more natural true figures."

Anna's words are very important, and the Marxist critic Georg Lukács could have aptly used them to bolster his claim that it is not Zola's naturalism, or Flaubert's estheticism, but the classical and critical realism of Tolstoy and the other Russian masters that developed the tradition opened by Balzac and Stendhal.[19] Yet those words, which reflect so fully Tolstoy's thought, may also be seen as further proof of that writer's refusal to accept the main artistic trends of his age. This implies that Tolstoy was an eccentric not only as a man, but also as a writer and a critic. In this too he resembles Alceste, who prefers to follow other standards than the critical norms of his time. Alceste may violate the social code of his class by tearing Oronte's unlucky sonnet to shreds, but he also violates its literary code when he measures that sonnet by other yardsticks than those of Boileau. When he reads his sonnet, Oronte expects it to be judged by a critic of the traditional type. The most perfect manifestation of this type is the *arbiter elegantiarum,* or the "man in the know," who assesses the exquisite quality of a single detail with the same sureness of taste with which a gourmet appraises the delicacy of a dish, or a man of fashion judges the refinement of a piece of clothing. Oronte is instead suddenly faced with someone judging his sonnet as a whole, and condemning it not on formal or technical grounds, but for the total failure of its inspiration. Even when he points out a few minor blemishes, Alceste's aim is not to help the author to correct or to improve his sonnet, but to force him to acknowledge the "original sin" of his own creation.

In this, Alceste may indeed go beyond his creator's conscious intent, and seems to anticipate esthetic and critical attitudes yet to come. Thus, for instance, when he says:

> *ce n'est point ainsi que parle la nature,*
>
> nature never spoke in such a way,

he seems to speak with the voice of Diderot and Rousseau, rather than that of the writers of his century. By "nature" Alceste means something more lively and spontaneous than was generally meant in his tradition or age; in brief, an inspiration ruled not so much by *goût* as by *génie. Génie* must be understood in the preromantic, rather than in the romantic sense of that term, or in a meaning already very close to that it acquired in the *Sturm und Drang,* a period which was also called *Geniezeit.* For the men of that epoch, *génie* meant both creativity and personality. Tolstoy seems to share their view of art and poetry as a "voice of nature," as the self-expression of the psyche. This is why Tolstoy the critic follows no other criteria than those of sincerity and insincerity. Like Alceste, Tolstoy condemns an artistic work at first glance, merely because it fails to produce on him an impression of naturalness and simplicity; only later, as he does in *What is Art?* with a few poems by Verlaine, he analyzes at length all the external symptoms that may prove that he was right in his diagnosis. The greatest artistic malady is for him what one might call emotional atrophy, and often he defines the works he dislikes as "works *à froid,* cold drawn, without feeling." In the sonnet scene Alceste attacks not only Oronte as a false poet, but also Philinte as a false

critic; and Tolstoy indicts in mass, for the same reason, the critics as well
as the artists of his time. He considers the former no less responsible than
the latter for the falseness of modern art, and treats them as if they were not
merely the Philintes, but the Tartuffes of literature: "Every false work of art
extolled by critics serves as a door through which the hypocrites of art at
once crowd in."

By "hypocrites of art" Tolstoy doubtless meant the exponents and sup-
porters of the two main artistic and literary currents dominating the culture
of his age: on one side the "decadents," and on the other, the "naturalists."
He always felt that both groups sinned against nature, the one through its
pathological subjectivism and morbid artificiality, the other through a passive objectivity and a sordid acceptance of reality. It was in reaction against
an art enslaved by either our brains or our senses that Tolstoy, in his early
youth, proclaimed an art based on "the understanding of the heart." In the
preface to *Childhood* he contrasted that kind of understanding with the
purely mental one by means of a felicitous simile:

> One may sing in two ways: from the throat or from the chest. Is it not true
> that a voice from the throat is much more flexible than one from the chest, but
> then, on the other hand, it does not set on your soul. . . . It is the same in litera-
> ture: one may write from the head or from the heart. . . . It may be a mistake,
> but I always checked myself when I began to write from my head, and tried to
> write only from my heart. . . .

It is from the simple seeds of such thoughts that Tolstoy slowly developed
all the doctrines he finally set down in *What is Art?* That early page contains in a nutshell the main belief of his later literary creed: that, when
inspired by genuine feeling, art transmits itself to the hearts of all men with
the overwhelming power of an infectious disease, through the "contagion"
of its emotions. Despite its romantic appearance, this Tolstoyan view of
artistic communication is classical in temper. The empathy he advocates
is based not on a passionate but on an *understanding* heart. As for the
theory of "contagion," it presupposes a natural, spontaneous exchange, rather
than the operation of willful witchcraft. Yet it was through an artificial
sorcery that the literary artists of the new generation tried to convey to a
limited group of readers the cold magic of their private worlds. They considered form as the vessel, and words as the vehicle, of art. Tolstoy, however,
never believed in the suggestive or evocative power of a deliberate style, nor
in the incantatory power of the word. This made him one of the very few
modern literary creators who failed to play up the verbal side of their calling
or craft. The indifference or the hostility he felt toward poetry were in part

an effect of this neglect. As a writer, he ignored poetry, up to the point of hardly composing a single verse in his whole life, and as a critic, he turned to poetry only to find there examples of "bad art." He would have resisted the modern attempt to reduce prose to the condition of poetry as strongly as he resisted in his own time the attempt to reduce it to the condition of music. He treated the epithet "poetic" as a term of opprobrium, as a contemptuous synonym for falsity in art. In *What is Art?* he gave a negative definition of that epithet and of all it implies in style as well as in content. It is obvious, and yet significant, that he condemned as "poetic" what others prefer to condemn under such labels as "conventional" and "literary":

Thus, in our circle, all sorts of legends, sagas and ancient traditions are considered poetic subjects. Among poetic people and objects we reckon maidens, warriors, shepherds, hermits, angels, devils of all sorts, moonlight, thunder, mountains, the sea, precipices, flowers, long hair, lions, lambs, doves, and nightingales. In general all those objects are considered poetic which have most frequently been used by former artists in their productions.

"Poetic means borrowed": this is how Tolstoy concludes his indictment against any form of literary sham. By this denial of the "poetic" Tolstoy reasserts his esthetic ideal, which is that of a classicism based more on the imitation of nature than on the imitation of art. Tolstoy's classicism is based on the primacy of sense over sound, rather than of sound over sense, on the belief that even in poetry it is rhyme that must agree with reason, not reason with rhyme. In this too Tolstoy runs against the trend of modern literature, which from romanticism on has tended more and more to treat prose as if it were verse, while the classical ages have done exactly the opposite. This is why, while many of his contemporaries would have chosen "prosaic" as the most negative of all critical terms, Tolstoy chose "poetic" instead. Such a choice was natural on the part of a writer who considered prose the natural idiom of both life and art.

Yet even though he was, so to speak, the great Monsieur Jourdain of modern writing, Tolstoy was always able to distinguish between the prose of life and the prose of art. While despising the esthetic bent of French realism, he knew as well as Flaubert and the other masters of the *écriture artiste* that literary creation is the art of taking infinite pains, that perfection is elusive, and may escape the writer unless he pins it down with the help of *le mot juste,* or through the right cadence and turn. Tolstoy stated this principle in a famous page of *What is Art?*

I have elsewhere quoted the profound remark of the Russian artist Bryulov on art, but I cannot here refrain from repeating it, because nothing better illustrates what can, and what cannot, be taught in the schools. Once when correcting a pupil's study, Bryulov just touched it in a few places and the poor dead study immediately became animated. "Why, you only touched it a *wee bit,* and it is quite another thing!" said one of the pupils. "Art begins where the *wee bit* begins," replied Bryulov, indicating by these words just what is most characteristic of art. The remark is true of all the arts, but its justice is particularly noticeable in the performance of music . . . so that the feeling of infection by the art of music, which seems so simple and so easily obtained, is a thing we receive only when the performer finds those infinitely minute degrees which are necessary to perfection in music. It is the same in all arts: a wee bit lighter, a wee bit darker, a wee bit higher, lower, to the right or to the left, in painting; a wee bit weaker or stronger in intonation, a wee bit sooner or later in dramatic art; a wee bit omitted, over-emphasized, or exaggerated in poetry, and there is no contagion. Infection is only obtained when an artist finds those infinitely minute degrees of which a work of art consists, and only to the extent to which he finds them.

Even in this statement Tolstoy fails to emphasize, as Flaubert would have done, that the artist's quest for perfection is an ordeal and a strife, a torture or a martyrdom. Tolstoy prefers to think that the artist is guided in that quest by an inborn wisdom or by an inner grace: more simply, by the sure feeling of what is right and what is wrong. That feeling was once called *goût.* By this deference to the authority of taste, Tolstoy here speaks again as a classic, rather than as a modern, artist. The words just quoted seem to recall La Bruyère's claim that the genuine artist or critic instinctively recognizes the ineffable and imponderable values of form. The gift of recognizing those values is negative and subjective, but the values themselves, although intangible, are objective and absolute. The miracle of art may be a *je ne sais quoi,* but that *quoi* is a *quid*:

> There is in art a point of perfection, as there is a point of goodness and maturity in nature. Those who feel and love it have a perfect taste; those who do not feel that point, or whose likings fall short of its mark, or overshoot it, have a defective taste. Thus there is both a good and a bad taste: and one argues about tastes with good reason.[20]

VIII

A comic archetype is to be taken no less seriously than a tragic one. While doing so, one must, however, avoid the temptation to change the former into the latter. This is precisely the mistake Rousseau made in his critique of *The Misanthrope,* where he presumed to understand Alceste better than Molière ever did. That critique should be discussed for no other reason than that Tolstoy would have more readily recognized his own likeness in Rousseau's distorted reflection than in Molière's original picture.

This is hardly surprising when we realize that Rousseau redrew Alceste's portrait in his own image, and that often Tolstoy himself, a long time before books were written to prove this point, felt he was a moral twin of Rousseau. The young Tolstoy patterned his life and ideas on the model of the Swiss master as soon as an early reading of *The Confessions* made him fall in love with the author of that book. In his late years, in a conversation reported by Paul Boyer, he recalled his youthful infatuation for Rousseau with the following words: "I worshipped him. I wore on my neck his portrait in a locket, as if it were a holy image." [21] It is true that with the passing of time he turned against his idol, whom in his old age he judged rather harshly, as shown in his statement to Gorki that "Rousseau lied and believed his lies." Yet one cannot deny that without Rousseau Tolstoy would have been a far different person than he was. Rousseau's misinterpretation of Alceste's misanthropy may be far from misleading if applied to the misanthropy of Tolstoy himself. Alceste becomes more like Tolstoy if we look at him through the eyes of Rousseau rather than of Molière.

Rousseau's critique of *The Misanthrope* can be found in his polemical epistle to D'Alembert, generally known under the title *Lettre sur les Spectacles*. The whole letter is an indictment of the theater, which the author condemns on the same grounds as Tolstoy, for being both conventional and immoral. The critique itself is but a part of the section on comedy, which Rousseau considers more dangerous than tragedy, since it portrays passions and vices all too accessible to the average man. With good strategy, Rousseau concentrates his attack on Molière as the recognized master of the genre. The assault opens with the rhetorical question: "Who will . . . refuse to admit that the theater of this Molière, whose talents I admire more than anyone, is but a school of vice and bad morals?" After a few more generalities, Rousseau turns to *The Misanthrope*, as Molière's acknowledged masterpiece. All he does in his re-examination of that play is to re-evaluate Alceste at the expense of Molière. While praising the edifying and exemplary morality of the ideal character Molière had chosen to represent, Rousseau blames the playwright for having drawn not a portrait, but a caricature. Rousseau undertakes to redress this wrong, and starts his apology with an almost romantic praise of the misanthrope as a critic of society, as the moral conscience of his generation: "What is then Molière's misanthrope? An honorable man detesting the mores of his age and the wickedness of the men of his time; who, precisely because he loves his fellow men, hates in them their reciprocal evildoings, and the vices producing them."

In brief, Rousseau separates the creature from his creator, and deals with

Alceste as if he were a real person, whom Molière had supposedly libeled. According to Rousseau, Molière chose to emphasize not Alceste's major qualities, but his minor foibles. By phrasing this accusation in seventeenth- rather than in eighteenth-century terms, one could say that Alceste's creator criticized an *homme de bien* merely because he was not at the same time an *honnête homme.* (Rousseau, however, uses *honnête homme* in its modern sense, as a synonym of *homme de bien,* and prefers to convey the same meaning through the less flattering formula *homme de monde.*) What Rous- seau claims is simply that Molière was unfair to his character, since he mocked his social shortcomings without paying the tribute due to the nobil- ity of his soul. What's even worse, the final effect of all this was that Molière made fun not only of Alceste's defects, but also of his virtues:

> He did not endeavor to form an honest man, but a man of the world: consequently, he aimed at correcting not what is vicious, but what is merely ridiculous; and, as I have already said, he found in vice itself a suitable tool to help him in doing this. Thus, intending to expose to public laughter all the short- comings contrary to the qualities of the sociable and likable man, after having made fun of so many foibles, the only one still left to him to play up was that which the world least forgives, i.e., the ridicule of virtue: and this is what he did in the Misanthrope.

The chief argument of Rousseau's apology for Alceste deals with his would-be misanthropy. Rousseau claims that Alceste's misanthropy is but the reverse side of the love he feels for his fellow men. Since men are all too ready to commit evil, or unwilling to resist it, misanthropy is both just and necessary; and it testifies to the moral nobility of the all too rare beings who hate mankind for its vices: "Thus only a great and noble soul may be affected by it. . . . There is no honest man who is not a misanthrope in this sense." Rousseau rejects the general opinion that Alceste may be right in theory, but that he is wrong in practice; that his extreme idealism leads him to commit the error, and even the injustice, of condemning as absolute evils the most venial sins. A really honest man, after all, should forgive and forget. Rousseau instead praises Alceste even for his worst exaggerations, since they are but the logical consequence of the fanaticism of virtue: "Truly enough, it is not worth while to remain a misanthrope if you are one only by half. . . ." Attack is the best defense, and Rousseau strikes with savage irony at Philinte, who plays the role of Alceste's antagonist, while acting at the same time as the mouthpiece of Molière, or as the spokesman of the society for which Molière wrote:

This Philinte is the sage of the play: one of those gentlemen of high society whose principles look very much like those of the scoundrels; of those people so sweet and amiable as to find that everything goes well, since it is in their interest that nothing go better. . . .

How easy it is to recognize in this portrait of Philinte, as redrawn by Rousseau, the perfect and eternal model of all those wise men of the world whom Tolstoy judges in *Anna Karenina* and *Resurrection* through the critical eyes of Konstantin Levin and Dmitri Neklyudov! And how equally easy it is to admit that Tolstoy looks far more like Alceste now that his likeness is compared not with Molière's original, but with a copy corrected by the hand of Rousseau!

Rousseau finds inexcusable in Molière his having forced such a "forthright and upright" character as Alceste "to cut a ridiculous figure." He condemns the author through the character himself, who, according to him, "hates calumny and detests satire." Calumny and satire are equally alien to high comedy, which is serious in temper; and they are wholly absent from this portrayal of Tolstoy as Alceste, whether *secundum* Rousseau or *secundum* Molière. The modern mind, however, may prefer to look at Tolstoy according to the first rather than to the second alternative. This is only natural. Tolstoy's misanthropy, after all, was of a kind conceivable only within a culture placing the individual far higher than his own society. Yet even so, Tolstoy's plight cannot be understood in the key of tragedy, but only of tragicomedy. It is in this key that the romantic mind reinterpreted the type of the misanthrope, as well as his plight. Such a reinterpretation reverses the original comic situation, since it is society that now becomes the butt of the satire.

Romantic criticism is full of such paradoxical reappraisals of Molière's masterpiece, yet it fell upon Russian culture to rewrite an inverted version of *The Misanthrope*. This is what Griboyedov did in *Woe from Wit,* a comedy of great interest on literary, as well as on historical, grounds: above all, for its almost perfect fusion of new values and old views. This fusion is evident even in the play's original title, *Gore ot uma,* where *um* is used, like the English "wit," as a double synonym for seventeenth-century *esprit* and eighteenth-century *génie.* In brief, what the title intended to convey is that it is a misfortune to be endowed with an original mind and with a singular personality. The play's protagonist, Chatski, is a Russian Alceste who returns home after having spent a few years abroad. Experience suddenly disappoints his naïve enthusiasm. His fiancée prefers to him a vain and vulgar opportunist, while the pillars of society mock his unpractical idealism. Unable to readjust himself to the corruption of this world, Chatski condemns that corruption with such violence as to leave society no other way out than to declare officially insane the only one of its members who is endowed with a lucid mind and a noble soul. Modern society likewise treats misanthropes as more or less dangerous fools, but from romanticism on, the poets of that society have preferred to consider the Alcestes and the Chatskis as either heroes or victims, rather than as misfits. This is only natural, since those poets like to play the misanthrope's role, and cannot fail to feel love, admiration, and pity for the Alceste or Chatski in themselves. Tolstoy himself was a far more realistic Alceste, and a far less romantic Chatski, and did not need to go into the world to know that society would treat him like a fool. Like all modern misanthropes, he hated society a priori, even before experiencing its falseness and deceit.

Society, in its turn, need not be deceived by Tolstoy's misanthropy, of which one could say what Rousseau said of Alceste's: "A convincing proof that Alceste is not a misanthrope in the literal sense is that despite all his temperamental excesses he still remains interesting and likable. . . . Although there are in Alceste some real shortcomings which deserve being laughed at, we cannot however help but feel respect for him in the bottom of our heart. . . ." This is perhaps the only point where Rousseau understates his case. As for our own Alceste, he was far more than merely interesting and likeable. He was a genius in the romantic as well as in the Rousseauistic definition of that term. By *génie* Rousseau meant not the originality of the active mind, but the originality of the passive soul. Tolstoy shared Rousseau's belief in the supreme value of the Self. The greatest paradox of his life and work is perhaps that, while being the outstanding creative mind of his age, he still exalted psychological originality to the detriment of esthetic originality. For him a man could become an artist only by remaining the kind of man he was born to be.

IX

A portrait painter, when he wishes to convey more than a physical likeness, represents his model against the background best suited to him. If he chooses to portray his subject wearing a costume or playing an assumed role, then the artist projects the human image against an ideal landscape. Background and landscape provide the portrait with the proper atmosphere, and place the character within a broader frame. The portrait painter is a kind of emblematic biographer, and like all biographers, he must satisfy the conflicting demands of psychology and history. This applies also to this literary portrait, which up to now has, however, represented its model with the help of psychology alone. Now history must come to the portraitist's aid. After all, Tolstoy resembles Alceste psychologically because he resembles him historically. Truly enough, Tolstoy looks more like Alceste when the latter is contemplated through later reinterpretations, rather than through the original version, of his character. This simply means that Tolstoy may be understood better through the cultural perspective of the eighteenth century than through that of the seventeenth. The task of the following pages is to prove this point, which could be summed up by saying that Tolstoy resembles in Rousseau's age other figures than Rousseau, and that, in a far more limited way, he resembles also, in Molière's age, other figures than Molière. While fulfilling this task, we may seem to lose sight of Alceste. This is not true: even if Alceste reappears only at the end of this essay, he will remain ideally present also in this particular inquiry, at least as a cultural symbol, if not as a psychological type.

Tolstoy is one of those rare figures who represent a cultural span far greater than that of their age. Like Goethe, whom Friedrich Schlegel defined as both the Shakespeare and the Voltaire of his own nation and time,[22] Tolstoy was a child of both the enlightenment and the nineteenth century. He was one of the few great men of his generation who was deeply rooted, and felt always at home, in the culture of *le siècle des lumières*. The cultural hero of *le siècle des lumières* had been the man of letters, understood not as a magician of words (like the poet for the romantics), or as a craftsman of style (as the novelist for Flaubertian realism), but as a critic and a teacher of life, as a shaper of thought and as a spreader of truth. Nothing conveys such a conception as fully as the names of *philosophe* and *Aufklärer,* by which the great masters of the eighteenth century chose to label themselves. Besides being a modern literary artist, Tolstoy was also a *philosophe* or an *Aufklärer* in the old-fashioned sense of those terms. This justifies the traditional parallel between him and Rousseau on historical, as well as on psychological, grounds. Yet Rousseau was not the whole of eighteenth-century thought. As for Tolstoy, he was not only the Rousseau of his age, but the Voltaire too.

Both paradoxically and properly, the Voltairian cast of Tolstoy's mind is nowhere so apparent as in the polemical side of his religious writings, although it is evident even in some of his less ideological works. In the *pars construens* of his religious doctrine, Tolstoy follows the example of Rousseau's *confession de foi,* by listening predominantly to the dictates of his conscience and heart. In the *pars destruens,* however, he adopts quite naturally the Voltairian method, cutting to shreds with razor-sharp reasoning and savage mockery all ecclesiastical sham. The cry "écrasez l'infâme" seems to re-echo continuously in the religious controversy of this would-be evangelist. There is no better example of this than the concluding page of a work to which he gave an almost Kantian title: *A Critique of Dogmatic Theology.* There, with impeccable logic and with devastating irony, he sums up all the hollow answers organized religion gives to man's tragic questions about life and death:

He asks that, and God by the mouth of the Church gives him this reply: You want to know what this world is? It is this: There is one God, all-knowing, all-good, and almighty. He is simply a spirit, but He has will and reason. This God is one, and at the same time three. The Father begot a Son, and the Son is in the flesh, and sits at the right hand of His Father. The Holy Spirit proceeded from the Father. All three of them are God, and they are all different and all the same. . . .[23]

In the rest of this page Tolstoy, with bitter sarcasm, doubly criticizes the vain reply the church gives to the "why's" man eternally asks. On one side, he confronts that reply with the Rousseauian demands of our heart, which needs the living spirit of faith and belief, while it is offered instead the dead letter of the dogma, a cold and rigid doctrine which confuses and repels. Our soul hungers for bread, and is given a stone. On the other side, he shows that that answer contravenes the Voltairian claims of our reason, the laws of logic, the requirements of what Dostoevski's Ivan Karamazov would call our "Euclidian mind." And it is with the lucid, even cynical, skepticism of such modern Biblical scholars as Strauss or Renan, as well as with the biting irony of a Voltaire, that Tolstoy points out further on the natural and logical impossibilities of God's creation of the world, as reported in Genesis: "There was a morning and an evening for the first day. If there was no sun during the first days, God himself shook the illuminating matter that there might be a morning and evening." It is significant that Tolstoy found it proper, without fear of being accused of either plagiarism or vulgarity, to point out again the most obvious of all scriptural absurdities, which so many minds had observed even before modern science and modern Biblical criticism. No better demonstration could be found of Tolstoy's tendency to think in eighteenth- rather than in nineteenth-century terms. The truth of this may be confirmed by a negative proof: by showing, for instance, that one of his greatest contemporaries used the same Biblical reference to teach a contrary lesson, and to affirm opposite values. In an episode of *The Brothers*

Karamazov Dostoevski caused one of his characters to underscore the same scriptural absurdity; yet he did so only to prove that that critical observation was a sign not only of intellectual immaturity, but even of a wicked and twisted understanding. While drawing a retrospective portrait of the bastard Smerdyakov, a scoundrel and a flunkey, Dostoevski reports a telling incident of his childhood. The aged, stern, and pious servant Grigori, who had taken the foundling Smerdyakov into his house, was one day teaching the Scripture to his ward, then a boy twelve years old. They were reading the first chapter of Genesis, when Grigori noticed an impious grin on the boy's face. This is how the clever and blasphemous child answered the old man's indignant question why he was smiling: "Oh, nothing. God created light on the first day, and the sun, moon, and stars on the fourth day. Where did the light come from on the first day?" [24] As any reader of Dostoevski's novel is well aware, Smerdyakov is but a caricature of Ivan Karamazov, who symbolizes the disloyalty of intelligence, with its Luciferian rebellion not so much against the Creator, as against the world He created. As such, Ivan Karamazov transcends the protest of Voltaire, although he himself quotes the name of that old sinner, with ambiguous sympathy, at least once in the story. Beyond the Voltairianism he shares with Smerdyakov, and perhaps even with Fyodor Karamazov, Ivan represents modern scientific rationalism, with its proud challenge to anything that is mysterious and sacred. Thus Dostoevski condemns in Smerdyakov and Ivan Karamazov the Western notion of reason, the absolute claim of the logical spirit.

Tolstoy, however, fully agreed with that notion, although he saw in the logical faculty a critical power, rather than a creative one. Thus he agreed with Rousseau in refusing to consider reason the best instrument to discover the meaning of life, but agreed with Voltaire in viewing it as the aptest tool to reveal what is unreal and untrue. And he used that weapon, as naïvely as Alceste, and as consistently as Voltaire, any time he wished to attack anything that looked to him like a lie, even if others saw there revealed truth or myth. The idea that man cannot do without reason, although reason by itself is not enough, is after all the position of Kant; and there is an important page in *A Confession* where Tolstoy restates that position as his own: "I wish to recognize anything inexplicable as being so not because the demands of my reason are wrong, but because I recognize the limits of my intellect." Thus, exactly like Kant, Tolstoy conceived of reason as a critical tool; but, being more of a *philosophe* in the French manner than a philosopher in the German sense of that term, he preferred to confuse *Vernunft* and *Verstand,* and refused to distinguish logic from intelligence. In this, he was like Voltaire, although the comparison may be a misleading one, since Tolstoy was a critic of society, but not a reformer, and also because the God he tried to believe in was not the God of Voltaire, but the God of Rousseau.

One could even say that Tolstoy's God was the God of Pascal, since he saw in Him a Supreme Being speaking directly to man's heart. For Tolstoy, as well as for that great contemporary of Molière, religion and faith were to be primarily rooted in the faculty of feeling. This does not mean that the believer must reject the help of intelligence, which may serve as a guiding light in his attempt to penetrate the divine truth hidden under the all too human veil of myth. Both Pascal and Tolstoy felt that there is only one faculty which could hinder man in his quest after God. To this faculty, which he considered equally opposed to feeling and understanding, Pascal gave the name of "imagination." For him imagination played in man's life the role of *la folle du logis*. In brief, Pascal conceived of imagination in psychological rather than in esthetic terms, and viewed it as a form of daydreaming and wishful thinking, leading us to self-deceit. Reason, instead, if used widely, strengthens, rather than weakens, the faith of man. With almost classical moderation, the religious mind must avoid both the "two excesses" of "excluding reason, or of admitting nothing besides it."

This is all the more necessary since God's revelation seems to fail to satisfy what one might call the Cartesian demands of reason itself, because "God fails to reveal Himself to men with all the evidence at His disposal." Such evidence, by which Pascal means the unequivocal logic of a direct statement, is particularly lacking in the Old Testament, where God, to reveal his truth to a primitive people like the Jews, who could understand only the material language of things, had to speak in images, or, as we would now say, in mythical terms. This is why Pascal says, "the Old Testament is only figurative." Pascal sees a great danger in this, since metaphorical and mythical imagery may strike our fancy, without convincing our mind or conquering our soul. This appeal to our imagination, as a matter of fact, may lead astray our sentiment even more than our intellect, since "men often mistake their imagination for their heart." God's revelation is happily not limited to the Hebrew books. One of the blessings of the new tidings was that the Gospel spoke not the language of the letter, but the language of the spirit. For Pascal, the Saviour redeemed man from his errors, as well as from his sins: Jesus Christ "came to take the figures away, and to put truth in their place." Christ was "the light that shines in the darkness," and Pascal conceived of that light in moral as well as in logical terms, as shown by his claim that "all that does not go toward charity is mere figure." Yet he often treated Christ not only as the Redeemer, but also as a spiritual *Aufklärer,* or as the Divine Being who dissipated the barbaric obscurity of the ancient religion and replaced it with classical clarity, as the prophet who resolved the confused poetry of the Old Testament into the lucid prose of the New.[25]

Strangely enough, Tolstoy took toward the Scriptures the same position as Pascal did. He too overemphasized the spirit to the detriment of the letter. He too distrusted the imagination and its power to distort even the Holy Writ. Quite naturally, he took an even more extreme stand than Pascal's, and denied to the Old Testament even the symbolic significance which no Christian apologist could fail to attribute to it. In short, he dared to reinterpret the faith of the Messias without taking into account the books that had prophesied His advent. He did so from the very earliest among his many evangelical tracts, in the preface of which he spoke thus:

> I do not consider the Old Testament, for the question is not what was the faith of the Jews, but in what does the faith of Christ consist. . . . The faith of the Jews, foreign to us, is as interesting to us as is, for instance, the faith of the Brahmins.

In brief, Tolstoy accepted the Pauline distinction between the dead letter and the living spirit at least as fully as Pascal, and claimed even more fully that that spirit breathes in the New Testament alone. He said so in the introduction to *The Gospel in Brief:* "The source of Christian teaching is the Gospels, and in them I found the explanation of the spirit which guides the life of all who really live." Finally, acting in this case more like Voltaire than like Pascal, he maintained that even in the Gospels the letter all too often deadens the spirit; that the fictions of imagination, or the importance of superstition, all too often obscure even there the light of faith, or the mirror of truth. Tolstoy did not hesitate to state this view with a repellent image, and in strong words:

> But together with this source of the pure water of life I found, wrongfully united with it, mud and slime which had hidden its purity from me: by the side of and bound up with the lofty Christian teaching, I found a Hebrew and a church teaching alien to it. I was in the position of a man who receives a bag of stinking dirt, and only after long struggle and much labor finds that amid that dirt lie priceless pearls: and he understands that he was not to blame for disliking the stinking dirt. . . .

As soon as he realized this, Tolstoy decided to be the man who would sift the pearls of Christ's faith from tradition's mud. With blasphemous daring, he did so by following both a medieval precedent and a modern example, and compiled an "evangelical harmony," [26] or a fusion of the Four Gospels into a single one. But while "evangelical harmonies," whether inspired by a mystical or a critical spirit, are generally produced through a process of accumulation and consolidation, with the reluctant omission of only those details that stand in glaring contradiction with the whole, Tolstoy adopted a far more stringent and rigorous canon: he expunged from the text as inane interpolations all passages offending either his sentiment or his reason. Thus he gave us a Gospel *secundum* Tolstoy, devoid of irrationality, deprived of metaphysical and mystical vision, despoiled of metaphors and symbols, mutilated of its miracles, and sometimes of its parables as well. By killing the letter, he killed also the spirit; and the outcome of this was that he finally dispensed not only with religion, but even with God: "I regard Christianity neither as a divine revelation nor as a historical phenomenon, but as a teaching which gives us the meaning of life. . . ."

Thus, by using the weapons of reason with neither pity nor piety, Tolstoy destroyed not only religion but science itself. His radical historical skepticism led him to deny not only sacred history, but human history as well. To do so, he had to be all at once a new Pascal and a new Voltaire, a new Kant and a new Rousseau; he had to be a skeptic and a believer, an idolater and an iconoclast, a classicist and a realist, in brief, Leo Tolstoy himself. To achieve this supreme paradox of his work and life, he had to be a new Alceste, equally unwilling to submit either his conscience to his consciousness, or his consciousness to his conscience. Refusing to be servant of the two spiritual rulers of his time, which were science and faith, he became their master, and forced them to do the bidding of both his mind and heart.

X

One could say that Tolstoy's achievements and failures proceed in part from his psychological dilemma, that they derive from the inner dualism of his problematic nature. On one side he strikes us with his liberality of mind, with an unmatched power to grasp the whole range of life. On the other, he surprises us with the one-sidedness of his concern not with human existence but with "what men live by." Two souls fight in his breast, one asserting the primacy of thinking, and the other, of being. Now, like Dmitri Karamazov, he would love life above anything else; now, like Dmitri's brother, Ivan, he would worship merely "the meaning of life." Isaiah Berlin adumbrated this conflict in a paradox he derived from a line by Archilochus. A sentence preserved among the fragments of that poet claims that the fox may know many little things, and the hedgehog only one, but big. Mr. Berlin extends this antithesis to the world of the spirit, dividing all writers and thinkers into "hedgehogs," who "relate everything to a single central vision, one system more or less coherent and articulate, in terms of which they understand, think and feel," and into "foxes," who "lead lives, perform acts, and entertain ideas that are centrifugal rather than centripetal, seizing upon the essence of a vast variety of experiences and objects for what they are in themselves." After having so defined his two categories, Mr. Berlin advances the hypothesis that "Tolstoy was by nature a fox, but he thought he was a hedgehog." If this were true, it would mean in political terms that in Tolstoy the liberal fox was stronger than the conservative hedgehog, or, in religious terms, that his pagan consciousness was stronger than his puritan conscience. This would also deny the schism of his soul, and reduce it to a matter of mere appearance. That schism, however, was his destiny, and the token of his greatness. Tolstoy himself saw contradiction and conflict as part of the human condition, as the lot of that feeling and thinking reed which is man. In his moods of Olympic serenity, when he could master or transcend his inner rifts, he considered contradiction as the most precious of man's gifts. Gorki once had the privilege of catching the old man in one of these moods, and of fixing that instant forever, to posterity's benefit. The aged master and the younger writer were sitting together among the cypresses of Crimea, listening to the song of a chaffinch. Tolstoy talked a while about the extreme jealousy which that bird seems to feel for its mate, and this led him to discuss human jealousy as well. Tolstoy concluded his talk with the remark that man becomes love's slave when woman holds him not by his lust, but by his soul. By way of objection, Gorki reminded Tolstoy that his *Kreutzer Sonata* was the very contradiction of what he had just said. All he got in reply was the radiance of a sudden smile beaming through Tolstoy's beard, and the single retort: "But I am not a chaffinch."

No, Tolstoy was not a chaffinch, nor was he a fox or a hedgehog, or, rather, he was both. He was perhaps more of a hedgehog as a man, and more of a fox as an artist; and this is why he smiled with Philinte's indulgence toward life, and frowned like Alceste on his fellow men. Yet this does not mean that we can sever in him the Philinte from the Alceste, the hedgehog from the fox, or the man from the artist. It was the inner discord of his personality that made him unique. Only by realizing this may we solve the most vexing question of Tolstoy's biography, which is whether the unrelenting warfare which as a convert and a doctrinaire he waged against the poet and the creator within himself ended in victory or defeat. The outcome of that issue was obviously a double triumph for the man and the artist. Rainer Maria Rilke was one of the few who saw this, as shown by the letter in which

he re-evokes, almost a quarter of a century later, the visits he had paid to
Tolstoy in his youth:

His very figure appeared to me like the personification of a fatality, of a misunderstanding: and in the end it moved me, since, despite all the obstinate
wrongs that fiercely unruly man did to himself, and was always willing to do to
others, he still seemed to remain touchingly valid and safe even when rebelling
against his greatest and most evident duties. It was in this way and no other that
a young man like me, who had already decided to devote all his life to art, could
understand that self-contradictory old man, trying to stifle within his soul what
had been divinely imposed on it; who with tireless effort foreswore himself even
in his own blood, but who failed to control the immense energies inexhaustibly
renewed by his artist's nature, being repressed and denied by him. How lofty
(and how pure!) stood he above all those, the majority in Europe, who, unlike
him, doubting those energies all their life, had resolved to hide with skill and
deceit (with "literature") the temporary decline, or the absence, of their creative
powers! [27]

What Rilke says here is simply that Tolstoy never played any stock role,
that in all he did he acted, like his Levin, out of "a perfectly new, unexpected view of things." This perpetual freshness of outlook was rooted in his
very being, and the artist expressed it simply and directly without ever
trying to enhance it. The classical simplicity of his writing achieved very
often the opposite effect, by attenuating the singular novelty of his vision,
and by reducing to the level of the natural the almost unnatural wonders of
his unique Self. This is why, unlike so many of the artists of our time, he
never attempted to correct, improve, or transform himself as an artist. The
only "counsel of perfection" he sought to follow was, if not religious, chiefly
ethical in character. Yet this "counsel of perfection" never implied, even
after the so-called conversion, the notion of a personal metamorphosis or a
radical psychological change. In early Christianity, the pagan convert considered himself a new man, as if he were reborn. But Tolstoy, who always
reacted against both death and life with the stubborn "I don't want to" of
his own Ivan Ilich,[28] was never seduced by the idea of rebirth. He wanted
to remain eternally who he was, or perhaps to become more fully what he
had always been. He could have said of himself what he said once of his
hero Levin: "He felt himself, and did not want to be anyone else. All he
wanted now was to be better than before."

It is perhaps in this paradoxical ability to reconcile within himself the
contrasting demands of becoming and being that there lies the greatest
difference between Tolstoy and Alceste. The latter has settled forever all
moral problems in his intransigent code of behavior, as well as in his in-

tolerant mind, and it is this weakness that makes him a comic type. In a high and noble sense, Alceste always remains the extreme and rigid manifestation of the hypochondriac "humor" which is the basis of his character. In other words, he will play to the end the role of the crank and the "eccentric" in a social and moral milieu which does not value exception and eccentricity. Tolstoy's character, however, was never fixed into a rigid mold; his, to use Montaigne's term, was an "undulating" nature. In brief, while Alceste cannot stand contradictions, which deny or destroy his very being, Tolstoy seems to prosper and grow stronger amidst them. Such a contrast is not merely psychological, but also historical in character. The culture that created Molière's misanthrope considered society, rather than itself, as the supreme value, and looked askance at any form of introspection and nonconformity. But Tolstoy lived in a culture partly shaped by Rousseauistic and romantic ideas, and therefore he was inclined to take the side of the individual in his struggle with the body social and politic. He did so in *Anna Karenina,* where he sided with the person against the group (but not, as Anna's destiny shows, against a morality standing higher than both the person and the group). In that novel practically everybody condemns the splendid isolation of Levin, his absolute absorption in himself, his total disrespect for all social standards and forms. As in the case of Alceste, all his friends consider Levin *un grand extravagant.* His older brother Sergey upbraids him for this: "Come, really, though . . . there's limit to everything. It's very well to be original and genuine, and to dislike everything conventional. . . ." It is the author alone who sympathizes with an "eccentricity" which all other characters either resent or scorn. Some of them see in such "eccentricity" a social danger so great as to imperil civilization itself. It is in reply to Levin's indictment of luxury and hedonism that Stiva accuses Kostya of savagery and barbarism:

"Why, of course," objected Stepan Arkadyevich. "But that's just the aim of civilization—to make everything a source of enjoyment." "Well, if that's the aim, I'd rather be a savage." "All you Levins are savages. . . ."

Stiva's accusation sounds like a replica or an echo of the line by which Philinte rejects, as both uncivil and uncivilized, Alceste's dogmatic and doctrinaire misanthropy:

Ce chagrin philosophe est un peu trop sauvage.

This philosophic rage is a bit extreme.

The intent of Philinte's words is merely to point out the uncouthness of his friend's pedantic moralism. By accusing of "savagery" the "philosophical wrath" of Alceste, Philinte restates on the author's behalf the moral and intellectual ideal of the *honnête homme*. Yet Molière could not realize the almost prophetic quality of that line, which seems to announce the culture of the following century, when the civilized common sense of the Philintes was to be replaced by the Alcestian savagery of a new "philosophic wrath." The *philosophe* will take the place of the *honnête homme,* and the former will convert into a virtue what was a vice in the latter. This is the reason why the following century will rehabilitate Alceste beyond Molière's intention, and against his will. Through the mediation of eighteenth-century thought, Tolstoy will inherit this "philosophical wrath," sharing it with Levin and all his autobiographical characters, and spreading it over all his works. The objects of that wrath will be numberless: not only such great entities as civilization and society, art and culture, state and church, but even things as small and petty as those which are often the occasion of Alceste's misanthropy, or its pretext.

What Tolstoy has in common with his archetype is that there is method in his madness. Like Alceste he obeys almost without self-control the heedings of his "inner voice," the dictates of a conscience denying all values but those of the self. Yet he feels at the same time the compulsion of seeking the rationale of both his denial and his stand. When he believes he has found a general principle satisfying at once the demands of his mind and his heart, Tolstoy applies it to life, without regard for the consequences. Molière makes fun of what one would now call Alceste's "intellectual radicalism." Yet "intellectual radicalism" was to dominate modern culture from the eighteenth century on. Tolstoy himself is an extreme manifestation of this trend, since he never hesitated to follow an idea to its bitter end, wherever it might lead him. Romain Rolland praised him for his "heroic logic," in terms which would have been hardly acceptable to the century of Molière and Descartes, when logic was identified with common sense, and the latter was considered "la chose du monde la plus répandue." Yet Tolstoy deserves that praise, even though he used the sharp razor of logic a little irresponsibly, with Voltairian amusement and Shavian mischief.

The nemesis of an originality of this kind, based on the *concordia discors* of the two opposite "inner voices," on the conflicting claims of reason and sentiment, is self-righteousness, to be understood not only in its normal, moral sense, but in the intellectual as well. Tolstoy could not be satisfied except by being Tolstoy and right at the same time. He did not care much to convert others to his own way of life, but he had to convert them to his views. In doing so, he showed little regard for human feelings, and even for the truth, being all too prone to confuse what he felt inwardly truthful with the objectively true. George Orwell noticed this trait of Tolstoy's character, which he defined as a sort of "spiritual bullying." Chekhov pointed out even more harshly "the boldness with which Tolstoy treats what he does not know and, out of sheer stubbornness, refuses to understand." [29] On another occasion, Chekhov went so far as to assert that Tolstoy was a spiritual tyrant, who used his prestige and eminence to behave with a boorishness which public opinion would allow to nobody else:

All great sages are as despotic as generals, and as ignorant and indelicate as generals, because they feel secure. Diogenes spat in people's faces, knowing that he would not suffer for it. Tolstoy abuses doctors as scoundrels, and displays his ignorance in great questions because he's just such a Diogenes he won't be locked up and abused in the newspapers. And so to the devil with the philosophy of all the great ones of this world.[30]

Chekhov was a doctor, and what stirred his indignation in this case was Tolstoy's Molièrian scorn for medicine and its practitioners. Yet this indictment transcends the immediate occasion that dictated it, and brands forever the great man's one-sidedness and wrongheadedness. The very allusion to Diogenes seems to imply that Tolstoy, while playing all too consciously his role as a critic of society, sometimes acted unconsciously as society's clown or fool. This, however, is not true, and the Chekhovian parallel between Tolstoy and Diogenes cannot be reduced to the ferocious caricature it seems to be. Tolstoy was a sincere and suffering Diogenes; even though he was unwilling to leave his family and house to live within a barrel, he was at least able to use the lamp of his mind to look for an honest man not only without, but also within himself.

The spectator of *The Misanthrope* never knows whether Alceste will make good his word and retire forever from the community of his peers, or whether he will yield to the entreaties of his friends and remain among his fellow men. He merely knows that Alceste will never become a cynic, although he will never cease to be a misanthrope. This is equally true of Tolstoy, who will direct his misanthropy toward man as a social animal, but whose cynicism will never involve man as a person or soul. This is why Tolstoy's main commandment may be summed up in two Alcestian utterances, one taking an imperative, and the other a negative, form. The first one is: "Je veux que l'on soit homme" (Let men behave like men), and there is no need to elaborate what such a principle meant for Tolstoy himself. The second is: "Plus de société" (No more conversation), which, as the translation clearly indicates, means simply "no more talk." Yet one should not forget that *esprit de conversation* and *esprit de société* are one and the same thing,[31] that all the misanthropes who start by requesting the abolition of social intercourse end by asking the abolition of society itself. Since society refuses to abolish both its talk and itself, the misanthrope has no other alternative but to withdraw "du commerce des hommes" (from the commerce with mankind).

Man may, however, lose his life in the attempt to save it; while trying "de fuir dans un desert l'approche des humains" (to flee into a desert land unfouled by mankind), he may die in solitude and despair far from his family and home, like Diogenes or King Lear. Yet sometimes a misanthrope like Tolstoy may be able to find, if only for a while, in life and not in death, if not in Yasnaya Polyana at least within himself, a secluded corner

> *Où d'être homme d'honneur on ait la liberté.*
>
> Where he'll be free to have an honest heart.

Society will in the end recognize the nobility of such an attempt, whether successful or not. And this is why posterity should engrave on Tolstoy's tomb, as an ideal epitaph, Eliante's simple praise of the misanthropic Alceste:

> *Et la sincérité dont son âme se pique*
> *A quelque chose en soi de noble et d'héroïque.*
> *C'est une vertu rare au siècle d'aujourd'hui,*
> *Et je la voudrais voir partout comme chez lui.*
>
> The honesty in which he takes such pride
> Has — to my mind — its noble, heroic side.
> In this false age, such candor seems outrageous;
> But I could wish that it were more contagious.

NOTES

1. The main vehicle of the indictment was Tolstoy's late pamphlet "Shakespeare and the Drama," which had also roused the attention of G. B. Shaw. Orwell's essay, amusingly entitled "Lear, Tolstoy, and the Fool," appeared in *Polemic,* VII (March 1947). Before Orwell, Romain Rolland had described the tragic episode which closed Tolstoy's life as "the flight of the old and dying King Lear across the steppe" (*Vie de Tolstoï,* Paris, 1928).

These two texts are the first of the many primary or secondary sources referred to more than once in the course of the present essay. To avoid taxing the patience of the reader with an excessive burden of notes, I give the full title, and other pertinent or biographical information, only at the point where each one of such texts is mentioned for the first time. For the sake of brevity, I have omitted giving page numbers for the passages cited or quoted.

2. Isaiah Berlin, *The Hedgehog and the Fox, An Essay on Tolstoy's View of History* (London, 1953).

3. Maxim Gorki, *Reminiscences of Leo Nikolaevich Tolstoy.* Translated by S. S.

Koteliansky and Leonard Woolf (New York, 1920). All other quotations from Gorki are taken from this work.

4. In a letter to A. S. Suvorin, dated December 11, 1891. This and all Chekhov's other letters are quoted as translated by Constance Garnett in *Letters by Anton Chekhov,* partly reproduced in *The Personal Papers of Anton Chekhov* (New York: Lear Publishers, 1948).

5. This, and all passages from the same work, are quoted from *What is Art?* and *Essays on Art* by Leo Tolstoy, as translated by Aylmer Maude, and as published in the Centenary Edition (New York: Oxford University Press, 1929).

6. All quotations from *Childhood, Boyhood, and Youth* are taken from the translation by Louise and Aylmer Maude, in the Centenary Edition.

7. The truth of this may be proved not only by internal evidence, but also by the external sign of the name of Nikolenka's friend. It is not anachronistic to argue that the latter too must be at least in part a self-portrait, in view of the fact that Tolstoy will give again and again the same name and surname to characters created to project some of his own autobiographical experiences. It may suffice to mention that he did so with the protagonist of such an early fragment as "A Landowner's Morning," and, in his old age, with the hero of his last novel, *Resurrection.*

8. All quotations from *Anna Karenina* are given in Constance Garnett's translation, as published in the Modern Library edition.

9. In a letter to A. N. Pleshcheev, written on February 15, 1890 (see note 4 above).

10. *Maximes,* no. 182.

11. Quoted as translated by Louise and Aylmer Maude, Centenary Edition.

12. Quoted as translated by Louise and Aylmer Maude, Centenary Edition.

13. David Riesman, *The Lonely Crowd* (New York: Doubleday Anchor Books, 1953; abridged edition).

14. *War and Peace* and *Domestic Happiness* condemn romantic love directly and indirectly, mainly through the celebration of family life and conjugal love. *Anna Karenina* contrasts tragically to the latter an adulterous passion, which breaks the barriers of the moral code and the social norm. *The Kreutzer Sonata,* "The Devil," and "Father Sergius" are outright indictments of sexual love, whether lawful or not.

15. See Dmitri Merezhkovski, *Tolstoy i Dostoevski,* 2 vols. (St. Petersburg, 1912). An earlier, abridged version was translated into English under the title *Tolstoy as Man and Artist, with an Essay on Dostoevski* (New York, 1902).

16. Some scholars attribute Oronte's sonnet to the *précieux* poet Benserade. This would mean that it was originally written with a serious intent.

17. André Suarès, *Tolstoï* (Paris, 1899).

18. To add scorn to injury, Tolstoy claims to have chosen his pieces at random: "To avoid the reproach of having selected the worst verses, I have copied out of each volume whatever poem happened to stand on page 28."

19. Georg Lukács, *Studies in European Realism,* translated by Edith Bone (London, 1900).

20. This aphorism is to be found in the introductory section of La Bruyère's *Les Charactéres* ("Des Ouvrages de l'Esprit").

21. In an interview published in *Le Temps* on August 28, 1901.

22. Friedrich Schlegel made this statement in *Die alte und neue Litteratur.*

23. This, and all other quotations from Tolstoy's theological works, are given as translated by A. Maude, Centenary Edition.

24. From *The Brothers Karamazov* as translated by Constance Garnett.

25. I have already developed the same idea in an essay on Pascal's classicism, pub-

lished originally in Italian: "Classicismo di Pascal," *Letteratura* (Florence), IX, 3 (May–June 1947).

26. A similar "harmony" was compiled in his spare time by Mr. Pontifex, Sr., as any reader of Samuel Butler's *The Way of All Flesh* well knows.

27. Rainer Marie Rilke, *Briefe aus Muzot* (*1921–1926*) (Leipzig, 1935); letter no. 98, written to Prof. Hermann Pongs on October 21, 1924.

28. "I don't want to": these words are continuously repeated by Ivan Ilich during his agony.

29. From a letter to A. A. Pleshcheev written on February 15, 1890 (see note 6 above).

30. From a letter to A. Suvorin, dated September 8, 1891 (see note 6 above).

31. This idea was stated by Madame de Staël in *De la Littérature,* and, above all, in *De l'Allemagne.*

Storytelling in a Double Key

I. A CRITIQUE OF SIX CHEKHOV TALES

CHEKHOV's early stories are of some interest to the critic only inasmuch as they anticipate the accomplished master, destined to mature a few years later. Otherwise, their importance is slight, although it would be wrong to despise pieces that are still able to amuse and intrigue the reader. They were written in the early eighties, or about seventy years ago; and it is rare for any kind of writing, especially at the popular level, to survive with any effectiveness for such a long interval. This is even truer when one considers that the writing in question was never taken too seriously by the author himself. Both the critic and the reader should never forget that the young Chekhov wrote to entertain, and to add a little to his own income in the bargain.

The periodicals for which Chekhov wrote his early tales wanted to give their public cheap and easy laughter, rather than rare and thoughtful humor, and Chekhov the budding writer readily complied with his editors' demands. He did so without indulging in vulgarity or coarseness; yet at that stage of his career he dealt only with stock situations, to which he gave, half spontaneously and half mechanically, stock responses. In brief, what distinguishes Chekhov's literary beginnings from his mature work is their relative lack of quality — the banality of the stuff, the uncouthness of the style, and the conventionality of the outlook. The ideal of the early Chekhov is the commonplace; the muse of his youth is the muse of commonness. Yet shortly afterwards he was able to grow into a genuine and original writer, and to raise his own inspiration, even within an odd and comical framework, to a level of "high seriousness." Many critics and readers have seen in Chekhov the dramatist a more accomplished artist than in Chekhov the storyteller, and, even without sharing such an opinion, one can easily acknowledge the great merits of the dramas he wrote at the end of his life. Yet one must also remember that the artist who ended his career with plays such as *Three Sisters* and *The Cherry Orchard* had started his apprenticeship as a man of the theater by composing the one act play *The Boor,* which is mere vaudeville. His early stories and sketches may be likewise considered as miniature farces in narrative form, and they differ in value from the tales of his mature period as much as *The Boor* differs from the controlled and profound dramas of his late years.

Strangely enough, the vaudeville element was fated to disappear completely from the work of Chekhov the playwright, while remaining a lasting, or at least a recurring, ingredient in his narrative work. It is true that even there the vaudeville element reappears only as an initial presupposition, to be finally discarded or forgotten. This suggests an analogy between his growth as a man and his progress as an artist, as well as between the unconscious workings of his own imagination and his conscious artistic method or creative process. Some of his best tales seem to reproduce *in parvo* the pattern of his career: each one of them ends by changing what at first looks like an unpromising seed into a bitter, and yet ripe, fruit.

Thus, according to the norm of the art and the life of this master, Chekhov's short stories often open in a low key only to close on a higher one. These pages will put this general feature to a detailed test, consisting of a close analysis of some characteristic products of Chekhov's storytelling craft. The examples will be chosen from stories written between the middle and the late eighties, in the transitional period between the writer's youthful apprenticeship and his mature mastery. The closing section will deal, however, with a piece written at the end of the following decade, when Chekhov reached the zenith of his powers and the sunset of his life.

During this transitional period, the new Chekhov slowly unfolds, like a larva, from the old one. This can be seen early in the case of "Vanka" (1886), a story which develops the all too obvious comic theme of the peasant's letter: a theme which will appear again, with varied effects, in the fiction of this master (see, for instance, "The Letter," 1887, and "At Christmas Time," 1900). The story at first gives the impression of having been written only to exploit all the fun implied in that situation, as shown by Chekhov's use of the rather worn-out motif of the letter mailed with an address understandable to the sender and perhaps to the addressee, but meaningless to the postmaster. As is to be expected, the greater part of the story is taken by the letter itself, which is supposed to amuse the reader by revealing the ignorance and the naïveté of the writer, and to reach its funny climax at the end, when its full and yet incomplete address, "To Grandfather in the Village," is finally reported.

The usual pattern, however, is completely transformed by the presence of a few very simple, and yet new, elements. First of all, the ignorant letter writer is not an adult, but the child Vanka, who has been apprenticed to a shoemaker in Moscow. In the second place, the letter is not merely a commonplace communication, with the customary inquiries about the health of the correspondent, or with the conventional season's greetings (the message is penned at Christmas time). The letter is far more than this, since it conveys all the anguish and agony of a lonely orphan in the big city, who wants to be rescued from an alien and cruel world, and begs his grandfather to take him back to the country. Furthermore, by punctuating the letter with the intermittent flashbacks of the boy's recollections, full of vain longings for a better and irrevocable past, Chekhov reveals in even starker outline the present plight of the letter writer, and all the misery filling his childish heart.

This undercurrent of pathos gives the story a moral dimension incommensurate with the central anecdote, and destroys it as such. The story operates against those comic traits which are its very roots. The effect is achieved by what could be paradoxically defined as a kind of pathetic relief. Thus, when ultimately submitted, the absurd address no longer amuses us. In a sense, the punch line falls flat; in another, it becomes far too sharp. Instead of provoking a smile on our lips, it stirs a pang in our hearts. The words on the envelope, "To Grandfather in the Village," fail to sound funny as soon as we realize that they will prevent the letter from reaching its destination, thus making all Vanka's efforts futile, and his sorrow fruitless. This example may suffice to prove that Chekhov achieves his creative intent through the technique of a sentimental counterpoint: more precisely, by attuning to each other a few discordant, and even dissonant, strings.

The same contrapuntal technique operates in a story like "Polinka" (1887), where it achieves an effect of suggestive charm, of poetic irony. Polinka, a girl still in her teens, is shopping in a bazaar, and is being served by her favorite salesman, who is also one of her boy friends. During their long and complex business transaction, which is highly comical, since it deals with ladies' things, incongruous for seller and buyer alike, she confesses to the salesman-suitor that she is in love with a student, and asks for his help and advice. This part of their conversation is softspoken, while their more practical exchanges about clothing materials and notions are made aloud. As for the orders passed by the salesman to other sections of the shop, they are shouted at the top of his voice.

The salesman tries to talk Polinka out of her infatuation, but his lower social position, his feeling of awe before the rich young customer, the sense of his own inferiority before an unknown and more glamorous rival, force him to become resigned to the inevitable. All the complexities and perplexities of the young man's mind are made evident by the exaggerated respect he shows to such a young thing as Polinka, whom he addresses very formally as Pelagheya Sergeevna, as well as by his lack of experience, which makes him take her calf love far more seriously than she does herself. His pain is too real for him to realize that Polinka is playing with joyful fun the role of an accomplished lady, in the grand manner of her shopping, as well as in the small talk about the troubles of her heart.

Here the sentimental counterpoint becomes musical as well, by alternating the running *sotto voce* of the private talk, and the resounding *staccato* of the public one. The whole effect of the story derives from the amusing contrast between the sentimental nonsense of the intimate conversation, and the objective, official character of the questions and answers concerning laces and trimmings, buttons and beads. Yet all these solid things become vain trifles when compared to the unsubstantial feelings now agitating their souls, which, however, never meet. The counter is at the same time a bridge and a fence, making for both separation and contact; and as such it symbolizes Chekhov's great theme, which is the failure of communication between human beings, even when they are as close and as friendly as these two. In this case the failure of communication is not due to an external accident, as in "Vanka," where the letter will never reach its destination merely because of a wrong address; but it proceeds from human nature, and is rooted in the inner substance of life itself. Human relations are often based on a misunderstanding, and the misunderstanding is the more tragic when it is neither reciprocal, nor caused by either party's ill will. The young salesman sees the woman in his customer, but Polinka does not see the man in the youth serving her. In itself the contrast is rather comic; its kernel, as usual, is a mere *qui pro quo*. Yet the final effect is one of pathetic irony, precisely because what is happening is far more, and far less, than a business transaction, than an exchange of money and goods. This is what Chekhov has been able to do with a story which perhaps was initially written only to exploit the ridiculous situation of the man serving women in a notion shop.

Among the tales of this period, there are two that stand out: "The Chorus Girl" and "A Gentleman Friend," both written in 1886. Each one describes a petty and yet painful incident, a "vile tale," to use the term which Dostoevski's fiction offers us ready-made. The protagonists are two prostitutes, both playing a victim's role, and seeing in the incident affecting them an outrageous symbol of their wretched lot. The author, as well as the reader, is aware of the pathetic significance of the grotesque events on which these pieces are centered. Each one of these two "vile tales" becomes what James Joyce would have called an "epiphany," although a negative one, since it reveals not the noble meaning, but the cruel nonsense of life.

In the first of these two tales, the "chorus girl" Pasha is entertaining her current friend, who is a married gentleman, when someone suddenly rings the bell. The gentleman withdraws into the room nearby. The visitor is a lady, the gentleman's wife. She starts by calling Pasha all possible names, and ends her tirade by demanding that the chorus girl return all the presents she has been receiving from her lover, who must pay back the money he has been embezzling from his office. Pasha complies and returns two cheap trinkets. The lady refuses to believe that those trifles are the entire lot. By insulting and threatening Pasha, by moving her to compassion and by humiliating herself, she succeeds in obtaining from the chorus girl all the far more precious jewels and presents she had been given by other, more generous, friends. After the lady has left with her booty, the unfaithful husband, who has overheard everything, runs after her, blaming Pasha, and pitying his wife for having humbled herself before such a "low creature" as the chorus girl.

This marvellous story is, in a certain sense, Chekhov's "Boule de Suif." But in Maupassant's tale the righteous indignation, on the part of her train companions, toward the prostitute who has saved them from annoyance by complying with the wishes of a Prussian officer, derives from the author's satirical view of the hypocrisy of society in matters of sex. In his story, however, as is usual with him, Chekhov displays little interest in the sex angle as such. His main concern is with the human soul, especially when it is misunderstood, misjudged, mistreated by another soul. The conflict at the base of "The Chorus Girl" revolves not around jealousy and love, but around the bourgeois values of respectability and interest. It is highly significant that the betrayed wife never reproaches Pasha for the alienation of her husband's affection; she blames the chorus girl only for having made him squander his money, thus depriving society and his family of their due.

By the tragic irony of the story, it is not shame or pity, but a sense of awe before the elegant and respectable lady, that forces the chorus girl to surrender all she owns, although she owes nothing to her. And to add insult to injury, the enraged wife calls her a "mercenary hussy" for all that. The tale reaches its climax, both pathetic and absurd, when the lady unknowingly chooses to refuse, among all the things "returned" to her, the pair of baubles her husband had given the chorus girl: "What are you giving me? . . . I am not asking for charity, but for what does not belong to you. . . ." [1]

Unlike the indignant and furious lady, Pasha accepts with dumb resignation her shame, as well as her loss. The tragicomedy of life forces Pasha and her like to behave passively, to undergo what life, or other human beings, *do* to them. But bourgeois wives, even when they are wronged, know how to act, and how to set right their wrongs. The contrast between the parts played by protagonist and antagonist is concretely symbolized by the *physique du rôle* of each one of the two principals. The wife is gaunt and tall, while Pasha, like the heroine of "Boule de Suif," is small and soft. The contrast is further emphasized by their difference in grooming and dress.

The moral superiority of Pasha over the lady is made evident by the very fact that she is the only one of the two women fully aware of the impression she makes on the other. She knows all too well that if she could look differently, she would be treated better, as a human being worthy of love and respect:

Pasha felt that on this lady in black with angry eyes and white slender fingers she produced the impression of something horrid and unseemly, and she felt ashamed of her chubby red cheeks, the pockmark on her nose, and the fringe on her forehead, which never could be combed back. And it seemed to her that if she had been thin, and had no powder on her face, then she could have disguised the fact that she was not "respectable," and she would not have felt so frightened and ashamed to stand facing the unknown, mysterious lady.

The sad moral of this fable is of course that the Pashas will never change, and will be ever dressed, and treated by men and women alike, as "chorus girls." Yet the tale carries another lesson, perhaps a wiser one, teaching that it is not dress that makes the man, or even the woman, at that. This truth, which applies equally to her rival, to that "mysterious lady" who is hardly mysterious to us, is unconsciously uttered by Pasha herself, in her single complaint or protest. While giving away things rightfully belonging to her, because she had got them, as she says, "from other gentlemen," Pasha bursts out: "Take them and grow rich." We doubt that the lady will grow rich, while knowing all too well that Pasha will grow even poorer than she now is. Yet she is right in what she says, and it is from these words that we realize that the wronged wife is now a wrongdoer, that, even more than the "mercenary hussy" she despises and despoils, she becomes a "gold digger" herself.

The heroine of "A Gentleman Friend," being a streetwalker, is, at least for bourgeois society, a creature even lower than the chorus girl. We meet her when she is leaving the hospital, and we may easily guess why she has been there. We must not overstress this detail: Chekhov, although more affected by the naturalistic strain than other Russian realists, certainly did not write such a story to point out the dangers of sexual promiscuity, or the horrors of social diseases. Notwithstanding his medical training and the keenness of his social conscience, Chekhov the artist could not but understress a point like this. The writer has no special cause to plead: what interests him is not the sordid side of his case, but its human poignancy and truth.

Thus, at the beginning of the story, he reduces the prostitute's plight to the particular strait she is in: to the immediate practical problems she must face now that she is again on her feet (and *only* on her feet). The poor girl is without shelter, and, even more important, she has no money with which to buy a new dress. She pawns a ring, but she gets only a ruble for it. She is as much aware as Pasha that the role she plays in life depends on how she is groomed and dressed, but while the sad tale of the chorus girl ends with Pasha's realization that her physical and sartorial appearance will never allow her to play any other role but the one fate assigned to her, this sorry story begins with the heroine's frantic attempts to procure the only proper attire for acting and living as she is supposed to. "What can you get for a ruble?" she thinks. "You can't buy for that sum a fashionable short jacket, not a big hat, nor a pair of bronze shoes, and without those things she had a feeling of being, as it were, undressed. . . ."

All the unconscious irony of the last sentence will be made evident if we consider that this woman, so preoccupied with the clothing she wants to have, is a professional stripteaser, who is paid to undress. The shabbiness of her apparel makes her more ashamed than nudity itself; it makes her feel as if she were nude in the street. In order to buy the trade costume she needs, she decides to visit one of her gentlemen friends, and to borrow from him. She picks a dentist: but while climbing his stairs, and lingering in his waiting room, she loses all her pluck. She thinks that the unfashionable dress she is now wearing makes her look like the beggar she now is, or even worse, like the working girl she is no more. While the chorus girl feels degraded by the sudden appearance of a lady looking respectable, if not in her actions and manners, at least in her aspect and dress, the streetwalker realizes her loss of status merely by drawing an invidious comparison between her present appearance and her former, more glamorous self.

Chekhov dramatizes the conflict between the two opposite self-images within the prostitute's mind, by contrasting her professional name, the fictitious and exotic Vanda, with the prosaic Nastasya, the real and legal one, as testified by her "yellow passport." And Vanda's feeling of humiliation reaches its climax when she suddenly sees her own present image as reflected in the immense mirror by which the writer's provident imagination, with realistic as well as with visionary insight, has furnished the splendid staircase leading to the dentist's office. Here, unknowingly, Chekhov uses the Dantean symbol of "other people's stairs": the climbing and descending of which is such a "bitter path" for the poor and the needy, when they beg for charity and help. To this the author adds the symbol of the looking glass, as if to suggest that the postulant knows all too well that at a given stage of her quest she will sooner or later discover her own wretched likeness on the inward mirror of shame, or on the outward mirror of truth.

Here is the central scene of the story, as the author reports it: "The staircase impressed her as luxurious and magnificent, but of all its splendors what caught her eye most was an immense looking glass, in which she saw a ragged figure without a fashionable jacket, without a big hat, and without bronze shoes." With marvellous intuition, the writer imagines that, at first sight, Vanda fails to recognize herself, because the figure she is looking at is deprived of the objects she longed to see. But when she takes a second look, she identifies in that shabby reflection her own true self. And for a while self-recognition gives place to self-knowledge. With a painful shock, the street walker realizes that she has become another person, or rather that she has changed back into the kind of person she once was: "And it seemed strange to Vanda that, now that she was humbly dressed and looked like a laundress or sewing girl, she felt ashamed, and no trace of her usual sauciness remained, and in her own mind she no longer thought of herself as Vanda, but as the Nastasya Kanavkin she used to be in the old days. . . ."

Only a writer endowed with keen psychological and ethical insight could have thought of this: a prostitute ashamed of being ashamed, feeling dishonored for thinking, behaving, and looking again like the better human

Storytelling in a Double Key

being she had been before. Nothing is more tragic than such an inverted perspective, such a reversal of values, which the writer, however, sets right without gnashing of teeth, without even lifting a finger to point out the moral of his unadorned tale. Those who lower themselves will be exalted, and the reader glimpses a sign of redemption in the very fact that the prostitute perceives her own indignity when she recovers, if only for a fleeting instant, the sense of her identity.

If such is the climax of the story, its ending cannot be but an anticlimax. When she is admitted into the dentist's office, the girl is taken for a stranger, and treated as if she were not a visitor, but a patient. The dentist obviously fails to recognize in Nastasya the Vanda who, for a full evening, had been his lady friend. Open-mouthed and speechless, the poor streetwalker lets one of her teeth be pulled, and pays the dentist with the only ruble she has left. Like Pasha, she is one of those creatures to whom things are done, and who are done for. But while Pasha is the victim of a foulness masquerading as retributive justice, Nastasya is the victim of something even colder and cruder: of our mechanical indifference to, or perfunctory interest in, not only the suffering but the very being of our fellow men. Thus the incidents reported in these two stories end on the same note of despair. Poor Pasha wails aloud, with her feelings deeply hurt: "She remembered how three years ago a merchant had beaten her for no sort of reason, and she wailed more loudly than ever." As for Nastasya, "she walked along the street, spitting blood, and brooding on her life, and the insults she had endured, and would have to endure tomorrow, and next week, and all her life, up to the very day of her death."

The chorus girl cries because she has no more illusions. She knows that her appearance, as well as the substance of her life, will never change, and that she will be forever wronged by unknown, respectable ladies, and by less respectable gentlemen friends. Nastasya, although equally aware of her fate, fails to weep only because she still hopes to become Vanda again. And at the close of the story she changes again into Vanda, as soon as she is able to buy and wear "an enormous red hat, a fashionable jacket, and bronze shoes." The list of these three pieces of apparel reappears here for the third time in the story (at the beginning, in the middle, and at the end), and this repetition gives those three concrete objects the obsessive quality of an *idée fixe,* which, despite its absurdity, has finally succeeded in materializing.

Chekhov is but one of the many writers who attempt to interpret the comedy of life in pathetic rather than in comic terms. One could say that he tends to reverse Gogol's formula, trying to give us "tears through laughter" instead of "laughter through tears." Yet even so, unlike Gogol, he never changes his laughter into a sneer, or his smile into a grimace. He constantly avoids the temptation of the grotesque, as if he knew that its nemesis is to degrade the comedy of life into a farce. While tragedy is self-sufficient, and can get along quite well even without comic relief, comedy is always a mixed genre, and needs a certain amount of tragic sense to achieve the catharsis of its own pathos and form. Thus, as both "The Chorus Girl" and "A Gentleman Friend" amply prove, Chekhov is quite right in looking for inspiration in what, twisting Maeterlinck's phrase, one may call *le tragi-comique quotidien.* And perhaps nothing is as tragicomic in our daily experience as that highly serious comedy of errors, moral and spiritual in character, constantly falsifying social relations and human intercourse.

Chekhov pays great attention to all those mistakes or equivocations that prevent the establishment of a communion of feeling between different human beings. Our own reciprocal misunderstandings are due not to material appearances or optical illusions, but to internal blindness. What Chekhov is primarily interested in is what one might call, perhaps too technically, a failure of communication. Such failure, which takes place mainly on the moral plane, may operate on both sides, although the author attributes it preferably to the party at the receiving end. Thus the comedy of errors becomes pathetic and tragic, deriving from a defective condition which the message sender can hardly improve or correct: in brief, from a fault in the reception. No situation lends itself so well as this one to the countrapuntal technique characteristic of Chekhov's method of presentation and development, and no story brings this point more movingly home than the one entitled, simply and eloquently, "Heartache" (1886).

The story opens with a static scene: something like an impressionistic landscape, built around two motionless figures, an animal and a man. The vision gives the eerie feeling of a *tableau vivant,* obviously recapturing a real life experience, which must have vividly caught the imagination of Chekhov, since he reproduced it almost verbatim in the later "Kashtanka," a tale about a child and a dog. Here is the scene, in Chekhov's words:

> Evening twilight, large flakes of snow are circling lazily about the street lamps which have just been lighted, settling in a thin layer on roofs, horses' backs, people's shoulders, caps. Iona Potapov, the cabby, is all white like a ghost. As hunched as a living body can be, he sits on the box without stirring. . . . His nag, too, is white and motionless. . . .[2]

The inertia of both the man and the horse is suddenly broken by the arrival of Iona's first fare, and Chekhov describes with great artistry the sledge's slow and difficult start. The driving man, the pulling nag, and the dragging sledge seem to be a caricatural replica of such noble visions or figures as the Centaur, or Lohengrin's swan. The human and the animal component of the team act with a rigid and mechanical parallelism, showing their pain and effort, and become almost as heavy and wooden as the sledge trailing after them: "The driver clucks to the horse, cranes his neck like a swan. . . . The nag, too stretches her neck. . . ."

The aged cabby is a grieving father who has just lost his son. He feels the poignant urge to pour out his sorrow, and wishes to tell somebody of his misery and loss. Only the compassion of a fellow man may console his heart. So "he turns his whole body around to his fare to talk." But the indifference of the customer, as well as the snares of the traffic, prevents him from getting his words and feelings across. The vain attempt repeats itself again and again, and the entire story is punctuated by a series of failures, succeeding each other through the same motions and gestures by driver or horse, or by both: the craning of their necks at the start, Iona's turning around during the ride, the team's return to a deathlike immobility at the ride's end. Then, while waiting for another fare, Iona "sits motionless and hunched on his box."

The last fare is a party of revelers, whom Iona will drive up to "a dark entrance," only to be underpaid by them. One of the riders is a hunchback, bent by nature as cruelly and permanently as Iona by his exposure to the biting cold. The revelers derisively force their crippled friend to stand up in the sledge. To show his indignation at their slow progress, or rather, to vent his resentment on another human being, even more wretched than himself, the hunchback gives Iona a blow on his shoulders. The blow falls on the neck of Iona just when he turns his head forward, after a vain attempt to talk.

The entire story is based, simply and powerfully, on this sort of graphic and dynamic symbolism: on the recurrence of the same tortured gestures by these two creatures, the man and the horse, as well as on the sledge's intermittent jerks. Finally, Iona decides to go back to his yard, where he tries his luck with a young fellow driver, who refuses to listen, and falls asleep. So, in the animal heat of the stable, while feeding his nag, the bereaved father tells his grief to the only living being who seems to lend a willing ear to his tale of woe. The story thus ends almost good-humoredly, relieving the almost unbearable tension, and relaxing the strings of pathos, which were about to snap.

Communication theory takes into account also those failures of understanding which are due to semantic confusions, to wrong assumptions about the agreed or conventional meaning of a given sign, especially a verbal one. Such a confusion is the more frequent and intense when the sign is loaded with an excessive emotional charge, or is one of those "shocking words" which may all too easily become "scandal's stones," or stumbling blocks. Literature generally deals with situations of this sort in a light comic vein, as if impropriety were a matter of misuse rather than of abuse. The usual intention is thus to contrast the outrageous implications of the utterance with the innocence and ignorance of the speaker. The young Chekhov was not above exploiting farcically verbal equivocations of this sort, but in his middle period he wrote at least one noble tale on what in the hands of another writer would have remained a vulgar *double entendre:* the flimsiest of all comical pretexts. Such a story is "The Service of the Dead" (1886), in which the shocking word, like a rock thrown into a pond, suddenly stirs the still waters of our soul.

On a Sunday morning, the shopkeeper Andrey Andreych leans on a railing in the church. He has just sent a note to the altar, asking that a mass be sung for the repose of the soul of his daughter Maria (or Matushka, as he still calls her). Chekhov characterizes him in a Gogolian manner, that is, by deducing his typical psychological traits from the concrete details of his behavior and aspect. Thus we get to know what kind of man he is as soon as we learn that he wears "the huge clumsy galoshes only seen on the feet of practical and prudent persons of firm religious convictions." While waiting for the requiem mass, the shopkeeper notices that Father Grigori is acting strangely near the altar, and then he realizes that the priest's "twitching eyebrows and beckoning finger might refer to him."

This slight, initial misapprehension prepares the reader for the profound misunderstanding which is the story's central theme. Andrey Andreych walks toward the altar, tramping with his heavy galoshes, which, although representative of his solid beliefs, still seem incongruous and indecorous in the church. When he reaches the altar, he is harshly reproached by the priest for what he had "dared" to write. At first, he fails to comprehend, but he finally understands that the priest objects to one word he had used in his written request for the mass: "For the soul of the servant of God, the harlot Maria." The word suddenly resounds in the mind of the reader with a more incongruous and indecorous thud than the heavy galoshes on the church's floor. The shopkeeper justifies himself by quoting the lives of the saints, and by citing Mary of Egypt, who had been forgiven by the Lord, and explains that he had added the epithet to the name of his daughter to follow the use of the martyrology, where the martyrs' names are always accompanied by terms designating their station or calling in life. The priest insists that the word is unseemly, reminding the shopkeeper that his daughter had been a "well-known actress," and that her death has been mentioned in the press.

From what Father Grigori tells the old man, the reader understands all too well the ambivalence of the priest's attitude toward the glories and the vanities of the world. He thinks of the dead sinner with an outraged sense of righteousness, but also with a feeling of involuntary respect. After all, through her fall, and even her ruin, she rose high in the eyes of men. It is for this, as well as for the dignity of the church, that he objects to the use of that term. Her guilt must be not only forgiven, but forgotten too. If the veil of the priest's well-meaning hypocrisy is easily lifted, the intention which led the shopkeeper to call his daughter a harlot will forever remain under a cloud of obscurity. The writer fails to solve this ambiguity, leaving in doubt whether Andrey Andreych really knows what "harlot" means: thus we remain unsure whether by mentioning that word he intends to refer to his daughter's exceptional career, or merely to her sin. We cannot even be sure of his naïveté, and the priest accuses him, not without reason, of being too subtle, and of presuming to read the Holy Writ better than a clergyman. True enough, the old man sticks to his own opinion, and during the mass, he lets drop again the forbidden word from his praying lips.

With his usual method, Chekhov accompanies the audible chant of the rite by the silent antiphony of Andrey Andreych's reflections, reminiscences, and thoughts. Suddenly the reader relives with him a forgotten episode of his life. The shopkeeper rehearses again in his memory his last walk with his daughter, and suddenly recalls how, at her enraptured enthusiasm for the loveliness of the local landscape, he had replied rather ineptly that farming did not pay on a soil like that. This flashback reveals immediately how and why those two hearts and two minds, with their opposite concerns for beauty and utility, were destined never to meet. Now the problem whether the father did or did not know the real meaning of "harlot" does not matter any longer: the point is that he misunderstood his daughter, to be misunderstood in return. The semantic confusion thus becomes merely a sign of man's inability to know himself, as well as others, including his next of kin. And we see that such inability persists even when we bury our dead. Yet in his last and greatest period, Chekhov was able to find within life, almost unconsciously, that sense of redemption that this somber story fails to find even in death. This is particularly true of the more important of the two stories discussed below.

II. "PSYCHE; IT'S A FINE SUBJECT"

In Chekhov's canon there are two tales, written at different times, which, starting from the opposite poles of pathos and irony, and following divergent paths, end by giving us parallel transfigurations, in realistic terms, of the same myth. This myth is the ancient story of Psyche, which remained lively and meaningful for the artists and writers of so many centuries, but which our commercial culture has mummified into the everlasting indignity of a soft-drink ad. Chekhov used the Psyche legend not openly, but obliquely, as a furtive hint that even in the profane prose of life there may lie hidden poetry's sacred spark. The grimness or the grayness of our daily lot seems to dominate both of these tales, but the sudden appearance of Psyche redeems their somber or dull view of life with a vivid, and not too unreal, flash. The first tale discloses the vision within the span of a simple image; and the second, of a mere name. That image and that name reduce in their turn the whole legend to a single symbol, hiding, rather than revealing, the myth it transcribes in quasi-hieroglyphic form. The symbol itself, eclipsed by the cloud of the letter, buried under the matter-of-factness of a naturalistic report, has escaped all scrutiny, thus making even less visible the presence of the myth it suggests and for which it stands. Yet in the end the beauty and poetry of the ancient legend triumph over all obtuseness and absurdity, over the obscurity of life and the disguise of art; and Psyche's face shines forth again, in one case through tragedy's, and in the other, through comedy's, mask. It is mainly such a passing and fleeting allusion to Psyche and her story that, beyond all appearance, makes these two tales what they really are; yet a detailed examination of their plainest and lowest level of meaning is required to reinterpret them within the higher, and deeper, frame of reference of both symbol and myth.

The first of these two tales is "Anyuta," which was written in 1886. The story seems to have been conceived in a mixed mood, half pathetic, half morbid; and it lies halfway, so to speak, between Mürger's *Scènes de la Vie de Bohême* and the most sordid tales of the early Dostoevski. At least at first sight, its protagonists impress us as the conventional seamstress and the conventional student, sharing their poverty and love in the same barely furnished room. Yet, from the very beginning, we surprise them in a highly unconventional situation. The student is preparing himself for one of the examinations he is about to take at the Medical School. In order to get his anatomy straight, he asks Anyuta to take her blouse off, and starts counting her ribs. A while later, a friend drops in. A student at the Academy of Fine Arts, he has come to take Anyuta away, since he needs a model, and wants her to pose for a painting he is working on. Anyuta retires to dress, and in the meanwhile the visitor reproaches his host for his slovenly life. When left alone, the medical student decides that he and the seamstress must part; he tells Anyuta of his decision as soon as she comes back from her sitting, bringing in the sugar she has just bought for the tea of her penniless friend.

Here Chekhov's contrapuntal technique acts, so to speak, negatively: the words and thoughts of the student fail to break the inarticulate silence of the girl. She is the only mute and passive figure of the story, acting with the resigned dumbness of a sacrificial lamb. The author adds his own silence to the silence of the heroine, pretending to look on her from the outside, which is exactly what the other two characters do. Thus all the references to Anyuta, while remaining external and objective, become highly symbolic. This kind of implied, and, so to speak, inert, symbolism grows more and more important in the creations of the late Chekhov. Here it finds expression not only in Anyuta's silence, but also in the parallel indifference of the two students, both of whom treat the seamstress, even if for different ends, as if she were merely an anatomical specimen.

In this story, the obvious love angle is completely overlooked. With unobtrusive but penetrating irony, Chekhov makes Anuyta's body serve the higher purposes of art and science. In reality, she serves, with both her body and soul, the blind selfishness of two human beings who consider her an inferior creature, while she is morally far superior to them. As for the ribs, says the medical student, "they are like the keys of a piano: one must study them in the skeleton and in the living body." Yet in reality he treats her as if she were a corpse on a slab. The art student is even more matter-of-fact: he handles Anyuta as if she were something neither living nor dead, but only a thing, a piece of property of so little value that it is better to borrow than to own it. "Do me a favor," he asks his friend, "lend me your young lady for just a couple of hours! I am painting a picture, you see, and I can't get on without a model." He asks for her as he would ask for a plate of fruit, to be discarded or returned, because he needs it to paint, not to eat. Yet the supreme irony of the story is that the young artist wants to produce something far nobler than a mere study. He is not one of those naïve painters who are satisfied with representing either a nude or a still life. He aims far higher, as we learn from the answer he gives to his friend's question about the theme of the painting he is working on: "Psyche; it's a fine subject."

Neither the students nor, for that matter, Anyuta, will ever realize that the only Psyche of the story is she herself. Yet this is the feeling conveyed to the reader by the tale's closing vision, when the abandoned seamstress returns noiselessly to the corner window of her lonely room, like a Cinderella without beauty, without a prince, and without a magic wand. While treating the scène de vie de bohême as if it were a "slice of life," Chekhov succeeds in changing the story into a tragic fable without words. And he does so by projecting on the shabby walls of a bohemian garret, beyond the falsity of a painted image which remains unseen, the true likeness of poor Psyche of old, as she was when she lost her lover, and was left like an orphan alone in the darkness of this world.

The second tale is "The Darling," which Chekhov wrote more than ten years later, in 1899, at the decline of his years, when his art was gradually changing the tragicomedy of life into something far too noble for pity, and far too pure for contempt. The change is particularly evident in this story, of which one could say, to paraphrase Milton's words, "nothing is here for tears." Nothing is here for laughter either, because "The Darling" ends by "saying yea" to life, by judging it "well and fair." Yet if the critic will go back to the text, so as to recapture the impression of his first reading, he will undoubtedly conclude that the final esthetic outcome transcends the tale's original intent. And he will do so even more confidently if he learns that his conclusion is supported by the authority of Leo Tolstoy, who was a great admirer of this story, as well as of Chekhov in general.

The protagonist, Olenka, is "a gentle, soft-hearted, compassionate girl, with mild, tender eyes, and very good health." Everyone feels captivated by her good nature, and exclaims: "You darling!" at the sight of her pleasant looks. She lives in her father's house, and watches from her back porch the tenant living in a lodge they rent. The tenant, whose name is Ivan Kukin, is thin and no longer young; he manages an open-air theater, and complains constantly about the rain which ruins his business, and about the public which fails to appreciate his shows. By listening to his misfortunes, the "darling" falls in love with him. She marries Kukin, works in his office, and accepts all his views as her own, repeating all he has to say about the theatrical arts. Despite her total identification with her husband, Olenka grows stouter and pinker, while Kukin grows thinner and paler. After a year has passed, he goes to Moscow on business, and within a few days Olenka receives a misspelled telegram informing her of Kukin's sudden death.

The poor widow loses all interest in life, but after a three month interval she meets at mass Vasili Pustovalov, a dignified gentleman working at a timber merchant's. In a day or two Pustovalov proposes, and Olenka marries again. The "darling" helps her new husband in the shop, and absorbs herself in the timber trade as fully as she had previously done in the theater world. For six years, her husband's ideas become her ideas, but her mind returns to emptiness as soon as her second husband follows the first into the grave. Yet within half a year she finds happiness anew, this time with an army veterinary surgeon, by the name of Vladimir Smirnin, now renting her lodge. Smirnin is married and has a son, but lives separated from his wife and child. Everyone realizes what has happened as soon as Olenka goes around discussing sanitary questions and the dangers of animal epidemics. "It was evident," as Chekhov says, "that she could not live a year without an attachment," and yet nobody thinks ill of the "darling" for this.

But Smirnin is suddenly transferred to a distant place, and Olenka is left alone again. Time passes, and she becomes indifferent, sad, and old: "what is worst of all . . . she had no opinion of any sort." Like all old lonely women, she has a cat, but does not care for her pet. Suddenly her solitude is broken again: Smirnin, looking older and wearing a civilian suit, knocks again at her door. He has left the service and has come back with his family, to start life anew. Olenka yields her house to the newcomers, and retires to the lodge. With this change of perspective, her life seems to take a new turn. And this time she falls in love with the little Sasha, who is ten years old. Soon enough, the father starts working outside, and the mother departs to live elsewhere. Thus Olenka mothers the boy, who calls her auntie, and tells her about his studies, and his school experiences. Now the "darling" goes around discussing teachers and lessons, home assignments and class work. And everybody understands that there is another man in her house and in her life, even if this time he is another woman's child, whom she loves like the mother she was born to be.

This résumé fails to do justice to the story, and to point out the internal contradiction already alluded to. Tolstoy's commentary fulfills, however, both tasks almost perfectly. In the opening of the critique of this piece, which he collected in *Readings for Every Day of the Year,* Tolstoy recalls the biblical story of Balaam (Numbers, 22–24). The King of the Moabites ordered him to curse the people of Israel, and Balaam wanted to comply with this command. But while climbing the mountain, he was warned by an angel, who at first was invisible to him, while being visible to his ass. So, when he reached the altar at the top, Balaam, instead of cursing the Jews, blessed them. "This," Tolstoy concludes, "is just what happened with the true poet and artist Chekhov when he wrote his charming story, 'The Darling.'" Tolstoy then proceeds to develop his point:

> The author evidently wanted to laugh at this pitiful creature — as he judged her with his intellect, not with his heart — this "Darling," who, after sharing Kukin's troubles about his theater, and then immersing herself in the interests of the timber business, under the influence of the veterinary surgeon considers the struggle against bovine tuberculosis to be the most important matter in the world, and is finally absorbed in questions of grammar and the interests of the little schoolboy in the big cap. Kukin's name is ridiculous, and so even is his illness and the telegram announcing his death. The timber dealer with his sedateness is ridiculous; but the soul of "Darling," with her capacity for devoting herself with her whole being to the one she loves, is not ridiculous but wonderful and holy.[3]

Nothing could be more exact, or better said: yet one may wonder whether Tolstoy is equally right in identifying the motive that had led the author of "The Darling" to take the pen. "When Chekhov began to write that story," says Tolstoy, "he wanted to show what woman ought not to be." In short, what Chekhov meant to do was to reassert his belief in the ideal of woman's emancipation, in her right and duty to have a mind and a soul of her own. While acknowledging the artistic miracle which had turned a satirical vignette into a noble human image, Tolstoy seems to enjoy as a good joke the implication that the author had to throw his beliefs overboard in the process. Being strongly adverse to the cause of woman's emancipation, Tolstoy speaks here *pro domo sua,* but the reader has no compelling reason to prefer his anti-feminism to Chekhov's feminism. Tolstoy has an axe to grind, and his guess is too shrewd. One could venture to say that Chekhov sat down to write "The Darling" with neither polemical intentions nor ideological pretensions: what he wanted to do was perhaps to exploit again at the lowest level a commonplace type and a stock comic situation, which, however unexpectedly, develops into a vision of beauty and truth. If D. S. Mirsky is right in claiming that each Chekhov story follows a curve, then there is no tale where the curve of his art better overshoots its mark.

What must have attracted Chekhov was the idea of rewriting a half pathetic, half mocking version of the "merry widow" motif: of portraying in his own inimitable way the conventional character of the woman ready and willing to marry a new husband as soon as she has buried the preceding one. That such was the case may still be proved through many eloquent clues. No reader of "The Darling" will fail to notice that Olenka calls her successive mates with almost identical nicknames: Vanichka the first, Vassichka the second, and Volodichka the third. These familiar diminutives, although respectively deriving from such different names as Ivan, Vasili, and Vladimir, sound as if they were practically interchangeable, as if to suggest that the three men are interchangeable too.

This runs true to type, since in the life scheme of the eternal, and eternally remarrying, widow, nothing really changes, while everything recurs: the bridal veil alternates regularly with the veil of mourning, and both may be worn in the same church. It is from this scheme that Chekhov derives the idea of the successive adoption, on Olenka's part, of the opinions and views of each one of her three men, and this detail is another proof that the story was originally conceived on the merry widow motif. Yet, if we look deeper, we realize that a merry widow does not look for happiness beyond wedded bliss: that she asks for no less than a ring, while offering nothing more than her hand. But Olenka gives and takes other, very different things. She receives her husbands' opinions, and makes them her own, while returning something far more solid and valuable in exchange. And when she loses the person she loves, she has no more use for his views, or for any views at all.

This cracks the merry widow pattern, which begins to break when she joins her third mate, who is a married man, without a wedding ceremony or the blessing of the Church. And the pattern visibly crumbles at the end, when Olenka finds her fourth and last love not in a man, but in a child, who is the son of her last friend. "Of her former attachments," says Chekhov, "not one had been so deep." Now we finally know Olenka for what she really is, and we better appraise in retrospect some of the story's earliest, unconscious hints. Now, for instance, we understand better her girlish infatuations for such unlikely objects as her father, her aunt, or her teacher of French. For her, almost any kind of person or any kind of love can do equally well, and it is because of this, not because of any old-maidish strain, that she fails to reduce love to sex alone.

Chekhov explains this better than we could, at that very point of the tale when the lonely Olenka is about to find her more lasting attachment: "She wanted a love that would absorb her whole being, and whole soul and reason — that could give her ideas and an object in life, and would warm her old blood." For all this one could never say of Olenka, as of Madame Bovary, that she is in love with love: she cares only for living beings like herself, as shown by the ease with which she forgets all her husbands after their deaths. Her brain is never haunted by dreams or ghosts, and this is why it is either empty, or full of other people's thoughts. This does not mean that the "Darling" is a parrot or a monkey in woman's dress, although it is almost certain that Chekhov conceived her initially in such a form. She is more like the ass of Balaam, who sees the angel his master is unable to see. Olenka is poor in spirit and pure in heart, and this is why life curses her three times, only to bless her forever, at the end.

Tolstoy is right when he reminds us that, unlike Olenka, her three men and even her foster-child are slightly ridiculous characters, and one must add that they remain unchangingly so from whatever standpoint we may look. The reminder is necessary: after all, the point of the story is that love is a grace proceeding from the lover's fullness of heart, not from the beloved's attractive qualities or high deserts. In the light of this, the parallel with Balaam's ass must be qualified by saying that Olenka sees angels where others see only men. Thus the double message of the story is that love is a matter of both blindness and insight.

While the whole story seems to emphasize Olenka's "insight," her "blindness" is intimated by a single hint, hidden, of all places, in the title itself. Since the latter is practically untranslatable, the foreign reader cannot help missing the hint. The "Darling" of the English translators is the Russian idiom *Dushechka,* meaning literally "little soul," and used colloquially as a term of endearment, a tribute of personal sympathy, a familiar and good-natured compliment. Chekhov never pays the compliment himself, except by indirection or implication: he merely repeats it again and again, in constant quotations from other people's direct speech. Thus the artist acts as an echo, reiterating that word as if it were a choral refrain, a suggestive *leitmotiv*. Yet, as we already know, everybody addresses Olenka in that way only when she is contented and happy, having someone to love and care for. As soon as she is left without a person on whom to pour the tenderness flowing from her heart, everybody ceases calling her Dushechka, as if she had lost her soul, as if she were no longer a soul.

Thus, even though intermittently used, that term becomes, so to say, Olenka's second name: and the reader finally finds it more right and true than the first. What one witnesses is a sort of transfiguration, both symbolic and literal: by changing into Dushechka, Olenka ends by personifying the very idea of the soul. We are suddenly faced by an allegory and a metamorphosis, turning the story into a fable, which, like all fables, partakes of the nature of myth. With startling awareness, we now realize that Du-

shechka, after all, is one of the Russian equivalents of the Greek Psyche, and
that what Chekhov has written could be but a reinterpretation of the ancient
legend about the girl who was named after the word meaning "soul."

The legend, which Apuleius first recorded for us,[4] tells how the youthful
Psyche became the loving wife of a great god, who was Eros himself. Eros
never showed her his face or person in the daylight; yet Psyche was happy
as long as she could take care of her little house in the daytime, and share
in night's darkness the bed and love of a husband she could neither know
nor see. What the legend means to say is that love is blind, and must remain
so, whether the loved one is mortal or an immortal creature. This is the truth
which the Greek Psyche had to learn, while the Russian Dushechka seems
to have known it, though unconsciously, all the time.

That Chekhov must have thought of this legend while writing "The
Darling" may be proved by the fact that the name or word Dushechka is but
a more popular variant of the literary *Dushenka,* after which Bogdanovich,
a minor Russian poet of the eighteenth century, entitled his own imitation
of La Fontaine's *Psyché,* which, in its turn, is a rather frivolous version of
the same old myth. This slight difference in the endings of what is practically
the same noun may have greater significance than we think. Both endings
are diminutive suffixes; but while in Bogdanovich's "-enka" there is a connotation of benevolent sympathy, in Chekhov's "-echka" there is an insinua-
tion of pettiness, and a nuance of indulgent scorn. This obviously means
that Chekhov's serious tale is as distant from Bogdanovich's light poem as
from the original legend itself: the distance may be considered so great as to
preclude any relationship. We realize this, and we realize as well that our
proof that such a relationship exists may be considered a verbal coincidence
and nothing more. In reply to this objection, we could observe that Chekhov
testified elsewhere about his knowledge of the legend itself. As we already
know, he did so in "Anyuta," by simply stating through the mouth of his
student-painter that Psyche is "a fine subject."

The student-painter is right, even if he is fully unconscious of the irony in
what he says. Aware as he was of the irony he himself had put in those words,
Chekhov must have been equally aware of their truth. Yes, Psyche is a fine
subject, even when the artist deals with it so freely as to completely change
its background and situation, lowering its fabulous vision to the level of a
bourgeois and provincial experience, and transcribing its poetic magic into
the plain images and the flat language of modern realism. This does not imply
that the tale is deprived of wonder: there is no greater wonder than to make
luminous and holy the inner and outer darkness in which we live, even

against our will. And there is no greater miracle than to have changed into a new Psyche, with no other sorcery but that of a single word, this heroine of the commonplace, this thrice-married little woman, neither clever nor beautiful, and no longer young.

D. H. Lawrence recommends that we never trust the writer, but only the tale. This is what one should do even with Chekhov, although he is one of the most trustworthy of modern writers, precisely because he builds on a broad moral structure, which compensates for the restrictions of his chosen literary forms. If this is true, then one must reject Leo Shestov's statement that Chekhov's is a creation *ex nihilo,*[5] always returning to the nothingness from which it sprang forth. It would be more proper to define it a creation *ex parvo,* producing from humble beginnings a somber and yet beautiful world.

NOTES

1. This, and all quotations from Chekhov's stories, unless indicated otherwise, are taken from Constance Garnett's translation of Chekhov's works, published in several volumes by the Macmillan Company.

2. Quoted as translated by Avram Yarmolinsky, in his *Portable Chekhov* (Viking Press).

3. Quoted as translated by Aylmer Maude in his edition of Tolstoy's works (Oxford University Press).

4. In his *Metamorphoses,* better known under the title of *The Golden Ass.*

5. In the essay "Tvorchestvo iz nichego" (Creation from nothing), which can be read in English under the title "Creation from the Void," in *Anton Tchekhov, and Other Essays,* by Leo Shestov, translated by S. S. Koteliansky and J. M. Murry (London, 1916).

The Art of Ivan Bunin

I

THE Western reader who turns his attention to modern Russian fiction often seems to think that the whole is limited to a single name. Yet Maxim Gorki, while remaining the outstanding historical figure of his age, is by no means a lonely master, or even an exemplary one. And none of Gorki's contemporaries is as different from him as his main rival and only peer, the younger Ivan Bunin, who was for a while considered Gorki's pupil. Gorki, however, felt otherwise, and proclaimed more than once that Bunin was the supreme living craftsman of Russian prose. The false opinion that he was merely a disciple of his older and more famous colleague was due in part to Bunin's early association with the *Znanie* (Knowledge) group, which Gorki had founded with the purpose of publishing realistic fiction by younger and less known authors, and which attracted all those writers who, for one reason or another, literary or otherwise, did not feel at home in the "idealistic" or "esthetic" camp.

While Gorki had come from a petty bourgeois, even plebeian, environment, had lived in his early youth the existence of a tramp and an outcast, and became later perhaps the only truly self-made man of Russian letters, Bunin, like almost all the masters of the classical age, was born a member of the landed gentry and was raised in a "nest of gentlefolk." The Bunins, however, like many families of the landowning nobility who had failed to adjust themselves to the changed times, were no longer well-to-do; and it is quite possible that the writer had in mind the history of his clan, and the decline and decay of his own class, when he wrote the poetic chronicle *Dry Valley*. Yet the line was still proud of its past and even counted some literary figures among its ancestors: Anna Bunina, a minor poetess of the early nineteenth century, and the great romantic Vasili Zhukovski, the natural son of one of the members of the clan.

Gorki came from the eastern provinces of European Russia, while Bunin's home was in the very heart of old Muscovy, from that region which is a kind of Russian Tuscany, and which at the beginning of the same century had produced so many mighty masters of the word. He was born in the year 1870, in the city of Voronezh, not far from the places where Tolstoy and Turgenev were born. While Gorki was self-taught and learned everything he knew from what he called his own "universities," which were life and the world, Bunin had his start in life with regular schooling — first at home; later in the provincial capital of Elets, which, with its own immediate surroundings, was going to become the locale of so many of his tales; and, finally, without graduating, at the University of Moscow.

While Gorki began his career as a prose writer and a storyteller, the literary beginnings of Bunin were more academic and conventional. He started as a poet and translator of verse, choosing for his versions texts that belonged almost exclusively to the narrative form, the romantic tradition, and the English tongue: for instance, Byron's dramatic poems, and The Song of Hiawatha, Longfellow's Amerindian pastiche, of which he gave a masterful rendering. Recognition of his merits was slow but steady from the start; it could not be compared in either quality or scope, being more official in character, with the popular success of Gorki, which was a triumph without parallel or precedent. Yet in 1903 Bunin received the Pushkin Prize, awarded by the literary section of the Russian Academy, which in 1909 honored him again by raising him to its ranks.

Like Gorki, Bunin migrated in search of warmer climates and settled for a while on the shores of Capri. But he went even farther than the Mediterranean and sailed through the Indian Ocean toward the South Seas for a stay on the far greater and more distant island of Ceylon. Unlike Gorki, he made literary use of his experience with non-Russian ways of life in faraway lands and wrote several exotic tales, with African and Oriental backgrounds, with colonial or tropical settings.

While Gorki always remained faithful to his proletarian upbringing, to the humanitarian and radical ideologies which had attracted him in his youth, Bunin always looked at political activity and at revolutionary agitation with aristocratic distaste, with the inborn skepticism of a conservative mind. Gorki, the "petrel" of the coming storm, accepted enthusiastically both the "little" and the "great" revolutions, the coup d'état of October not less than the uprising of February; Bunin, who had remained aloof from any form of social or practical action, took in 1917 a firm anticommunist stand. While

Gorki was destined to return home for good, Bunin took the road of exile, choosing France as his haven and dividing his time between Paris and the Maritime Alps.

Thus Bunin became the undisputed literary leader of the *émigrés,* while Gorki was enthroned as the dean of red letters and exalted to the role of cultural hero of the Soviet Union. Although Gorki had always enjoyed an immense international reputation, and for more than a third of a century had been as famous in Europe and in America as in his homeland, it was Bunin, still not yet well known abroad, who was destined to become, after Tolstoy's refusal and Gorki's failure, the first and only Russian to receive the Nobel Prize for literature, which was awarded to him in 1933. Now over eighty years old, this hard and splendid worker remains, since Gorki's death, the only living monument of the silver age of Russian literature.[1]

Besides his early volumes of verse and his early collections of stories, the literary heritage that Bunin will leave to posterity includes the novel *The Village* (1910), and four volumes of tales, which often contain at the end a few compositions in verse. The earliest of these volumes was *Dry Valley* (1912) which, like the others, opens with the title piece; it was followed by *Iounn the Weeper* (1913), *The Cup of Life* (1914), and, finally, by *The Gentleman from San Francisco* (1916). These works are the creation of Bunin's maturity, and contain all his masterpieces. The production of his years in exile is uneven, and in recent times all too often marred by writings full of a senile obsession with sex; yet it includes an outstanding novelette, *Mitya's Love* (1925); an excellent collection of tales, *A Sunstroke* (1927); and, finally, what is Bunin's most ambitious undertaking up to date, the long narrative cycle started in 1927 under the title of *The Life of Arsenyev.*

As any reader slightly acquainted with a few of these works can see, Bunin has written far more consistently and faithfully than Gorki in the straightforward tradition of Russian classical realism. His real masters are Goncharov, Turgenev, and Tolstoy; in the case of the last, Bunin was especially influenced by such pieces as "The Death of Ivan Ilich." It has been said that without the precedent of that Tolstoyan work Bunin would not have written his story "The Gentleman from San Francisco," which is nonetheless a highly original creation, not only the masterpiece among his tales, but one of the greatest ever written in the Russian tongue. There is no doubt that Bunin's "Happiness" is reminiscent of Tolstoy's *Domestic Happiness,* as the very title implies. Bunin acknowledged in the same way his debt to Goncharov by writing "The Dream of Oblomov's Grandson," and no Rus-

sian reader will fail to notice the attempt to reproduce the qualities of Turgenev's mood and style in such stories as "Conversation at Night" and "The
Grammar of Love."

Yet very often Bunin follows less obvious models or less classical examples:
for instance, the tale "A Spring Evening" (1913), where a peasant kills a
beggar to rob him of a few cents, is clearly reminiscent of a strange and cruel
true story which Dostoevski relates in *The Idiot,* the story of a merchant
killed in a hotel by his roommate for the sake of a gold watch. It is equally
evident that Bunin paid great attention to the "extravagant" writings of a
peculiar master, Leskov, whom he imitated in structure, but not in the
uniquely colorful texture of his style. Bunin's tale "A Goodly Life" (1910) is
certainly modeled on Leskov's narrative "The Amazon"; while another story,
"The Cup of Life," is clearly related to one of the favorite subjects of Leskov,
the provincial clergy, so keenly portrayed in Leskov's novel, *Cathedral Folk.*

It has been said that Bunin learned lessons also from Chekhov and Gorki,
but their influence was more vague and less lasting. This is perhaps due to
the fact that Bunin was predominantly interested in a social environment
which, even in his youth, belonged to a past almost completely dead, but
which had been a primary object of observation for Tolstoy and the other
classical realists — Russian country life, as exemplified by both the landed
gentry and the peasantry. Gorki, instead, paid far greater attention to the old
class of provincial merchants and to the newly risen urban proletariat, while
Chekhov devoted the best of all his creative energies to the portrayal of the
intelligentsia and the petty bourgeoisie. This is why the atmosphere of *The
Village* is so un-Gorkian and un-Chekhovian, despite the fact that the protagonists of that novel are a shopkeeper forever intent on amassing property
and money and a plebeian intellectual, always intoxicated with ideas and
words. Perhaps there are more traces of a Chekhovian than of a Gorkian
influence in Bunin's writing. It can be located, however, only in his very
early or his very late works. In his youth, Bunin often imitated the more
lyrical side of Chekhov's genius, as expressed, almost uniquely, in "The
Steppe." In his old age he was again attracted by the less typical Chekhov,
by the unsentimental recorder of such pathetic cases as the one which is the
theme of "The Lady with the Pet Dog," a tale which left its imprint on
Bunin's story "A Sunstroke."

This absence of any significant Chekhovian or Gorkian influence may be
explained also by the powerful attraction which Bunin felt not so much for
the literary theories as for the stylistic practices of French realism, especially
in its Flaubertian brand. Russian classical fiction had been strongly affected

by the examples of such masters as Stendhal and Balzac, and from the end of the nineteenth century to the beginning of the twentieth, the late realists were bound to feel, although in their own way, the impact of Zola's work and of French naturalism. But the teachings of Flaubert and the Goncourts had never been received in Russia with great honor or favor, and we can safely assert that Bunin is the only Russian realist who was ever won over to the French method of the *écriture artiste* and to the Parnassian ideals of impersonality and impassibility.

This "esthetic" mood strongly differentiates Bunin on one side from his beloved masters, the great novelists and storytellers of the classical age, and on the other from the outstanding figures of his own generation — in other words, from Chekhov and Gorki, to whom he was otherwise bound by the strong ties of a common loyalty to the national tradition of literary realism. This particular attitude produced the paradoxical effect of making Bunin closer than Chekhov and Gorki, and far closer than he and his critics ever supposed, to the esthetic revival of the beginning of the century. In Bunin there is a decadent strain, which, however, as in the case of Flaubert, operates in harmony with the conventions of realism and within the rigid framework of a world clearly perceived with the mind and the senses. Yet this does not make that world intelligible and sensible; what is logical and meaningful is only the artificial order imposed by the artist on the chaos of nature and of human existence.

Within the macrocosm of the universe and within the microcosm of man's experience, Bunin contemplates, like Flaubert, only the workings of cruel and blind forces. His interest in the morbid and pathological in nature and life expresses itself with a kind of unimpassioned and objective detachment, which spurns the pathetic involvement so characteristic of the Russian decadents, and spurns even more the otherworldly longings of the Russian symbolists. Bunin's distaste for the esoteric and the occult, for the eclectic and the composite, for the mystical and the metaphysical: in brief, his artistic integrity and unswerving loyalty to the demands which his talent makes on an artist's will, have transformed into an authentic master a writer who at first seemed fated to play merely an epigone's role.

Bunin's mastery is fully revealed even by his poetry, which is far less original than his prose. Without sharing the minority opinion that Bunin's verse is superior to his fiction,[2] one could still say that his craft as a poet, which he has almost ceased practicing for the last quarter of a century, proves even better than his artistry as a prose writer the uniqueness of Bunin's position among the Russian men of letters of his time. As is the case with his

stories, the themes of his poems, almost always very short and traditional
in form and content, are primarily scenes of Russian life and nature, although here also there appear not too infrequently foreign backgrounds and
exotic subjects, sometimes even classical motifs. The impersonality of the
tone, the plastic rigor of the style, the lucid order of the structure sharply
distinguish Bunin's verse from the suggestive and musical diction, from the
pathos and subjectivity of the Russian poetry of the same period. There is
less of a decadent strain in his verse than in his prose, and no trace of symbol-
istic mist. His poems may seem to anticipate the neoclassical and neo-Parnas-
sian revival of such poets as Kuzmin and Gumilev, but Bunin's taste is more
simple and solemn, less decorative and illustrative than theirs.

Bunin is more faithful than any other Russian poet of his generation to
the lesson of Pushkin and Tyutchev, the two national classical masters; the
lesson remained for many of his rivals an all too conscious ideal, while he
practiced it without pedantry or fuss. Perhaps his poetic keyboard is too
narrow and the strings of his lyre are too few: his music is so monotonous
as to seem almost monochordal. The range of his poetry is limited on the
one hand by obvious and transparent allegories built around a single situation or anecdote, and on the other by timeless and crystal-clear representa-
tions of the ever changing seasons of nature or of man's soul. In brief, the
limitations of Bunin's lyrics are the same as those of any verse predominantly
narrative or evocative in character. Yet his descriptive poetry is more self-
contained than those purple passages, in the form of detailed landscapes or
of exuberant natural spectacles, which often mar and unbalance his otherwise
masterful narrative works.

II

Despite the fact that his prose, even more than his verse, is frequently
patterned after examples by other masters, Bunin is far from being a derivative artist — a truth that must be tested, since so far we have emphasized
how much his creation is dependent upon previous models and sources. This
re-examination of Bunin's fiction must thus begin with the task of showing
the originality of his tales in contrast with their sources, and the genuine
quality of an inspiration that relies on more than mere invention.

Let us start with the story "Conversation at Night" (1911), which charac-
teristically betrays, as already remarked, traces of Turgenev's influence. As a
matter of fact, it directly re-echoes "Bezhin Meadow," one of the most famous
pieces in A Sportsman's Sketches. Both stories pretend to be the direct report
of a conversation taking place among several people out-of-doors on a sum-

mer night. In both cases, the subject matter of the conversation is horror stories, terrible happenings which the speakers have experienced personally, either as actors or as witnesses. In their written versions, those horror stories are retold from the viewpoint of an outsider, one who overheard them by chance in Turgenev's tale, and one for whose benefit they were told for the first time in Bunin's.

In Turgenev the listener is an adult, a sportsman who regularly relates in the first person all the happenings he has witnessed in his hunting expeditions, and the storytellers are a group of youngsters who narrate a series of haunting visions of the supernatural, which their superstitious beliefs transform into real experiences. In Bunin, everything is reversed: the listener is a young nobleman keeping watch in the company of his peasants, while the storytellers are all mature, even aged, men. The happenings they relate are horror stories, not subjectively, but objectively true, and equally dominated by the sense of death. But death is now a human, not a supernatural agency: it is death by violence and murder, not menacing from above, but striking from below. Its presence is conjured up again by the matter-of-fact report that one of the narrators had once killed a fellow man in cold blood.

Turgenev's story, like practically everything he wrote, begins as an idyll and ends as an elegy. It is with a feeling of poetic sympathy that the writer relives in his adult mind the fairy-tale quality of the children's imaginations and fears, and it is with poignant sorrow and awe that he compares in retrospect their superstitious forebodings with the early death, a short time later, of one of them. But the only sentiment mastering the soul of Bunin's listener and infecting the reader is, rather, the psychological agony aroused by the instinct of self-preservation, by the sudden discovery that one of the men so casually befriended is a murderer and that he may strike again.

The comparison of these two stories, so related and yet so unlike, reveals immediately all the differences between a realism based on a sense of sympathetic affinity between the heart of the artist and the object observed by him, and another kind of realism in which the artist alienates himself from the human content of the experience he contemplates in order to represent it better. Turgenev's is the realism of grace, and Bunin's the realism of necessity. For this reason, while Turgenev's vision remains in the reader's memory like the shadow of a dream, the echo of a song, the nightmare of Bunin preserves even in recollection the rigid and static impression of a bas-relief.

The same effect of plastic composition, the same sense of massive solidity, is produced by "A Spring Evening," already described as the replica of a Dostoevskian "true story," as reported by one of the characters in *The Idiot*.

In Dostoevski the story has the quality of a conversation piece or newspaper account, of a "slice of life" which the author finds meaningful despite its sordidness, or because of it. Thus it contains a "sign of contradiction," a redeeming trait, the mystical epiphany of something higher, and even more real than reality itself. This is to be seen in the emphasis laid on the fact that the murderer, as a good Christian, prays before committing his crime. In the same way, Bunin's murderer addresses his victim with the Christian epithet "brother" and begs him to yield his money peaceably, so that both may be relieved of the dreadful necessity of killing and being killed.

But in Bunin's story that act and that word play the role of strange details or curious traits, of peculiar and yet meaningless idiosyncrasies. The knife of Dostoevski's murderer, who mercifully slaughters his friend in his sleep, is here replaced by a flagstone which the killer, lowering his "bull head," tears away from the pavement with a "crash," and it is with that "cold" and "heavy" object that he crushes the skull of his victim through the face. The entire story seems to be engraved on that very stone, as if it were chiseled in granite.

A similar impression is produced by "The Gentleman from San Francisco," which seems sculptured in a more polished and precious substance, like porphyry or basalt. It is the story of an American millionaire who has crossed the Atlantic with his family to enjoy a little fun and rest far from home, and who suddenly dies of a stroke, while dressing for dinner, in a Capri hotel. The management does both its best and its worst to hide the tragedy from the guests, and the corpse is snatched away in unseemly haste, without honor or respect. There is an obvious contrast between the plush glamor of the hotel, its luxury and comfort, and the cheapness and vulgarity of the millionaire's end; perhaps, also, there is the intent to relate significantly the prosperous materialism of the millionaire's life with the brutality of his death, which is not the death of a human being but of a brute slaughtered, like a bull, by a blow struck from nowhere. But what is far more important is the anonymity of that death, symbolized by the very fact that the hero, or rather the victim, remains nameless. He was the "gentleman from San Francisco," and nothing more.

This story differs basically from Tolstoy's "Death of Ivan Ilich," although there is some resemblance in several respects, especially in the emphasis on the callous indifference of the survivors at the spectacle of death. Ivan Ilich is an average man, a vulgar man, but one whom we know personally, almost intimately, as is shown by the use, even in the title, of his Christian name and patronymic, and with whom we get better acquainted during his illness, of which we know the causes and the progress. It is his malady, as a matter of fact, that makes even Ivan Ilich better acquainted with life and with himself, and humanizes and spiritualizes him. His death is as brutal as the death of the gentleman from San Francisco, but it is a gradual process; while the latter is struck by a sudden blow, Ivan Ilich is slowly sucked into the bottom of a sack, like a domestic animal which his master wants to get rid of. During his torture, Ivan Ilich utters human sounds, which only near the end become the meaningless whining of a poor beast. But the gentleman from San Francisco has time to utter only an inarticulate gasp.

Finally, in spite of everything, the ordeal of Ivan Ilich ends with a sense of illumination and redemption: death transcends its ugliness and becomes a vision of grace, even though only for a passing moment. But the death of the gentleman from San Francisco is an "act of God" only in the natural sense of the phrase: a stroke of lightning, without mysticism or tragedy. The human drama of the mortality of the body reconciles itself in Tolstoy's tale with the hope of, if not the belief in, the immortality of the soul, while in Bunin's story there is only the triumph of nothingness, and there resounds only the bell of doom. Yet this story, conveying so powerfully the sense of the fragility of life and the certainty of the annihilation of all things, is an authentic masterpiece, ancient, mysterious, and perfect as a monolith.

Bunin's skill in changing alien material into a substance of his own is equally evident in "A Goodly Life," which, as already stated, is derivative from Leskov's "The Amazon." In both pieces a cunning and scheming woman reviews, with complacency and self-indulgence, her own worldly career, and from her account we learn how, by using her wits and by exploiting her men, she has been able to feather her nest and to reach a position of prosperity and respectability. She is a self-righteous hypocrite, unscrupulous and unremorseful, who has sacrificed her friends for her profit, and even ruined her son. It is the old story of Moll Flanders, of the go-getter and the gold-digger, rewritten against the background of a provincial existence and the Russian way of life. Both Bunin and Leskov reproduce the idiomatic and personal peculiarities of her popular speech, but while Leskov, in doing so, aims at an effect of genial humor and amusing irony, the purpose of Bunin is more objective and functional. Leskov's piece is a vivid and grotesque caricature, as the title itself indicates, and it emphasizes the naïveté of the heroine rather than her duplicity, while Bunin's aim is to draw, without ethos or pathos, a lucid and merciless portrait.

As for "The Cup of Life," it bears the same relationship to Leskov's *Cathedral Folk* as *Le Curé de Tours* does to the longer novels of *La*

Comédie Humaine. Like Balzac's tale, Bunin's story is built around an ecclesiastical intrigue. While, in his great fresco of the life of the Russian clergy, Leskov aims both at producing the concrete and picturesque feeling of a unique milieu and at evoking the moral battle taking place within the walls of the church and within each individual soul, Bunin is interested only in the ironic contrast between the holy rituals of religious life and the mean passions of his frocked heroes. Balzac, with romantic exaggeration, raises the petty clerical plottings of *Le Curé de Tours* to the level of a military and diplomatic duel, to a high strategy so skillful and complex as to transcend the vulgar prizes of the victory, which are easy living and social prestige; the dry realism of Bunin lowers the rivalry between his characters to the plane of a struggle for life in the Darwinian sense.

The long warfare, without quarter or truce, between the two clergymen Iordanski and Selikhov, who are moved by identical ambitions and desires, by a reciprocal envy and by the same hatred, ends without conqueror or conquered, because the one dies while celebrating, almost triumphantly, the funeral rites of the other. The lady whom both had loved and whom one had succeeded in marrying is left a widow and dies without enjoying the house which she had long dreamed of owning. Everybody leaves the scene of the world without being able to drink fully from the "cup of life." Only Gorizontov, the giant, survives, by using his own energies sparingly and by exploiting even in life his future death, having already sold to the Medical School of the University of Moscow the skeleton which still supports his enormous body. The story closes in this way, with the unrelieved irony of bitter sarcasm.

Even exotic backgrounds and tropical settings are used by Bunin for the purpose of expressing with stern objectivity the cruelty of life and the absurdity of the world. Thus, in "Brethren" (1916) he describes the wretched existence of a Singhalese rickshaw-boy, pulling a tired and bored white man around the city of Colombo. During the tour, the boy discovers by chance that his girl friend has betrayed him, and he kills himself at the end of that day's work. In the second part of the story, Bunin reports the conversations of the same white man with the captain of the ship carrying him home, and from his words we learn that a different and yet equal burden of sorrow is oppressing the heart of the rich man, no less than it did the heart of the poor rickshaw-boy. Here Bunin aims at an effect of symmetrical parallelism and of symbolic contrast; the meaning of the story lies in the juxtaposition of two episodes which are related only by chance and by a common, but negative, trait: the mutual indifference of two sufferers.

The simple allegorical message which the narrative conveys lies in the composition itself, in the lucid arrangement of the artistic object, not in the human actors as such, or in any ethical judgment of the artist, who uses words for painting, not for preaching. The moral, if any, is contained in the title of the story, and in its epigraph, which is a quotation from the holy wisdom of India: "Look at these brothers who are killing each other; I do not want to utter words of grief." The artistic aim of Bunin is concisely and effectively stated in these very words; his intent as a writer is merely to point his finger in silence at the cruel wounds of life and at the cynical indifference of the material universe. If there is a lesson, it is taught to us by the things themselves. Such is the esthetic practice of a writer who is the master of what one might call a stoic realism.

Far less convincing is another famous exotic story, the one entitled "The Dreams of Chang" (1916). Here the past life of a retired sea captain who was once betrayed by his wife and who is now waiting only for death is evoked through the reminiscences of his old Chinese dog. This is not an "animal story" in the sense that Tolstoy's "Kholstomer" or Chekhov's "Kashtanka" are, because there is no attempt to understand or reconstruct animal psychology per se. Nor is it an "animal fable" in the traditional sense, like Cervantes' "Dialogue of the Dogs," where animals look at the human world with intellectual irony and philosophical wisdom. The weakness of Bunin's tale lies in the fact that it remains halfway between those two poles and that the perspective of the animal's reminiscences is essentially used as a dehumanizing and depersonalizing device, through which the various episodes of the captain's past life are deprived of their all too human content. The same device helps Bunin to adopt again his favorite method of a parallel juxtaposition of different scenes, which here, however, does not serve a higher artistic purpose. There are other exotic stories of Bunin, full of human insight, which recall the work of another storyteller of the sea, the Anglicized Slav Joseph Conrad.

Bunin's scorn for the pathetic does not prevent him from trying his hand at that kind of poetic and sentimental realism so frequently and lovingly practiced by the masters of the Russian classical age. One of the most charming stories of this kind is "The Grammar of Love," which at first reminds us of Turgenev at his best. It is the description of a visit made by a young man to the empty house of a dead relative who had lived there for twenty years completely alone, with only the company of his memories and souvenirs — memories and souvenirs of a fiancée who died young. It is a pilgrimage to a sanctuary of faith and love, and we expect from the devout pilgrim not only piety and reverence but also some idolatry and fetishism.

The poet, however, destroys immediately this mystical mood by an ambivalent and almost decadent attitude toward the objects of that pious worship. The reader himself is infected by this half moved and half amused reaction toward the obsolete quaintness of the trifles left by a past only recently dead. Thus the author contributes toward preventing the revival of that religion of remembrance which the visitor tries to conjure within himself. When the latter discovers the necklace of the woman who was loved so much and so long, the view of that object arouses in him "the same indecipherable sentiment he had once experienced, in a small Italian town, at the sight of the relics of a woman saint." This allusion to a holy or sacred thing must not deceive us; the relics, no less than the necklace, are evoked only as unfamiliar, bizarre *objets d'art*. In this way, those outmoded, old-fashioned keepsakes are forever deprived of all traces of human life, of the joy or sorrow they once bespoke. Thus they become ancient and archaic, as distant in space and time as a meteorite or a fossil.

It was only in his later years that Bunin wrote his first real love stories, dominated, unlike the earlier ones, by the sexual impulse alone. Even here, however, love is seen as a sudden flame rather than a slow fire, as a "sunstroke," to use the title of one of the best tales of this kind. In "A Sunstroke," an officer serving in a forgotten garrison on the Volga has a brief affair with a woman whom he meets by chance, never to meet again, but the ashes of that passion will remain forever in his soul, left as empty as the water stirred by the departing river boat. The situation is initially identical with the one in Chekhov's "Lady with a Pet Dog," where, however, the adventure started by chance is renewed by the will of the two partners, who bind themselves for the rest of their lives with the chains of affection and habit.

Completely un-Chekhovian is the atmosphere of another story, which, like the previous one, is among the best written by Bunin in exile: "A Light Breath." It is a "case history" reconstructed against the background of Russian "high life" before the revolution. A girl of the nobility, although in love with a young man, gives herself to a mature officer, who is also a distant relative of hers. The sordid adventure brings an aftermath of shame, and the girl kills herself. At this point the "case history" changes into a work of poetry and art: the image of the handful of dust, which is now suffocating even the memory of that lively breath which was the secret of her charm, symbolizes both the violence of fate and the sorrow of the soul for a creature of grace or a thing of beauty forever lost. Here there is a real feeling of pity for the "brief candle" of human life and feminine youth.

This sense of the fatality of Eros finds perhaps its highest expression in one of the best among Bunin's late works, the novelette *Mitya's Love,* where the protagonist is again a young person. It is an ordinary story: Mitya leaves the big city and his fiancée Katya for a brief stay on his country estate. For a long time he does not hear from his fiancée, and the first letter he receives is to be the last, for Katya writes merely to break the news to him of her decision to put an end to their tie, and Mitya shoots himself. The progress of passion and jealousy in a fresh, immature mind continually fed and tortured by love and desire, by trust and suspicion, by hope and despair, reminds us of the broodings of the Proustian protagonist over the shadow of his Albertine and over his own past. But in Bunin's narrative, as always, there is the candid and lucid vision of a mind which contemplates the human heart with compassion, but without illusion.

These last stories are more human and "softer" than the earlier ones, but not so solid and well constructed. They deal with more complex personalities and subtler feelings, while the earlier tales dealt with primitive psychologies and elemental passions. But even here we witness almost without exception the triumph of death, or at least the defeat of man. Life is still for Bunin a Pandora's box, even if now he does not look at it with the Gorgon's eye of his youth. He is no longer exclusively interested in crises and climaxes, in states of acute tension, in those moments when time seems to stand still. The catastrophes or cataclysms of our existence are now being replaced by more normal and human experiences, which Bunin contemplates as skeptically but not so cynically as before, with a touch of indulgent wisdom which is new in him.

Yet the stories of his maturity remain the best he ever wrote and constitute by themselves a high achievement and an imposing body of work, produced, like his novels, in the brief span of a few years, at the acme of his talent. Sometimes it may seem that they irradiate a light which is clear but too cold — that their colors are as bright and lifeless as the colors we see in the magic lantern or the kaleidoscope. But the best pieces are pure gold, and the skill of their maker is as perfect as the craft of the goldsmith. All too often, in regard to both his stories and his novel *The Village,* Bunin has been accused of treating the palpitating substance of life with the frigid efficiency of a surgeon. It has also been said that he pays excessive attention to the trifles of reality and the minutiae of physical experience by reproducing them with painstaking pedantry. The latter accusation is true, and this fault may be seen, even more than in the descriptive pages based on visual impressions, in those passages where he handles with exuberant detail the blind perceptions of the crudest senses. It is in such cases that we see Bunin at his worst, as shown by this almost ludicrous example taken from "Brethren," and referring to the poor rickshaw-boy of that story: "The smell of his body had become worse; it was a scent of boiling tea, mixed with cocoanut oil and some sort of spirit: it was the smell of a handful of ants crushed between one's fingers and palm. . . ."

Yet the best of his production as a short story writer, that dozen tales which he wrote in his early maturity and which culminate in "The Gentleman from San Francisco," will hold a place of their own in all anthologies, and their presence and permanence there will again attest to the singularity of Bunin's creation in his own nation and time. If there is anyone outside of Russia to whom we may compare the author of these stories, it is perhaps the Italian *verista* Giovanni Verga, and it is not a mere coincidence that the Sicilian and the Russian appealed equally, in the English world, to the keen and earnest mind of D. H. Lawrence.[3]

III

That Bunin is also a poet is a fact never to be forgotten by the reader of his prose, perhaps even less by the reader of his novels than by the reader of his tales. That the author himself was aware of the poetic quality of his most ambitious undertakings as a writer of fiction is shown by the subtitle "a poem," which he gave to the two novels of his maturity, beginning with *The Village*.[4] In this he followed the example of Gogol, who had given the same subtitle to *Dead Souls*. One must remember, however, that the Russian word *poema* indicates the epic poem or a poetic narrative of vast proportions; hence the use of that label ought to imply that the poetic quality of the novels so designated resides more in the imaginative design of the whole than in matters of diction and texture.

Yet Gogol, by calling his novel "a poem," may have intended to allude to the splendor of the lyrical digressions so frequent in its pages, and even more to the suggestiveness and ornamental magnificence of its style. Perhaps in the very choice of that label there was a touch of irony, nay, of "romantic irony" — after all, *Dead Souls* is an epic narrative in form but not in substance, using the grand style of heroic inspiration to evoke by contrast a mean and unheroic way of life. From this standpoint, we can assert that the subtitle is used more literally and traditionally by the author of *The Village*, even if in Bunin's term we may find also other, and more modern, overtones.

It is evident, for instance, that by the use of that term both Bunin and

Gogol wished to emphasize, among other things, their own deliberate attempt to transform the ugly matter of life into the beautiful substance of poetry. Yet Bunin wanted at the same time to underline the detachment with which the artist had contemplated and represented the reality thus transfigured by art. This does not mean that Bunin was more keenly aware than Gogol of that attitude of impartial serenity which, rightly or wrongly, is generally considered a peculiar trait of the epic poem, or of any kind of inspiration or narration which the term "epic" may designate. Bunin was probably thinking primarily in Flaubertian terms and aiming at writing a novel so elaborate and exemplary as to produce the effect of a poem. Yet in Bunin's case we cannot avoid recalling Nietzsche's statement in *The Birth of Tragedy* that, while lyric and tragic poetry are dynamic and musical in character, the epos is essentially plastic and static. There is no doubt that the last two epithets define perfectly the most characteristic elements of the creative imagination of Bunin, and that they are especially applicable to the particular case of *The Village*.

Besides this minor detail of a common subtitle, there is no other real similarity in quality, subject matter, or spirit, between *The Village* and *Dead Souls*. It is true that the reader of the former may be inclined to respond, as Pushkin is supposed to have done after a reading of the latter, with the sigh: "How sad is our Russia!" But one should not forget that the feeling of sadness aroused by Gogolian Russia is an unexpected by-product of a vision of romantic humor, of a grotesque distortion of reality through the lens of an imagination both pathetic and comic. The feeling of sadness aroused by Bunin's Russia is, instead, the effect of the "high seriousness" of this novel's inspiration, both so lucid and so detached as to give sometimes an impression of apathy.

Even objectively, the Russia of *The Village* is very different from the Russia of *Dead Souls* or of Gogol's time. Landowners and bureaucrats are replaced by peasants and by peasants alone; even those who have risen in station were once tillers of the soil, and their prosperity is based on exploitation of the peasants' toil. In Bunin's novel, there are no provincial capitals or country manors as there are in Gogol, but only the village with its huts and fields. Certainly Bunin's novel is not the only Russian narrative of this kind, and it is perhaps significant that the author gave it the same title assigned by Grigorovich three quarters of a century before to one of the earliest works of fiction exclusively devoted to the Russian peasantry. This word may have appealed to both Grigorovich and Bunin for the breadth of its

meaning: *derevnya* means both "country" and "village," and contains all
the possible allusions, positive or negative, to a mode of existence which is
the opposite of city life.

But the similarities between *The Village* of Bunin and *The Village* of
Grigorovich end here; the latter was written in the sentimental and humanitarian spirit of peasant fiction in the European literature of its time, as
treated by George Sand, Auerbach, and later in Russia by Turgenev in *A
Sportsman's Sketches*. Grigorovich's novel is, moreover, centered around an
individual character and a personal case, while Bunin's work is a large
composition and a complex portrayal, more aptly designated by its collective
title. Furthermore, Bunin's novel aims at being an artistic monument rather
than a social document and avoids all the dangers of "civic writing," which
leans so easily at one and the same time toward both idealization and ideology.

One should likewise bear in mind that the peasant Russia described by
Grigorovich was still the Russia of serfdom, while the action of Bunin's novel
takes place a long time after the emancipation of the serfs, in another and
even more critical age — in other words, in the tragic years immediately following the Russo-Japanese War and the "little revolution" of 1905. Since
it was published in 1910, *The Village* therefore describes Russian country life
as an immediate experience. This fact does not prevent it from being
dominated by the feeling that the village or the country it conjures up before
our eyes represents what is human and universal in Russia beyond any limita-
tion of space and time. The author, in fact, uses one of the characters as a
mouthpiece for his own symbolic intent when he causes the old peasant
Balashkin to tell Kuzma Ilich, one of the two protagonists of the story:
"Russia, all Russia, is but a village — fix this well in your mind!"

The composition of *The Village* is based on the usual devices of juxtaposition, parallelism, and symmetry. The quality of its inspiration and style,
the almost pre-established harmony of its plan, and finally, its division into
three equal, complementary parts, may justify the comparing of this novel
to what is called a triptych in the field of the visual arts. The structure is
highly contrived, and conveys, therefore, rather than a sense of easy and
graceful proportions, an effect of both restraint and constraint.

The first part describes the striving and struggling life of Tikhon Ilich,
a "rugged individualist" of peasant origin, who has become an innkeeper
and whose sole aim in life is to acquire property and to amass money. Aware
of his strength, he is harsh toward himself no less than toward others, including his family. Always ready to exact a hard bargain from life and his fellow
men, he is not, however, completely devoid of an elementary sense of justice.

Tikhon feels obscurely that he is being punished for his sins by the fatality or curse preventing him, through a fault of himself or of his women, from having any offspring.

The second part is centered in the life of his brother Kuzma during the years of their long feud. Kuzma is a self-taught peasant, a tramp and an outcast, a naïve idealist always unable to realize his dreams of a better life for himself, for other human beings, or for the Russian people; and who wanders everywhere, hopeless and helpless, searching vainly for happiness, and often merely for luck. The third part describes Kuzma's activities and experiences after his reconciliation with Tikhon, who entrusts him with the task of overseeing a piece of land he has acquired. The novel ends with the marriage of the "Young One," the mistress of Tikhon, with one of his dependents — a marriage which is wanted by her former lover, and which his brother vainly tries to prevent.

The victory in the practical and moral struggle between the two brothers falls, therefore, to the only one who really willed it, and this shows that there is no dramatic contrast between the protagonist and the antagonist. Yet this unbrotherly couple is a relatively new replica of an old psychological opposition, frequently treated in Russian literature, and generally conceived in terms of a friendly contrast, in a relationship of duality rather than of dualism — the opposition between the practical and the unpractical man, the active and the passive one, between the realist and the idealist, the doer and the dreamer.

That opposition had already been established between Stolz and the protagonist in Goncharov's *Oblomov*, or, even earlier, between the two peasants Khor and Kalinych in the opening piece of Turgenev's *Sportsman's Sketches*. Yet, unlike Goncharov, Bunin refuses to feel any indulgent sympathy for Oblomov-Kuzma, or any abstract respect for Stolz-Tikhon, and, unlike Turgenev, he is incapable of loving equally and fully each of his respective equivalents of Kalinych and Khor. His own impartiality is the impartiality of skepticism and cynicism, or at least the impartiality of an artist's mind looking at human reality from a distance or from above.

For this very reason, Tikhon and Kuzma, who avoid the dangers of becoming mere types, remain as characters so fixed in their own idiosyncrasies that they really fail to merge and to meet. They are contrasted statically, rather than dynamically, and this is why their opposition is more formal than substantial and there is no drama in their conflict. In a certain sense, these two "brother-enemies" have the same relationship to each other as the two protagonists of "Brethren."

On the other hand, it must be recognized that the aim of Bunin's novel was to create exactly such an effect. It is quite significant that he takes a different position from Goncharov's, for whom the real Russian is Oblomov, while Stolz is a German by origin and a Russian more by chance than by choice. Thus he follows the example of Turgenev's sketch in suggesting that in Russia there is room for both the Kalinychs and the Khors. That it is really so is shown by the fact that each of Bunin's brothers claims to be an authentic representative of Russian humanity. Paradoxically, it is Kuzma, in whom Bunin rehearses some of the most obvious traits of Russian literary psychology and who is such an evident replica, in modern surroundings and in peasant dress, of the stock figure of the "superfluous man," who claims to be a norm and an exception at the same time, when he describes himself as "a strange type of Russian."

Yet the same thing can be said of the more complex and contradictory figure of Tikhon, who often wavers between a matter-of-fact view of man's lot and an almost mystical boredom with the business of living, and who feels as much at home as his brother in the human gallery of Russian fiction. Of both one could say what Bunin says of one of them and of Russian psychology in general: "All colors in one soul!"

The greatest shortcoming of *The Village* may be seen in the fact, rather uncommon in Bunin's work, that the two principal characters, especially the antagonist, are unduly given to self-analysis and introspection, that they think, and even talk, too much. Both Tikhon, like the "hard" heroes of Gorki, and Kuzma, like the "soft" heroes of Chekhov, chatter too articulately and inconclusively about the absurdity of life and the contradictions of the human soul, about the tragic fate of Russia and the future destiny of her people. Even more unconvincing is the presence in this novel of a peasant equivalent to the type and role of Potugin in Turgenev's *Smoke,* the old Balashkin, who is not content to observe and condemn the ills of Russian reality, but who even writes them down in a little notebook of his own, and who, like Potugin, repeatedly curses the sleepy backwardness of Russia and her people.

As a matter of fact, Balashkin is even more of a stock character than Potugin himself; the writer looks at him without any special sympathy, just as he looks at Tikhon and at Kuzma without Gorkian pathos or Chekhovian indulgence. This is perhaps due to the fact that the ideological outbursts of the characters are treated more as documentary material than as the expression of the author's social or moral views. In truth, such a polemical and topical element appears here almost by exception and eventually disappears from Bunin's work. After *The Village* Bunin's characters will talk, if at all, rather too little than too much, and this applies also to *Dry Valley,* where people do not speak but sing.

Tikhon and Kuzma resemble each other in other ways, too. Bunin makes this similarity evident through the use of various devices: by the symbolical analogy between Tikhon's sterility and Kuzma's lack of will; by the parallelism between Tikhon's willful and Kuzma's wishful selfishness; by balancing the former's sins of commission with the latter's sins of omission. For these reasons the two brothers stand in this novel not opposite, but beside each other; like figures in a primitive painting, they look straight ahead, not around themselves. Nor is the power of this composite portrait too much weakened by the excessive emphasis of the author on the thoughts or words of his models, which after all are merely added, like the lettering of an ancient picture.

Yet those two figures do not stand alone; as a matter of fact, they act as caryatids supporting a greater structure. Around or against them stands the entire village, which, especially in the third part, becomes the real protagonist of the story, a collective actor rather than a passive chorus. The last panel of the triptych assumes, therefore, the shape of a poliptych of its own. The minor figures, who in the first two parts had occupied the background, now invade the foreground of the picture. Their very presence, by contrast, revitalizes the two protagonists, who end by standing out in a clear-cut separation from the compositional mass.

The secondary characters are less polished and finished, looking more like torsos than like complete statues, yet they are no less solid or perfect. While the protagonists are always designated by their patronymics, the peasants are distinguished only by their Christian names, like Denis and Yakov; or by nicknames, like Odnodvorka; or merely by descriptive labels, like the "Young One" and the "She-Goat." This makes for both picturesqueness and anonymity, and the elemental simplicity of their traits renders them common and peculiar at the same time. Thus, paradoxically, they become almost more real as artistic persons than Tikhon and Kuzma, whose portraits are more detailed and who have more developed personalities. In comparison with the two brothers, the peasants seem to be at the same time more particular and general, more national and universal. For the creative imagination of Bunin, what appears to be less glamorous and interesting on the plane of life may become more suggestive and significant on the plane of art.

The artistic result of *The Village* is achieved, as we have already said, by a skillful and exact craftsmanship which avoids any kind of idealization and sentimentality. Of these peasants and their lot, as of the two protagonists and their life, one could really say what Balashkin says of the contents of his notebook: "They are materials worthy of the devil." Bunin's novel is an attempt to evoke the inferno of peasant Russia: a real inferno, ruled by the Tempter himself, not the bizarre hell of Gogol's fancy, visited by a host of little demons who are merely mischievous and mean. And it is the firmness of the hand which had been able to draw such a picture that led his friend, Boris Zaytsev, to call Bunin "an Antonio Pollaiuolo of our time."

IV

In *The Village* there is no sense of change, no sense of time. The action takes place in a timeless present, without future or hope, without past or memory. For this very reason, that novel is far more representative and typical of Bunin and his creation than *Dry Valley*, which, from any standpoint, is the opposite of *The Village*, an exception or a paradox among the works of this writer and, without any doubt, his supreme masterpiece. It is really strange that Bunin gave the same subtitle, "A Poem," to two pieces so different in intent, in spirit, and in scope. Here, consciously or not, the subtitle seems to indicate a quality of lyrical nostalgia and suggestiveness, and the very fact that this novelette is extremely short (less than a hundred pages) may allow the reader to interpret the label to mean "a prose poem."

That quality and this definition imply quite clearly that the static style and the sculptural structure of *The Village* have been replaced by an inspiration which is musical in spirit and form. While we compared *The Village* to a triptych or a poliptych, to a visual or plastic composition, *Dry Valley* might be more properly likened to a symphony. *The Village* aims, perhaps unsuccessfully, at achieving that kind of artistic ideal which Nietzsche defined as Apollonian, while *Dry Valley* follows instead a Dionysian impulse. Since Nietzsche had based his esthetic mythology on the philosophy of Schopenhauer, we may state, with the help of the ideas of that thinker, that *Dry Valley* expresses, as only wordless music can, the cosmic will to live through man's death. In truth, the real theme of this tale is the curse of living and dying within the prison of time, a mood which is not conveyed in words but in sighs and tunes. The story itself is told not in speech but in weeping and song, while all the surrounding world seems to weep and sing with it. Here the poet is never afraid of what is called the "pathetic fallacy." Human grief infects creation itself, and in the pauses of the voice of the poet, when the tale is broken by a spell of oblivion or silence, it seems that we can hear the "tears of things."

Yet, even more than *The Village*, *Dry Valley* may appear at first sight to be a work intentionally or initially written in the realistic tradition, nay, in the very stream of naturalism. Like so many typical naturalistic novels, a genre within which we may include a few works which anticipated or readapted that form, *Dry Valley* is the story of the ruin of a family and it describes all phases and aspects of that ruin: the steady economic decline, the slow physiological and psychological degeneration, the gradual process of degradation of the ethos and the will, the dissipation of the last resources, and the final annihilation of the house or the clan. From this viewpoint the Khrushchevs of *Dry Valley* could be rightly considered as a link in that chain which in Russia includes the Golovlevs of Saltykov and the Artamonovs of Gorki and which in Europe starts with Zola's Rougon-Marquarts to end with Thomas Mann's Buddenbrooks.

Yet *Dry Valley* recalls also a more purely Russian series of literary works, which, from the title of a famous narrative of Sergey Aksakov, perhaps the earliest of its kind, one could call "family chronicles" — those splendid idylls or elegies in prose describing the patriarchal way of life of the landed gentry on their ancient lands and in their old manors, in their "nests of gentlefolk," left to us not only by Turgenev and Aksakov but also by Goncharov and by the great Tolstoy himself.

Sergey Aksakov had experienced that way of life at its best in his youth, even though he did not write about it until he was old. But when Turgenev, Goncharov, and Tolstoy were writing, it already belonged to the past and was about to disappear from the face of the earth. In Bunin's age, it was only a memory, and to re-evoke it, he had to turn backwards in time and could not help but choose as the period and theme of his book the very moment of the agony of that world. The final crisis of the Khrushchev clan, which owns, among other holdings, the village of Dry Valley[5] and its farmlands, is in fact historically placed at the time immediately following the Crimean War and the emancipation of the serfs.

However, we do not witness those events directly, but at a double remove. The narrator of the story is the last male descendant of the Khrushchevs: he and his sister are the only survivors of the family, and they have no heirs. We do not know exactly the date at which the narration takes place, although we may guess that it must be at the end of the past century or the beginning of the present. The narrator does not recollect the events themselves, but the reminiscences and reports of his old nurse Natalia, who, when he and his sister were in their childhood, used to retell the story of the old times.

The narration takes, therefore, the dual shape of direct and indirect speech, being spoken in both the third and the first person. The ruin of the family is thus projected in three layers of time, and in three different psychological perspectives: the perspective of Natalia, and the perspectives of the narrator both as a child and as an adult. Through these different perspectives we see the unfolding of the crisis, its climax, and its aftermath, but without following either the sequence of time or the chain of events. The various ages and generations merge together continuously, in a series of flashbacks, touched off by a spontaneous association of impressions and moods. Yet even this confusion of the chronology has a logic of its own, and it is the logic of the heart.[6]

That the perspective of the nurse is the most important of the three is evident from every point of view. Her central position as narrator and witness is symbolized by the fact that her name is continually repeated in the story, almost as frequently as the name of Dry Valley, while the person speaking in the first person remains nameless. As a sign of collective anonymity the narrator uses even more frequently the formula "my sister and I," while Natalia's remarks, when reported in the form of direct speech, are dominated by the plural "we."

This lack of the sense of any clear-cut individual distinction between the various members of the family and their household is poetic and natural, since *Dry Valley* is probably the only narrative of its kind where there is no differentiation between landowners and peasants, between masters and serfs. They may belong to different classes or ranks, but all of them belong even more to the same human breed. This is especially true of the domestic servants, who are practically undifferentiated from their masters. And all members of the family and the household base their reciprocal kinship on something higher than the tie of dependence and blood, that is, on their common bond with the land. This is why the real protagonist of the story is neither Natalia nor the Khrushchev clan, but the village and the country of Dry Valley. And its antagonist, who in the end will win, is time itself.

This feeling of attachment to an ancestral land is all the more powerful because it is not the human, perhaps all too human, feeling of the landlord or laborer who loves the earth because of the money or sweat he has shed on it and the wheat or wealth it produces for him. No, the Khrushchevs and their retainers are neither tillers nor exploiters of the soil nourishing them, for they live on it not like human beings, but like plants and trees, and thus are condemned to die as soon as that soil dries up, or they are uprooted from it.

It is not a mere figure of speech to say that the only possible mode of existence for the Khrushchevs, as for their dependents and heirs, is vegetative life. While the last branches are slowly withering away, their heart's desire is to be transplanted back into their native land and to grow there again for a brief time, lonely, unseen, and forgotten "as the crimson flower of the steppe." Since this is not possible, they wish at least to be buried there, and their most poignant sorrow is not that their immediate ancestors are sleeping forever in the oblivion of unmarked graves, which no one is able even to point out any longer, but that those graves were dug in an alien earth.

If the family and its mode of existence seem still to survive, it is merely because, thanks to Natalia's narrations as recalled by her former wards, their memory is not yet completely dead. The Khrushchevs and Dry Valley are still floating on the waters of time, into which they will finally sink, a long time after their shipwreck. The future will submerge everything into nothingness, both a past which was only an illusion and a present which is but a shadow. After all, nothing ever happened in Dry Valley, at least in the sense of events which are the effect of human action or of human will. Like the changes of the weather and the cycles of the seasons, every occurrence is there passively accepted, in joy or in sorrow, with patience or resignation.

In the present even less happens; there is only a continuous attempt to recapture the vision and the feeling of "the time lost," to revive "the remembrance of things past." And if there is a sense of absolute and final despair in the soul of the last of the Khrushchevs, it is not so much the awareness that the well of life is completely dried up on their land as the inexorable certainty that sooner or later no one will be left to shed tears on the abandoned ruins and the desert earth. This hopeless feeling that even the last memories will fade away forever, that no heart will survive where the religion of memory could be rekindled again, gives *Dry Valley* a sense of tragic pathos which no work of Bunin ever attained either before or after. This feeling is shared by Natalia who, however, accepts that destiny with the simplicity of a creature of the earth and who entrusts herself and her past to the anonymous memory of the race, through legends and songs. Her "folk soul" feels perhaps instinctively that no tradition is wholly lost.

The device of re-evoking the past of the Khrushchevs through a threefold projection, and at a double remove, is not a contrived literary convention, but a successful invention, which gives the story richness and color, passion and depth. It is this very device which helps to produce the musical pattern of the work, acting as a kind of choral accompaniment to the melody of *Dry Valley*. The solo in this melody is sung by Natalia, with her pure voice and solemn accents. The poet, through the narrator, has this to say of the

stories she tells: "There were in those narrations jokes, digressions, and
omissions; there were extraordinary vividness, simplicity, and imagination.
But there was something else beside: mystery, and a soft-voiced murmuring,
resounding and lofty. They were dominated by a kind of ancient melancholy."
No critic could speak better of the work itself.

Practically every one of the characters, Natalia even oftener than any
other, is frequently defined by the narrator as a "Dry Valley soul." The most
typical characteristic of the "Dry Valley soul" is an attitude of awe before
life and the world, a naïve belief that every small incident or happening is a
miracle or a curse, a wonder or a sign. In the page quoted above, the narrator
and the poet describe the presence of that sentiment in Natalia's tales with
the following words: "And all this was penetrated by the archaic or old-
fashioned belief in predestination, a sense confused and unexpressed, yet
constantly full of the feeling that everyone must take upon himself this or
that burden, in conformity with this or that destiny."

In other words, Dry Valley, its "souls," and the very story of their suffer-
ings, are obsessed by superstition and fatalism. Yet this character of theirs is
not treated by Bunin in a positivistic vein, or according to any kind of
naturalistic determinism. Nor does he handle this theme with mystical
participation or consent; superstition and fatalism are for him merely the
human and poetic expression of the primitive sense of the immanent presence
of the supernatural in man's life and within nature herself. It is a religious
feeling, albeit not a spiritual one, since it does not postulate, even in the
characters' minds, that creation is ruled by a benign hand, by a divine
providence, or by a cosmic design. Rather it presupposes the existence of
superhuman forces, obscure in character and evil in intent, which bring ruin
into life and chaos into the world.

It is this sense of the supernatural that led Prince Mirsky to the suggestive,
and yet misleading, parallel between this story and "The Fall of the House
of Usher" by Edgar Allan Poe.[7] But *Dry Valley* is neither a "horror story"
nor a "tale of wonder," but an ordinary narrative, filled with the sense of
habit rather than with strangeness and surprise, written in an atmosphere
which is more hypnotic than magnetic, fabulous because of its imaginative
richness, not because of any flight of fancy. Its sense of fatality does not
reside in the complexity of the passions or the exceptional destiny of its
characters, but in the things themselves and in their very substance, which is
the substance of the earth. This is why that fatality is not allegorized, but
expressed simply and directly, beginning with the title of the story, which is

also the name of its locale. That name is repeated continuously, as if it were a refrain or a spell, and all its suggestion is based on the etymological allusion conveyed by it, by the poetic irony suggesting that Dry Valley is also a "valley of tears."

The country of Dry Valley may be wild and poor, yet nature there is full of beauty and charm. The splendor of the landscape is so overpowering that not only the characters, but even the poet and the reader, seem to be overwhelmed by it. Yet here the descriptive passages play a far different role from the panoramas or dioramas which so often overcharge Bunin's work. Here the spectacles or manifestations of nature are dramatis personae, not stage sets. Each one of the different and yet harmonic visions of the village and the country around it, each one of the numberless evocations of a peculiar season or hour in nature or time, is a unique note in this poetic symphony that changes colors and words into music. Here the landscapes are really states of mind, and psychic moods.

It is primarily from the viewpoint of the realistic quality of its content that one should disapprove of Mirsky's likening of this story to the tale by Poe. The parallel shows that that critic interpreted this piece in purely romantic terms, while it is evident that it would be far more proper, historically and critically, to place it within the framework of symbolism. Probably *Dry Valley* is the only really symbolist novel ever written in Russia — a paradoxical feat, since its author was disdainful of symbolism and almost a Parnassian in temperament. Yet this short novel is a symbolist work from several points of view, especially in its highly subjective and yet almost impersonal mood. It is symbolist because its suggestiveness is based on intuition and insight, not on abstraction and allegory, and because it reduces the verbal art of the poet, generally conceived in plastic and figurative terms, to the "condition of music." It is thus that this story strangely ends as a kind of tragic pastoral.

The musical, suggestive, and intuitive vein of this little masterpiece is a rare, but not unique, manifestation in Bunin's work. Such a vein had appeared at the beginning of his career, and reappeared again at the end of it. So in "Antonov Apples," a story written as early as 1900, Bunin had anticipated Proust by at least ten years in using the device of the "intermittence du coeur": causing the peculiar scent of a particular kind of apple to recall in the mind of the protagonist all the forgotten memories of the past life of his family and of himself. The same evocative qualities can be found in *The Life of Arsenyev*,[8] which is a veiled autobiography, consciously yet freely constructed; it produces an effect of poetic remoteness rather than of esthetic distance. As such, it reminds us more of those Tolstoyan narratives which are based partly on invention and partly on direct experience than of the straightforward personal memoirs written by Gorki. This long novel, too, seems to have been dictated by an imaginative reminiscing, by the memory of the heart.

Yet, in spite of its quality, it is not *The Life of Arsenyev,* but the far shorter *Dry Valley* (along with "The Gentleman from San Francisco"), which must be considered the high point of Bunin's work. That "poem" in narrative form is destined to remain forever original and new, as no other Russian piece of writing of the same time seems to be, and it is strange, and yet illuminating, that it was written by an author whose dominant attitude was the "punctilio of tradition," as Vladimir Pozner put it.[9] This lesson may teach us that a sudden grace or a divine spark can change into a sorcerer and a wonder-worker even the skillful artificer, the cold virtuoso, or the studious artisan.

NOTES

1. When this essay was written, Bunin was still alive. He died in France in the spring of 1954.

2. Such an opinion was stated by Vladimir Nabokov in a chapter on *émigré* literature, which can be read in his charming autobiography in English, *Conclusive Evidence* (New York: Harpers, 1951).

3. D. H. Lawrence collaborated personally in making the best of all English versions of the most masterly of Bunin's short stories. See the title piece of the collection *The Gentleman from San Francisco and Other Stories,* translated by S. S. Koteliansky and Leonard Woolf (Richmond, England, 1927). Practically all Bunin's tales discussed in the present essay can be read in English in that collection, as well as in the selections listed below: *The Gentleman from San Francisco and Fourteen Other Stories,* translated by Bernard Guilbert Guerney (New York: Knopf, 1934), *The Elaghin Affair and Other Stories,* also translated by Mr. Guerney (New York: Knopf, 1935), *The Grammar of Love and Other Stories,* translated by John Cournos (London, 1935). The student interested in the more recent production of Bunin will find in English *Mitya's Love,* translated by M. Boyd (New York: Holt, 1926), and a collection of tales written in the last few years: *Dark Avenues and Other Stories,* translated by R. Hare (London: John Lehmann, 1949). Bunin's literary recollections, under the title of *Memoirs and Portraits,* in a translation by V. Trail and R. Chancellor, have been published by Doubleday and Company (New York, 1951).

4. *The Village* is available in English in the old translation by Isabel F. Hapgood, reprinted by Knopf in 1923.

5. This is how Mr. Guerney, who translated this work into English, rendered its original title, which is the place name *Sukhodol,* corresponding etymologically to the English "Dryvale." Mr. Guerney's translation, originally included in the selection entitled *The Elaghin Affair and Other Stories* (see note 3), has been recently reprinted in Philip Rahv's anthology, *Russian Short Novels* (New York, 1956).

6. This plurality and complexity of "points of view" makes us think that Bunin wrote *Dry Valley* under the influence of Leskov's short novel *A Decayed Family* (1874), where the past splendor and the present ruin of what was once a proud lineage are recalled through the combined recollections of its last feminine heir, of a lady companion, and of a maidservant. Leskov's story, however, stresses the ethos, rather than the pathos, of decay.

7. In his *History of Russian Literature* (New York: Knopf, 1949).

8. A self-contained fragment of this long narrative, entitled *The Well of Days,* was translated by Gleb Struve and Hamish Miles, and published by Knopf in 1934.

9. In his *Panorama de la littérature russe contemporaine* (Paris: Kra, 1929).

On the Works and Thoughts of Vasili Rozanov

THE students of Vasili Rozanov have concentrated their attention on his strange biography and morbid psychology, on the novelty in form and content of his literary work, on the most picturesque and suggestive intuitions of his asystematic philosophy, on his contradictory political opinions and social views, finally, and most extensively, on his paradoxical, and even shocking, views about religion and sex. All these aspects of Rozanov's personality and writings are extraordinarily important and interesting, but the task of this essay will be rather to attempt to isolate the substance, both common and unique, underlying all the different and contrasting components of the figure of Rozanov as a writer as well as a man. An investigation of this kind cannot be made without a previous recapitulation of several often superficial and even secondary facts, nor without frequent allusions to the most obvious traits of Rozanov's psychological and literary portrait.

To understand the biography and the psychology of this writer it may be worth while to begin by referring to his youthful infatuation for Dostoevski, which later became an almost pathological adoration, not merely for the author and the historical figure, but for the man himself. This worship of the great novelist lasted until Rozanov's death, and it is evident in practically every page of his writings and letters, as well as in the testimonials, oral and written, left by his friends. It was to the study of Dostoevski that Rozanov devoted his first important work, an essay of book length called *The Legend of the Grand Inquisitor,* which appeared in 1890: a landmark in the reinterpretation not only of that master, but also of the literary tradition to which he belongs, as is shown by, among other things, the opening pages, with their reassessment of Gogol's realism in both idealistic and nihilistic terms. For this and other radical re-evaluations of ideas and men, the *Legend* looks more like a philosophical essay than a piece of literary criticism.

As for the author of that essay, he appears to us less like a spiritual heir or son than like a younger brother of Dostoevski: his understanding of the mind of his master is so uncanny that it seems due to a kind of mysterious kinship. Even before writing those pages, Rozanov had tried to establish a vicarious relationship with the person of his hero by his own marriage, which had taken place a few years before, to Apollinaria Suslova, who as a young student had been the mistress of Dostoevski, and who is certainly the model for Polina (a diminutive of Apollinaria), the most important character in *The Gambler* besides its protagonist. Polina had stirred in Dostoevski a brief, stormy, and morbid passion, which survived in his memory and in his blood as a magic and evil spell, and which inspired the proud and cruel feminine figures he portrayed in his later works (Aglaya in *The Idiot,* Grushenka in *The Brothers Karamazov,* and so on). If the most important historian of this liaison was to be Lyubov, the daughter of Dostoevski, who narrated it in her father's biography, the proof of Polina's identification with the characters mentioned above was to be provided, amazingly enough, by Rozanov himself.

Rozanov later gave, as one of the reasons for his marriage with Polina, his desire to find a compensation for his failure to get personally acquainted with the great man who had once loved her. The matter, of course, was not so simple as that. We know that Rozanov had met Polina for the first time in his native city, when he was still an adolescent, but he married her a few years later, in 1880 (one year before Dostoevski's death), when he was still a student at the University of Moscow, and his age was twenty-four. If we know little more than this about the beginning of their relationship, we know enough about its outcome. Life with Polina was hell. Rozanov was not a Petruchio, and Apollinaria remained an untamed shrew. As a matter of fact, after six years of married life she walked out on him. Nor did she stop persecuting her husband even after their separation; she denied him a divorce, and prevented Rozanov from entering into legal wedlock with Varvara Rudneva, whom he had met in Elets while working there as a teacher. Despite this, Varvara became in 1889 the faithful companion of his life, and bore him five children. Many of the pages of Rozanov's later works are a constant hymn to her, whom he used to call his "friend." Both the experience with Polina and his deep love for his common-law wife were perhaps among the motives that led Rozanov to study and to discuss so eagerly the question of divorce and illegitimate offspring. A two-volume col-

lection of essays on this theme, entitled *The Family Problem in Russia,*
appeared in 1903.

This was not the only one of Rozanov's writings touching the problem
of the relationship between family and sexual life on one side, and ethics
and religion on the other. As a matter of fact, all the most important books
he wrote between 1890 and 1912 were concerned either with religion
or with sex, or, more frequently, with both. Practically all of them were
collections of articles originally written for the daily or the periodical press.
But before becoming a journalist and a publicist, Rozanov had been a teacher
of history and geography in provincial high schools. After devoting thirteen
years of his life to this task, he abandoned the teaching profession, in which he
had never felt at home, to enter for a while the civil service. He was a bad
teacher, not because he was a bad scholar, but because he had never been
a good student, as he gaily confesses himself: "How nice it is that I slept
through my university courses. . . . Every hour, and on every turn, the
'teacher' denied me, and I denied the 'teacher.'" Perhaps he was too much
interested in the fecundation of the flesh to be good at that "fecundation by
the spirit" which is the definition of teaching according to Plato. And he
was too easily infected psychologically to be able to infect others intellectually.

In the meanwhile his first published writing, an antiacademic and antira-
tional philosophical tract, *About the Understanding,* which appeared in 1886,
had aroused the curiosity and the interest of Strakhov,[1] who invited him to
settle in Petersburg and to write for the conservative press. This fact was
always considered by Rozanov as proof that he had "lived by chance"; in
any event, he was able or willing to follow that advice only several years
later. It was not until the mid-nineties that he became a permanent and
regular contributor to Suvorin's semiofficial daily *The New Times.* He wrote
freely, when, how, and about what he liked; and yet this freedom did not
prevent him from doing willingly several dirty jobs, flattering or pleasing
the obscurantist opinions of those governmental circles which had found
their organ in Suvorin's paper. Among other things, Rozanov approved in
print of Tolstoy's excommunication by the Holy Synod, and publicly supported the abominable prejudice, fostered by the tsarist regime, of the so-
called "ritual murder" ascribed to the Jews.

All these services did not help him very much, because the powers that
be looked at many of his articles and books with great distaste, considering
them not only pornographic, but blasphemous as well. Thus several of his
publications fell under the blows of religious, if not political, censorship. A

convinced reactionary, he was at the same time a skeptic and a cynic. As such, he was easily inclined to see all the sides of an issue. At times, like Dostoevski, he felt the seduction of subversive radicalism. It was therefore very easy for him to understand the opposite camp, and even to share some of its views. It was under the pen name of Varvarin (which means "barbarian" in Russian, but which may have been suggested to him by the Christian name of his wife), that he wrote not infrequently for a liberal newspaper, the organ of the cultural and political Left, *The Russian Word*.

The ambivalence of Rozanov's political ideas may be easily seen also in his books, even in those which are in the main but collections of the articles he originally wrote for the conservative press. Their predominant theme is sex versus religion, or religion versus sex; but at least one of his volumes, published in 1908 and inspired by the "little revolution" of 1905, is primarily political in character, and seems to take almost a radical stand. Yet, more than by any sympathy toward the revolution, the book was dictated by a scornful criticism of the administrative inefficiency and political impotence of the tsarist regime, as its significant title, *When Authority Went Away*, clearly suggests.

Rozanov's most important polemical activity, however, was directed against Christianity and the church. A suggestive denial of Christian metaphysics was attempted in *The Dark Face* (1911), while its sequel, entitled *Moonlight People* (1916), is a powerful indictment of monastic life, which he regarded as dangerously spreading to other sections of religion and society the contagion of its asceticism. Far less biased, and often full of admiration and praise for some aspects of the Orthodox faith and for the figure of the low clergyman, the Russian *pop,* had been Rozanov's previous work, *The Russian Church* (1909). Some of his scandalous, or at least equivocal, views about both Christianity and Orthodoxy had already been developed by Rozanov in the two volumes of *In the World of the Obscure and the Uncertain* (1901), the first of his publications to be censored because of some supposedly pornographic passages, and in another two-volume work, entitled *Around the Walls of the Temple* (1906). Even his travel notebooks, even works more cultural or literary in character, like *From Oriental Motifs* (1915 and 1919), are concerned with the same polemics against Christendom and its church.

We shall deal later with the literary production of the last period of his life, which begins in 1912. Starting with that year, he wrote a series of books which are in part a continuation of his earlier writings, but which in the main must be considered something completely unexpected and new. Before

studying them, however, we must get acquainted in some detail with the
sexual and religious vision of life which he had gradually and constantly
built in his earlier works.

II

Logically and sentimentally, Rozanov's system of ideas begins with the
identification of God and sex: "the tie of sex with God is stronger than the
tie of intellect, and even conscience, with God. . . ." Rozanov feels that
because of this tie, the man who does not accept God's existence is essentially
unable to recognize the value of sex. "The atheist is a sexless being," says he,
re-echoing and translating into his own terms Dostoevski's conception of the
atheist as a victim of abstract, lifeless thinking, as someone who has killed
his own personality through what Rozanov himself calls the "algebra of
spiritualism."

Such a view implies what Nietzsche would call a "transvaluation of all
values," not only in the fields of religion and sex, but also in the fields of
culture and history. First of all, Rozanov's attitude involves a new metaphysics. According to this new metaphysical outlook, Rozanov is on one
hand led to identify God with his creation, and to postulate a pantheistic and
naturalistic faith, divinizing the biological element in man's existence and
in God's universe. On the other hand he tends to consider the divine presence
as something physical, even corporeal, which man may perceive through his
senses. Ultimately, Rozanov's metaphysics spiritualizes, raising it to the level
of a hypostasis, sex itself. His philosophy could in brief be defined as a sort
of sexual transcendentalism. Rozanov almost said so in his own words:
"Because of its substance and function, sex belongs to the transcendental
and mystical order. . . . Sex transcends the limits of nature, because it is
anatural and supernatural. . . ." Often Rozanov affirms literally the holiness
of sex, not only in its idea and essence, but even in its instruments and organs,
the male and female genitalia.

Rozanov's "transvaluation" involves also a paradoxical reinterpretation
of the historical body of religious beliefs, a scandalous reversal of the accepted ideas about the "pilgrim's progress" of the faith of the West. Rozanov
does not see in Christianity the "highest religion": as a matter of fact, he
asserts the superiority of the creeds of the ancient world over that of modern
man. Not satisfied with this, he establishes an unresolved antinomy between
Christianity and all naturalistic religions, where the latter represent everything he considers good, and the former symbolizes everything he thinks

evil or bad. This antinomy is developed both literally and figuratively in his works.

When he speaks of ancient religions, Rozanov means primarily biblical Hebraism. This does not prevent him from placing under the same heading the faith of modern Israel, historical Judaism, or from including within the same category classical paganism, and even the archaic and exotic faiths of the East, especially of Egypt. When he emphasizes Hebraism, all old religions are symbolized in the figure of the Father; when he emphasizes pagan and primitive cults, their allegory is the Sun. For Rozanov, all ancient faiths are earthly and worldly in the good sense of these two terms; in them, marriage is really a sacrament, because sex is holy, being the treasure of the race, the Ark of the tribe, the "tree of life" given by God to man. He praises the religions of antiquity because they exalt procreation and fecundity, child-bearing and child-raising, the love of man and wife, the ties between parents and children, the continuity of the family and the perpetuation of the species. For him, it is when it preaches the immortality of life, rather than the immortality of the soul, that religion is really a sacred thing.

In this and other regards, Rozanov considers Christianity to be the very opposite of the religions of the ancient world. Unlike them, Christianity is unable to recognize that "the base of the family being animal and fleshly, it is mystico-religious exactly because animal and fleshly." At its best, or at its worst, Christianity regulates sex by mortifying it, by treating marriage and the family as necessary evils, and thus merely tolerating them. Christianity is the religion of Jesus, who is a degenerate or unregenerate Son, because He came to deny His Father, not for the salvation, but for the ruination of man. He was a prophet of renunciation and abstention, who denied earth for heaven; a preacher of asceticism and monasticism, of chastity and virginity; a killer of life, because for Him life was a sin, nay, the original sin. For Rozanov the Gospel is essentially a gospel of death: "How brief is the rite of baptism, how dull the ceremony of wedding, how hasty the sacrament of confession and communion! But man dies, and Christianity rises in all its power: what songs, what words, what thoughts, what poetry!" For this very reason the New Testament finds its culmination not in the Resurrection, but in the sacrifice of the Son of God: "In the Gospel the passion and the death of Christ are expressed in a more generous and exalted style and impress the heart of man more than the mystery of the Nativity." Rozanov finds it scandalous, and yet significant, that the highest mystery of Christianity is the very death of its God: "God in the coffin — what a mystery! God looking at man from the bottom of his coffin . . . ! " For Rozanov the tragic paradox of Christianity is revealed even by its symbology, since, as he says, "in the general, universal symbolism of graphic signs, the figure of the cross (✠) is the symbol of death."

Rozanov contrasts Christ as God of Death to the Father, or to the supreme gods of all ancient religions, through the symbol of the Moon. As for the members of his priesthood, who are the regular rather than the secular clergy, Rozanov calls them "moonlight people," the "dark rays" reflected on earth by the "dark face" of Jesus Christ: "It is this dark sun, it is this universal death and metaphysics of death that are the object of the adoration of the monks." Rozanov often develops this antithesis between the Son and the Father into an antithesis between the spirit and the letter of the Old Testament, and the spirit and the letter of the New Testament. Pascal and Nietzsche had already stated the same opposition, each one of them on different ethical and literary grounds. Whether or not he follows a path already opened by others, Rozanov praises the Old Testament and criticizes the New for the very reasons which had led Pascal to judge in the opposite way. Here is a typical passage in *The Apocalypse of Our Time:* "For what incomprehensible reason have men failed to notice that the Gospel is a book religiously cold, not to say indifferent? Where nobody sings, nobody rejoices, nobody is uplifted, nobody raises his eyes toward the sky? . . . And where is the supreme thing, the Psalm, the essence of all?" In other words only the God of the Old Testament is the real God: "God is the god of the living, not the god of the dead."

Sometimes Rozanov translates all these antinomies into a Manichaean opposition between two gods eternally at war with each other. The Son had said: "My kingdom is not of this world," and Rozanov replies: "But the world is God's. Why has Thou said: the Father and Myself are one? Not only You are not one, but Thou revoltest against Him. Thou doest unto Him what Saturnus did unto Uranus." Thus Christ becomes for him a new Ariman, or rather a new Lucifer, a seducer and a tempter: "Thou art beautiful, Lord Jesus. And Thou hast corrupted the world with Thy beauty." Like Ariman and Lucifer, Christ is a destroyer: "Where the fire of Christ has burned, there nothing will ever grow. . . . From the soil of Christianity no grass ever grows. . . ." Rozanov often expands his religious dualism into a metaphysical conflict between Christ and creation itself: "Is the solar system enclosed within the Gospel, or is the Gospel enclosed within the solar system? Christianity is not cosmological." And elsewhere: "The sun was lighted up before Christianity. And it will never be extinguished, even if Christianity comes to an end." Yet, despite this assurance that cosmology will ultimately conquer religion, Rozanov fears very often the opposite outcome, the conquest of the world by Christ, the triumph of the principle of death over the principle of life. This sense of defeat led him to pronounce many times, not only on his death bed, his own *Galilee, vicisti*. The truth is that he succumbed frequently to the Tempter himself.

Sometimes Rozanov fights against this charm by affirming that Jesus was not a prophet, but a rhetorician: "Christ is but eloquence, eloquence alone." In unconscious and yet indirect opposition to the view of Pascal, according to whom Christ is the pure logician who through the New Testament brought into the world that lucid truth of the spirit which the Old Testament had hidden under the veil of its figures and myths, Rozanov considers Christ as a sophist, or, as Nietzsche would say, as a decadent and a nihilist. Yet Rozanov's attitude toward Christ remains contradictory and equivocal, and may be summed up in his paradoxical definition of Jesus as "the sweetest and bitterest fruit in the world." Sometimes Rozanov seems to love Christ for the very powerlessness and impotence he imputes to Him; sometimes, for the powerlessness and impotence which is the lot of all men: "Only in tears He will manifest Himself. Who does not weep, will not discover Christ. But who weeps, will certainly see Him."

Rozanov's quarrel with Christianity derives not so much from the Christian denial of sex, as from the Christian denial of family life: "Christianity is outside of the family. Under Christianity and because of it, the family disintegrates, merely because Christianity does not need it. And the reason for this fact is that Christianity is superior to the family." It is true that often Rozanov exalts love not only within, but also without the conjugal bed; that sometimes he goes even further, defending the most abnormal manifestations of the erotic instinct. Thus for instance he praises the phallic cult of the Romans and the Egyptians' animal worship; and in a page which almost seems an inspired translation of some of the ideas of Freud, which of course were unknown to him, he justifies, or at least acknowledges, even the most extreme perversions of sex, or, as he says, "those awful and incomprehensible tempests which explode sometimes here on earth, and which empirical thinking calls 'sexual anomalies.'" This understanding of the psychic forces that lead man to violate the sexual taboos of the tribe was often the cause of the accusations of pornography leveled against him.

Yet what Rozanov really cares for is a normal acceptance of normal sexual life. He supports monogamy, in both theory and practice, with an enthusiasm not always shared by the average family man. He seems not to care about modesty, but he cares about chastity, which he defines not as a denial, but as an affirmation of sex: "Chastity is the irradiation of sex. . . . The supreme ideal of chastity is offered to us by the bride, not by the virgin. . . . Chastity is man's respect for his own sex, a discreet and prudent way to treat it as something absolutely holy." A pregnant woman is for him the most sacred being on earth.

Similar qualifications must be made in regard to his polemics against Christianity. This anti-Christian controversialist avoids any form of anti-clericalism, and shows instead great admiration for the traditions of Orthodoxy, especially in matters of rite and liturgy. This may also explain why he died reconciled with his church. His honesty and sincerity in this respect may be proved by the fact that he foresaw that he would do this very thing: "But naturally when I die, I shall die within the church; I need incomparably more religion than literature (which is not at all necessary): and after all the clergy is dearer to me than any other class." While it was in a fit of frenzy that the "Antichrist" Nietzsche invoked the "crucified Dionysus" with his last breath, it was in full possession of his faculties that Rozanov uttered the sacramental words "Christ has risen" on his deathbed.

III

The last of Rozanov's books, *The Apocalypse of Our Times*, was practically written on that deathbed. From the viewpoint of its apparent purpose, that book is related to *When Authority Went Away*, the most political of his previous works. From the standpoint of its content, *The Apocalypse* is a replica of what Rozanov had been writing up to 1912. But in terms of inspiration, structure, and style, it is far more related to the works written after 1912, where Rozanov had expressed his personality and genius at their finest.

Up to that time Rozanov had been primarily a journalist and a publicist, or, at best, an essayist. In other words, he had been writing for an audience with definite opinions, and on matters of public interest. All he had published up to 1912 had been highly personal, with a subjectivity which, however, was to be chiefly found in the author's perspectives and attitudes, and only secondarily in the work itself. His style had always been lively and fresh. Still, his early literary idiom had been little more than a highly individual version of the *koiné* of ideological, critical, and journalistic writing. As for the subject matter of his earlier works, it had been almost always given him by the moment and milieu in which he wrote. In brief, he had always written on social problems and public issues, on a range of questions perhaps too broad for the peculiar temper of his talent.

But in the works of his later period, excluding in part his last book, the only thing which really interests Rozanov is Rozanov himself. The journalist and the publicist, the essayist and the pamphleteer, becomes now the prophet of the only God, who is the Self. Now the writer addresses himself to a different group of readers, far more limited in number and higher in quality, than the subscribers of the newspapers or periodicals to which he had formerly contributed. With these new readers he establishes a relationship of intimacy and confidence, a kind of pathetic and pathological complicity, rather than a rational or cultural understanding. Even now his books are not written as books, but as series of fragments: yet, when published in book form, those fragments make a more consistent and compact whole than his previous collections of topical articles.

This fragmentary quality of Rozanov's late writings is nothing new in itself, nor is there anything new in the interest they seem to show in banal and vulgar details, nor in the use they often make of private and public documents (letters, reports, and so on). In *The Dark Face* Rozanov had already quoted in its entirety a medico-legal memorandum about a case of collective hysteria in a sect of religious dissenters; in *In the World of the Obscure and the Uncertain* he had already published a running commentary on letters by his correspondents, friendly or unfriendly, known or unknown. But in his early works Rozanov had given unity to his disparate materials through the external device of the question discussed. Now, however, his fragments are smaller, as well as unrelated and often irrelevant; and their novel and greater unity is directly contrived by the tone of his voice, by what he called himself the "passion" of his "talent."

Rozanov's is now no longer the language of discussion, argument, and controversy, which even at its best must be at least partially rhetorical and conventional; it is rather the idiom of conversation, confidence, and confession. In spite of its flowing ease, his new diction is highly poetic, while remaining colloquial in essence. To emphasize this effect of spoken naturalness, Rozanov adopts a series of typographical devices, such as interjections and suspension points, italicized and capitalized words, parentheses and quotation marks, hyphens and dashes, larger characters and thicker types. His intention in doing so is not to follow the example of what the poets of the advance-guard used to call "typographical relief," but to imitate and reproduce a heavily underscored manuscript, marking all changes of emphasis for the writer's personal use.

All this adds to the chaotic impression of the whole: formlessness now seems to become the only shape his thoughts can take. Yet, merely by yielding to the caprices of his inspiration, he succeeds in creating a form of his own. Such was the opinion of highly competent judges, for instance of Vyacheslav Ivanov, who saw in Rozanov's chosen medium a genre previously unknown, through which literature was both renewing and transcending itself. Aphorisms, meditations, recollections, dreams, loose thoughts: the writing of Rozanov is now made of the stuff life is made of. He treats everything on the same plane, from the loftiest spiritual contemplations to the most trivial details of the daily routine of human life. Both the ineffable and the unspeakable seem to find voice in his words. Rozanov was aware that his greatest achievement was to express the inarticulate, to utter what nobody had ever uttered, perhaps because nobody had felt it was worth saying. Once he said of himself: "In me there is a kind of fetishism for trifles. Trifles are my 'god.'" And in one of his letters to his friend Hollerbach we find the following statement: "There is generally a great deal of fetishism in me. Do you know which passage in your letter I liked best? That in which you say that you would like to see my material setting, and especially to see and touch my things and books. I think you would like to have a look at my furniture, on what and how I sit. . . ." In almost all his writings we find this extraordinary interest in banal and common things, even on the plane of thought. In view of this one could repeat about him the judgment of Coleridge on Sterne: "His originality lies in bringing forward into distinct consciousness those minutiae of thought and feeling which appear trifles, yet have an importance for the moment, and which almost every man feels in one way or another."

Rozanov, however, unlike Sterne, was not a writer of fiction, and this is why Russian critics preferred to compare his technical medium with Nietzsche's "aphorisms" and Pascal's "thoughts." Both comparisons are apt, although they must be qualified by the remark that every aphorism of Nietzsche and every thought of Pascal is classically self-sufficient and achieved in a sense that cannot be said of Rozanov's fragments. Moreover, Pascal's thoughts were originally part of an apologetic work, while Nietzsche's aphorisms are essentially cultural and intellectual in character, and concerned with values or issues far greater than the personality of the writer himself. In contrast to this, Rozanov's fragments are written without an over-all plan and on the flimsiest pretexts. Nobody, as a matter of fact, has described his medium better than Rozanov himself, in the opening page of *Solitaria*,[2] where his genre or technique found its first, and, as the author claims, perhaps its highest expression, a judgment with which we agree.

In that page, Rozanov describes his new literary medium in the following way:

> The wind blows at midnight and carries away leaves. . . . So also life in fleeting time tears off from our soul exclamations, sights, half-thoughts, half-feelings . . . which, being fragments of sounds, have the significance that they come straight from the soul, without elaboration, without purpose, without premeditation, without anything eternal. Simply, the soul is alive, that is, has lived, has breathed. . . . I have always somehow liked these sudden exclamations. Strictly speaking, they flow in continuously, but one can't succeed (there's no paper at hand) in putting them down, and they die. Afterwards one can't remember them for anything. Yet certain things I succeeded in jotting down on paper. The jottings went on piling up. And then I decided to gather together those fallen leaves.

Solitaria, as a matter of fact, was followed in 1913 by the first series of a similar work which took the very name of *Fallen Leaves.* A "second basket" of *Fallen Leaves* appeared in 1915. Both these volumes were written in the same style as *Solitaria,* and one is almost tempted to use their title as the best possible term to define those fragmentary notations which are Rozanov's most personal form. In the following work, which was also to be his last, Rozanov resumed, at least in part, the shape of his writings before 1912; the sections and divisions of *The Apocalypse of Our Times* often take on the external form of the newspaper article or of the journalistic piece. This was due perhaps to the fact that the subject matter of the book was a political and historical event, the "hard fact" of revolution, which even Rozanov was forced to consider a public issue, at least as important as his own person. Yet even in these pages he looked at history from the point of view of his most intimate and personal concerns.

All this was perhaps due to the particular circumstance from which *The Apocalypse of Our Times* was born. Rozanov wrote it in the city of Sergiev-Posad, not far from Moscow, while living in a private home. Later he spent some time in one of the most important sanctuaries of that town, full of convents and churches. It was indeed in the famous *Troitsa Lavra* or Trinity Monastery that this enemy of Christianity found temporary shelter from persecution, as well as from hunger and cold. The way *The Apocalypse of Our Times* was composed was also due to the writer's pressing financial needs. The book appeared in the form of a periodical; its ten installments were issued from November 1917 to the summer of 1918, and were sold to friendly subscribers, who sometimes paid not in money, but with shipments of clothing and food. (In several of its issues, the author begs his readers for alms, or for payments in kind.) The entire work was meant as a pamphlet against Christianity and the church, and against the revolution as well; yet it had been written and printed in one of the holiest places of Russia, and could be published only because of the revolutionary abolition of ecclesiastical censorship. Unable to continue working, Rozanov left the *Apocalypse* unfinished, and died at the beginning of the year 1919.

Not a single one of the Russian critics who have written on Rozanov since his death has failed to notice that *Solitaria, Fallen Leaves,* and *The Apocalypse of Our Times* are those of his literary remains that recommend him to posterity, and that will perhaps also grant a longer lease of life to the rest of his work.[3] So it was stated by his friend and biographer Hollerbach, and by such *émigré* writers as Prince Mirsky, N. Arsenyev, Vladimir Pozner, and Boris de Schloezer, all of whom devoted important pages to Rozanov's work. The merits of all of these critics are not lessened by the fact that they all too often chose to emphasize the most obvious and external characteristics of Rozanov's thought, and to view him as the apologist of sex rather than as the mystical seer of the soul.[4]

The main task of this essay is to concentrate the attention on the second of these two aspects and also to investigate the inner personality of Rozanov and to reconstruct his own conception of man. It is not true that Rozanov was concerned exclusively with sex, although he was more responsible than anybody else for the formation of this myth, as our survey has already amply shown. Since the real, or at least the greater, Rozanov is to be found only in his late works, our inquiry from now on will be based almost exclusively on *Solitaria, Fallen Leaves,* and *The Apocalypse of Our Times.* We shall make some use also of his letters, especially those to Hollerbach, and also of his commentary on Strakhov's letters, edited under the title of *Literary Exiles,* by Rozanov himself. This commentary, as a matter of fact, is almost an independent book, consisting of an immense series of footnotes, often longer than the letter they refer to. But before studying further those works of Rozanov which we might call the "books of the soul," we must begin by studying the psyche of the man who wrote them.

IV

We may begin by drawing the portrait of Rozanov the man from his least relevant traits, from his small idiosyncrasies, which, along with his more important psychological features, he reveals to the reader in his own words.[5] It is interesting, for instance, to note that he is affected by an inferiority complex in regard to his name and external appearance: "Surprisingly disgusting to me is my name. . . . Therefore, 'The Works of Rozanov' doesn't tempt me. It is even ridiculous. 'Poems by V. Rozanov' can't possibly be thought of. . . . This unusually disgusting name is mine in addition to a miserable appearance. . . ." He confesses that this feeling affected him especially because of his desire to love and be loved: "But in my heart I thought, 'No, that's settled. Women will never love me, not a single one.' What remains then? To retire into myself, to live with myself (not egotistically, but spiritually, for the future)." Sometimes, however, he reverses his position, claiming that he likes both his name and his appearance to be ugly. "Now I am even pleased that Rozanov is so disgusting. . . . Why do I need an attractive face or new clothes, when I myself (in myself, or the 'clod') am infinitely attractive?" This ambivalent stand, based on mixed feelings of sympathy and antipathy toward himself, is obviously apparent also in Rozanov's half embarrassed, half complacent awareness of his own lack of breeding and bearing, of ease of manner and bodily grace: "I was always clumsy. There is in me a terrible monstrosity of behavior, to the point of not knowing how to get up or how to sit down. I simply do not understand what it is to do all this."

Rozanov confesses that the same "monstrosity of behavior" affects not only his body, but also his soul: "My soul is a kind of imbroglio, from which I am unable to get my foot. . . . (All this, i.e., imbroglio, is revealed also by my style)." By the term "imbroglio" he seems to allude to the chaotic formlessness of his personality, which he avows with both shame and awe: "I simply have no sense of form (Aristotle's *causa formalis*). I am a 'clod,' a 'loofah.' But that is because I am all spirit and all subject. The subjective in me is indeed developed to an extent which I don't find and don't imagine in anyone else." He knows that this subjectivity may be a kind of fatal curse, which makes of him an outcast from the body of mankind. From this derives his frequent wish that that curse be cast away. He even claims that writing is for him but "an attempt to get out from that awful curtain, from which I wanted to and yet couldn't get out." In most cases Rozanov's subjectivity affects his own vision of things to such an extent that his spiritual sight becomes abnormal. He is aware that his eyes look for things which nobody sees, and find them where nobody looks: "It is as if my eye (my mind) were at a level with the table. The table is a thin sheet of paper. A little push, and I discover what is under the table. . . ."

Rozanov's obsessive concern with the Self leads him to love with equal intensity anything related to his own ego, whatever it is: "On myself, even mud is good, because it is I." It is with both self-pity and self-praise that he states elsewhere his own acceptance of the fact that his soul "is mixed with mud, tenderness, and melancholy." Precisely because even the slightest motion of his psyche may become full of supreme meaning for him, precisely because each one of his feelings and thoughts may acquire, even if only for an instant, an absolute value, does he consider all his thoughts and feelings, without taking into account any ethical or intellectual consideration, as both beautiful and good in themselves. He lovingly defines them as "some golden fishes gamboling in the sun, in an aquarium full of filth. . . . And they do not die from it. As a matter of fact, they feel well there. . . ."

Such a conception implies a deep interest in what one might call the passive rather than the active components of the soul. As a matter of fact, it is the inert side of the psyche that Rozanov loves most. He realizes that this is what sets him apart from other men. Thus he often speaks of his own spiritual solitude less with pride than with regret. He recognized that his destiny was to go through life companionless. And this prophet of sex once chose to describe his own loneliness in a suggestive and equivocal image, which, despite its literal meaning, beyond its very allusion to a peculiar grammatical term, seems to imply the asexuality, or even the homosexuality, of his soul. In that image he defined himself as "a noncopulative man. A man solo." If here Rozanov seems to speak out of a sense of grievance, or even of shame, he often makes the same avowal with a feeling of self-satisfaction. In a famous passage where he acknowledges that through his own indifference to public and social life he had too easily become the succubus of any outsider, of any external pressure, he claims with pride that the opposite would take place in the most intimate recesses of his own soul. This time, too, he uses, with similar equivocal effects, grammatical similes:

A perfectly different thing is my dream (life). As regards that, I never stirred one iota under anyone's influence whatsoever. It was the same in my childhood, too. In that respect I was a perfectly unbrought-up man, utterly unyielding to cultural influences. . . . To look at me, I am all-declinable. In myself (subject) — absolutely undeclinable, noncompatible. A sort of adverb.

Despite such a proud acceptance of the insularity of his nature, Rozanov feels continuously that his person must be not only insulated, but also protected, and from this standpoint he resembles very much "the man in a case" in a famous story by Chekhov. But while the Chekhovian hero wishes for a "shell" sheltering him from life,[6] and finds that shelter only in death's casket, Rozanov is able to satisfy his yearning after a snug security in a kind of vitalistic and biological nirvana, in the plasma of existence and in the femininity of the *Erdgeist,* in what he calls "the breasts of the world and the mystery of its belly." If Baudelaire dreamt of losing himself on the body of his *géante,* with a similar longing our writer thinks of himself not as a loving male, but as a fondled child, and dreams of "the baby Rozanov lost somewhere on earth's breasts." Sometimes he seems to complain of his psychological inability to reach adult status, to grow to a life of self-reliance and maturity: "I am the least born man, as though I still lay (as a clod) in my mother's womb"; but even more frequently he seems to rejoice in his own infant-like nature as if it were a heaven of bliss: "I am like a child in his mother's womb, but one who doesn't wish to be born: 'Here I have enough warmth'. . . ."

The only havens reality may offer to a man of this kind are private life and family life, and Rozanov is indeed the glorifier of both. Private life, of which he has the most extreme notion, is for him the supreme value. He is proud to have rediscovered this value, and to have attributed to it a significance and a relevance never acknowledged before. In a revealing passage he writes:

People, would you like me to tell you a stupendous truth, which not a single one of the prophets told you? . . . I am the first. Just sitting at home, and even picking your nose, and looking at the sunset. Ha-ha-ha! I swear to you: this is more universal than religion. . . . All religions will pass, but this will remain: simply sitting on a chair and looking in the distance.

This claim that sitting at home is the supreme ideal of being bares the hidden secret of Rozanov's life. Apparently he found some kind of compensation for his nostalgic yearning after the protective warmth of his mother's womb, in the warmth, both physiological and psychological, natural as well as artificial, of the home. For a Russian peasant that warmth may be symbolized by his oven; for a bourgeois, by a lived-in room; for Rozanov it is symbolized by the bed, or by the bodily heat of his wife and children. Since he cannot live forever like an egg in its shell, Rozanov settles for the best possible compromise, which is to spend all of his life in the nest. This is literally true and was stated by him in his own words: "But you, reader, be spiritually firm. Stand on your feet. . . . And remember: life is the home. And the home must be warm, nice and round (like a womb). Work for your round home, and God in heaven will not abandon you. He will not forget the bird making its nest." The significance of this passage will appear even greater when we realize that these lines, which close *The Apocalypse of Our Times,* are perhaps the last he wrote.

Rozanov feels tied to his nest by a kind of umbilical cord, like a baby to his mother's womb. He cannot even conceive of the open air, of the external world. His psychology is literally an indoor psychology, as he so readily avows: "In me there is probably some hostility toward free air, and I don't remember having ever gone for a promenade or a walk." Rozanov's naturalism is not earthly or cosmic, but vitalistic in the physiological and biological sense of the term; despite his many similarities to Rousseau, Rozanov was never a *promeneur solitaire*. Even outdoors, says he, "I would always try to find a hidden corner (out of people's eyes, out of the beaten path," which simply means that even in nature he would look for nests and wombs.

This explains why sex is for him the supreme manifestation of man's life in the microcosm of the family, rather than the supreme force of the macrocosm, as it was, for instance, in Schopenhauer's view. This also shows that the parallel with D. H. Lawrence, made by some of Rozanov's Western readers, is completely wrong. D. H. Lawrence's heroes and heroines do not need the sacrament of religion and society to embrace each other, yet they need the approval of Pan; and perhaps for this reason their sexual consummation takes place generally not in the privacy of a room, but under the indulgent eyes of Pan himself. The only thing Rozanov and D. H. Lawrence have in common is their equal scorn for hygiene, that kind of spiritual exercise of the body. But D. H. Lawrence scorns hygiene in nature; Rozanov, in the home, too.

V

Such a conception of family life is typically "proletarian" in character, as shown by the etymology of that term. Yet Rozanov states the opposite view: "The family is the most aristocratic form of life! . . . Yes! Despite misfortunes, mistakes, accidents . . . it is after all the most aristocratic form of life!" This paradoxical attempt to exalt and to ennoble the daily rut of family life shows Rozanov for what he really is: a petty bourgeois. He candidly makes the typical bourgeois boast of being able to raise a "bird's nest," to support a large family. The boast is made in a good-natured and amusing manner. He tells how, when he used to receive at home the "decadents," at the end of an evening party he would detain his friend, the teacher Viktor Proteykin, and "point to a place behind the door. . . . Behind the door stood such a multitude of little galoshes that I myself used to be surprised. To count them quickly was impossible. And both I and Proteykin would burst out laughing. 'What a lot!' . . . I always thought with pride; 'There sit down to my table ten persons, including servants. And all of them are fed by my labor. All of them find a place in the world round my labor'. . . ."

That Rozanov was a petty bourgeois is shown even more convincingly by the sequel to the passage just quoted, which is an attack against Herzen, whom Rozanov despises both as an aristocrat and as a radical. The gist of the attack is that it is not the Herzens, but the Rozanovs that have the right to say "Civis rossicus sum." It is this rejection of the intelligentsia, not so much on ideological as on social grounds, that reveals Rozanov as the strange monster or rare bird, he really was: the last example of a human species now completely extinct, called the Russian bourgeois. The dominant traits of that social and psychological type have been often described in Russian literature, and may be summed up in what Gogol called by the name of *poshlost*. In plain English *poshlost* means vulgarity, a vulgarity which is not merely a matter of taste, but of the ethos as well.[7] *Poshlost* rules the minds of men or of a class only when it has already dominated their souls. Thus, at least ideally, *poshlost* means a degeneration and corruption which are accepted with a sense of absolute innocence, as if they were facts of nature or acts of God. In brief, the *poshlost* of the Russian bourgeois or officeholder generally goes without that hypocrisy so highly regarded by their equivalents in the West. As a matter of fact, the Russian bourgeois is characterized by a cynicism not less naïve than the idealism of the intelligentsia. Rozanov possesses this kind of cynicism with a peculiar intensity: "The idea of law as duty never occurred to me. I only read about it in the dictionary, under letter D. . . . Any duty at the bottom of my heart always seemed comical to me. . . ." Rozanov knows, as well as anybody else, that "something is rotten in Russia," yet he seems to like the scent of that rottenness. "Russian life is dirty, yet so dear," he says in words which seem to re-echo the ending of a famous poem by Alexander Blok:

> My dear Russia, even if so,
> The dearest country you are to me.

It was only natural that both the radical or liberal wing and the religious and idealistic one of the Russian intelligentsia of his time would accuse Rozanov of resembling too much two of the most obscene figures of Russian fiction, Dostoevski's Smerdyakov and Sologub's Peredonov,[8] who represent Russian *poshlost* at its best, or rather, at its worst. It was equally natural for Rozanov to accept those identifications without qualms: "From the epoch of *Solitaria* there was firmly established in the press the idea that I am a Peredonov or a Smerdyakov. *Merci*." Curiously enough, both parallels seem literally true. It has been observed that Rozanov loved Dostoevski, even more than as a writer, as a creator of both real and unreal psychologies, and it is therefore both strange and significant to see that, personally, Rozanov reminds us of the most nauseating minor figures of Dostoevski's human gallery, not only of Smerdyakov but also of that "underground man," who is neither a hero nor an insect. Exactly because of this, Rozanov is sometimes able to dig as deep in autobiography as Dostoevski did in fiction. To requote a phrase which Rozanov must have known, we may recall that Dostoevski said once that "there are many, even too many, indecent things in the minds of decent people." [9] Now Rozanov's task was perhaps to reveal, with the utmost candor, his own personal lack of decency not only in thinking and writing, but in living too.

VI

Our reference to Freud reminds us that many critics, especially Boris de Schloezer, have considered Rozanov a typical Freudian case. Such a claim could be easily bolstered by recalling a few details of his biography and some of his psychological traits. His life started with a childhood spent under the guardianship of a rigid mother abandoned by her husband, and he was forever affected by a mother fixation, by an obsessive longing for the womb. We know that in his later years he was easily attracted, like Leopold Bloom by Gerty McDowell, by young girls. Thus even his phallic cult could be seen as a kind of compensation for some quite feminine traits in his phychosexual structure. Whatever psychoanalysis may say, there is no doubt that the Don Juan or the Casanova is in love with the other sex, while Rozanov was in love with his own, with a curious kind of narcissism, and in this context it may be worth observing that in ancient religions it was woman and not man who sacrificed to that cult.

All this, of course, makes him grotesque and ridiculous: nothing could be more distant from the idea of the "male animal" or the Don Juan than this paterfamilias, who, as a youth, was described by a woman friend, in a letter to Polina Suslova, as "forced to be a woman," and who in his later years could relate in print that a girl relative had once told him: "the only masculine thing in you is your trousers." The Suslova episode may show that he was masochistically inclined: his marriage to the former mistress of Dostoevski, considered as a spiritual father by him, could be easily explained by the psychoanalyst in terms of the Oedipus complex. To this we shall add that his own psychosexual traits inspired a good deal of his writing, that he sublimated his own phallic cult into an erotic religion, and, finally, that in his controversy with Christianity, he expressed perhaps his own conflicts with traditional morality and social taboos.

Yet, in spite of its plausibility, the hypothesis that Rozanov is a Freudian case is far from the truth. First of all, he is quite conscious of his own psychosexual processes, and he leans far more toward expression than repression. He tends to exhibit, not to inhibit, what is hidden in the lower depth of the Self. The main concern of his psyche is not abstention, but indulgence; he is not an ascetic, but an orgiast. He does not aim at mortifying the flesh, but at glorifying it. He wants to satisfy man's urges, not to restrain them. As for his strange spiritualism, Rozanov achieved it directly, by exalting rather than sublimating his own Self: or, to speak again in Freudian terms, through the Ego, not the Superego. Rozanov was undoubtedly a Narcissus who was in love with his sex precisely because he was in love with his soul.

It would perhaps be truer to see Freudian cases in his critics than in Rozanov himself. Too many of them have paid more attention to the ideal than to the real side of his personality, while they should have done the opposite. This is why they have taken too literally and too seriously, at its face value, his mystique of sex. Few realized that Rozanov elaborated that mystique to justify or glorify something more important, personal, and deep: but that something has nothing to do with psychoanalysis, exactly because it was a projection of his wholly unrepressed instincts. Rozanov the man and the writer was not the unconscious victim of those instincts, precisely because he both served and exploited them. That he was fully aware of this is to be seen in the proud and shameless answer he made to those critics who had reproached him for his venality and commercialism: "They say that I fix a dear price on my book *Solitaria:* yet my works are not mixed with water or even blood, but with human seed."

It is precisely because he is not a Freudian case that Rozanov often speaks like Freud, without knowing him, which is in itself the proof that he did not need to become the patient of any psychoanalyst. As we have already stated, neither his work nor his psyche is troubled by any deep-seated conflict with traditional morality. Being the kind of man he is, he does not know the pangs of the Calvinistic or Puritan conscience in matters of sex, nor does he feel any bourgeois scruples in matters of social ethics, in his attitude toward duty and the law. Morality in general, and middle-class morality in particular, do not hold any prestige for him. He expresses his indifference, and even scorn, toward morality and social ethics in the most ironical and trenchant way: "I am not such a scoundrel as to think of morality. . . . I don't even know how they spell morality, with one *l* or two. . . . I am not an enemy of morality: it simply never enters my mind. . . ." In brief, Rozanov is completely amoral. An English synonym for personal morality is uprightness, but Rozanov is amorphous, spineless, boneless. His own ethos is that of the amoeba, or of an inarticulate and invertebrate animal. There is no possibility of a conflict between instinct and conscience, between vitality and morality, when psychology itself is reduced to the level of biology, as mere consciousness of living.

His friend and biographer, Hollerbach, was thus wrong in trying to defend Rozanov from the accusation of immorality, maintaining that he worked "not against morality, but toward a new religion and morality." This is true of all "immoralists," from Nietzsche to Gide, but it is not true of Rozanov, who cannot be the founder of a new morality because he showed his scorn for the old one by not taking it seriously, by acting as if it were not even worth while to try to destroy it. It is with aggressive pride that he denounces the ethical smugness of his attackers, which he considers as proof of their inhuman unreality, of their lack of life: "Don't imagine that you are more moral than I. You are neither moral, nor immoral. You are merely manufactured things. A shop of manufactured things. And look, I am going to take a stick and break these things. Is a china shop moral or immoral?"

Although derived from the cave of our instincts, Rozanov's amorality, unlike Gide's or Nietzsche's immorality, never becomes an idealization or rationalization of its instinctive roots. The inner spring of that amorality is a kind of animal faith in the absolute freedom of the psyche, of our deeper will to live, as well as of our most fleeting wishes and whims. In other words, what one might call Rozanov's negative ethos is but an unexpected and yet natural consequence of his conception of private life, which is hedonistic from both the physiological and the psychological viewpoints, and which is neither moral nor immoral exactly because Rozanov's hedonistic vitalism has nothing to do with esthetic hedonism:

A million years passed before my soul was let out into the world to enjoy it, and how can I suddenly say to her: don't forget yourself, darling, but enjoy yourself in a moral fashion. No, I say to her: enjoy yourself, darling, have a good time, my lovely one, enjoy yourself, my precious, enjoy yourself in any way you please. And toward evening you will go to God. For my life is my day, and not Socrates' or Spinoza's.

It is easy to understand how and why a man like this, for whom human life did not differ in any way from the life of such ephemeral beings as a worm or a butterfly, and who at the same time was oppressed by the loneliness of his soul, would finally consider sexual intercourse as the only way to immortalize life, or at least to break for a while the despair of his solitude. And it is equally understandable that, without believing in the immortality of the soul and in the resurrection of the flesh, he could not do without some kind of religious belief. Religious thinking and feeling were for him as intimate and personal as sex, and yet he never completely identified religion and sex. One could say that in his system the religious moment follows the sexual one, as if to prove the eternal truth of the ancient saying: *post coitum animal triste*. In this sense, the religious Rozanov is the *animal triste* par excellence.

It is this melancholy or sadness that saves him, and that changes him from a satyr into a silenus. It was to a silenus that Plato and Rabelais compared Socrates, not only in the proper sense of that mythological name, but also in the figurative meaning of the noun derived from it, which designated a vessel full of spirits. Rozanov, of course, was not a Socrates: devoid as he was of any philosophical wisdom, or of any dialectical irony, he looks more like a barbarian than like a Hellene, a Marsyas rather than an Apollo. Yet this ugly, bearded, and dirty silenus, drunk with sex, obsessed by an all-embracing, heterosexual eroticism, was still able to reconcile what was earthly and heavenly in him. Like Dostoevski's Dmitri, whom he resembles as much as any other Karamazov excepting Ivan, Rozanov could not live without serving at once the opposite ideals of Sodom and the Madonna: yet, in a certain sense, he transcended their conflict. Perhaps this was due to the *anima naturaliter christiana* in him, which prevented this cynic from serving, except in form, other gods than his god, other masters than his soul. He knew every vice and sin, but, despite his betrayals, notwithstanding the ease with which he could change his allegiance and turn his coat, he was fundamentally incapable of duplicity and hypocrisy, simply because he never bowed to the idols of decency and respectability. His hatred of cant seems to redeem even his depravity and cynicism, and allowed him to remain supremely loyal to himself. Empty of piety as he was, he was full of pity; even his self-pity was but the personal expression of a deep feeling of compassion for the fate of man.

VII

If Rozanov is typically Russian in his class psychology and in many of his individual traits, there is no doubt either about the Russian quality of his artistic genius, about the Russian peculiarity of his literary temper. Notwithstanding all the usual and often valid comparisons to be made between him and such Western writers and thinkers as Rousseau, Pascal, and Nietzsche,

Rozanov's cultural and artistic ancestors are all Russian. In his somber political obscurantism, his interest in popular religion, even his diction and style, he belongs to a national school of thinking and writing little known in the West, the most extreme representatives of which are perhaps two figures of the late nineteenth century, the philosopher Konstantin Leontiev and the storyteller Nikolay Leskov. In the chain of that tradition he forged a new link, which was to be further strengthened by a few writers of the younger generation, especially the novelist Aleksey Remizov, who considered Rozanov his master, and who defined him as "the most alive of our contemporaries."

In that stream of the Russian literary tradition which is better known in the West, Rozanov naturally belongs, as we have stated before, to the lineage of Gogol and Dostoevski. He possessed not only the deep psychological insight of the latter, but also the former's malicious and indiscreet psychological curiosity. He shared Gogol's idea of literature as a kind of exalted gossip, of the writer as a glorified Peeping Tom: "The postmaster, looking into other people's letters (Gogol's *Inspector*), was a man endowed with excellent literary taste." Yet Rozanov belongs also to the literary tradition of Goncharov and Tolstoy, of *Oblomov* and *War and Peace* (he frequently praises the latter), with their exaltation of patriarchal life, of biological patience, of vitalistic laziness. Among the great Russian masters, only Turgenev and Pushkin (despite Rozanov's frequent praise of the greatest of all Russian poets) are completely alien to him. He must have found both of them either too classical and serene, or too clean and chaste. Yet the only national tradition he fully and scornfully rejects is the tradition of the intelligentsia, with its concern for social service, with its political activism and ideological radicalism: in his enmity toward Belinski and his followers he is even more uncompromising than Dostoevski himself.

Despite all these ties with the Russian cultural tradition, Rozanov's work gives an impression of isolation, especially in regard to his contemporaries. Although deeply rooted in the soil of Russian culture, he was out of tune with the *Zeitgeist* of his own generation: and he felt himself a "literary exile," not only from the camp of the intelligentsia, but also from the field of his own mystic, idealistic, and modernistic admirers, the decadents and the symbolists. This feeling of isolation had some basis in fact. First of all, the decadents and the symbolists were deliberate and conscious artists, who learned their craft at the school of the West; even when their inspiration was chaotic, their style was ornamental and formalistic. Notwithstanding their genuine sympathy for some of the manifestations of Rozanov's genius, they could not accept without reservation his formlessness, what one might call

the invertebrate character of his writing, about which, by the way, he himself used to joke good-naturedly. Once, for instance, in a kind of self-con-
scious literary parable, he described a pavement all dug up, only to ask this
rhetorical question, and to give this ironical answer: "What's this? Street
repairs? No: it is the 'works' of Rozanov. And on the iron rails freely rides
a streetcar." Skilled craftsmen as they were, good pruners and gardeners
of ideas and words, the esthetic and idealistic writers of his own age could
not accept easily the wild extravaganzas of Rozanov's style and thought.

The two masters of his generation to whom Rozanov may be less arbi-
trarily, although only partially and superficially, compared are Leo Shestov
and Dmitri Merezhkovski. Rozanov had in common with Shestov the
tendency to dissociate ethics from religion; with Merezhkovski, to conceive
of man and of the world dualistically, as an interplay of opposites, where
the adoration of the Holy Ghost generated the idolatry of sex, and the idolatry of sex generated the adoration of the Holy Ghost. Shestov and Merezhkovski, like other metaphysical thinkers and mystical writers of their generation, including Rozanov himself, indulged in their personal version
of what Huysmans would have called *érudites hystéries,* but their apocalyptic mythologies were far more allegorical and visionary than Rozanov's.
Unlike them, he derived his ideas not so much from his mind as from his
temperament.

Culturally, all the most important of Rozanov's contemporaries were far
more European than he, yet Rozanov seems more universal than they, despite his literary parochialism and provincialism. While the decadents and
symbolists were well versed in ancient and modern lore, in the most important literary movements and traditions of the West, Rozanov had done
very little reading outside of Russian literature, which he knew very well.
Thus it is not surprising that his numberless judgments on the Russian
literary tradition are often fresher and keener than theirs. Unlike his decadent and symbolist colleagues, he speaks of Western thinkers and writers
only when he wants to show his antipathies, for instance for Herbert Spencer
and his brand. The few foreign literary monuments with which he is well
acquainted are the Holy Writ and other sacred books, and they include
practically no "classical" works. In this he deeply differed from his contemporaries, who were literary cosmopolitans, cultural "men of the world."
He differed from them also for other reasons. They were professional men
of letters; he was a pamphleteer and a journalist. They were, *de facto* and
de jure, members of the aristocracy or of the upper bourgeoisie, and it may
be because of this that Rozanov, half plebeian and half petty bourgeois, dis-

liked the decadents and used to call them "sterile men." Yet, like Nietzsche, another enemy of decadence, he was a decadent himself, at least in the psychological sense of the term; he was that kind of a decadent which only an outcast can be.

It is highly interesting to see what meaning and value literature could possess for a man and a writer of this sort. He hated literature when he found that, instead of being a calling or a gift, it was merely an attitude, as it seemed to him was the case with most authors. "Not literature, but literariness is awful: the literariness of the soul, the literariness of life," he once said. If this is true, then literature is a burden and a curse: "I endure literature as my grave, I endure literature as my sorrow, I endure literature as my disgust." In contrast to this view, he always held that literary talent, at least as far as he himself was concerned, was something physiologically personal and intimate, like one's shirt: "I feel literature like my own trousers, equally close, absolutely as something my own." Literary talent was thus for him more than a vocation or a spiritual calling; it was a physical grace, an inborn instinct, as unconscious and spontaneous as a nerve reflex: "The secret of writing is in one's fingertips, and the secret of the orator is on the tip of his tongue." It was perhaps because of this view that he had no illusions about the durability of his work. In love as he was with any bad or good quality of his own, he was still able to acknowledge that "there is something disgusting in my style. The disgusting is not eternal. I shall therefore be temporary. The disgusting consists in a certain satisfaction, in something like a kind of enchantment in front of oneself." Certainly, there is nothing antiseptic in the style of Rozanov: his writing is so full of living matter that it seems destined to go the way of all flesh.

In view of this highly personal, almost physiological conception of literature, Rozanov could not conceive of writing except in the form of the page written by hand. He hated the printed word, and believed that the personality of the author is retained only by his manuscript. Rozanov extended his "fetishism for trifles" to anything handwritten, either documents or letters, by himself or his friends. Such a fetishism is all the more significant in view of his avowed lack of interest in printed books, which he often sold after having left them unread and uncut:

It is as though that damned Gutenberg has licked all writers with his copper tongue, and all of them have lost their souls in print, have lost their face, character. My "I" is only in manuscript, as is the "I" of every writer. I have a superstitious fear of tearing up letters, notebooks (even my children's exercise books), manuscripts — I don't tear up anything.

After all, a manuscript reveals to us the voice of a writer through his script, that very voice which one hears with far more difficulty while reading his books. "What is new is the accent," says Rozanov, "the accent of the manuscript, pre-Gutenberg, for itself." It was perhaps to suggest that there is a difference between a self-penned text, and a text copied or set in print, that Rozanov inserted after the title of the book the words "pochti na pravach rukopisi," which Prince Mirsky translated as "almost privately printed."

This is the reason for the use on Rozanov's part of the typographical devices already mentioned, by which he changes printed books almost into facsimiles of his drafts, hoping that this may help the reader to read the work as if it were a musical score. This obviously implies the notion of literature as something spoken and chanted, as well as written. It is only to preserve this actual or virtual oral quality of literary inspiration that man writes it down: "Every movement of the soul is accomplished by utterance. And every utterance I want without fail to write down. It is an instinct. Was it from such an instinct that (written) literature was born? . . . Literature was born by itself (silently) and for itself. . . ." His own writing is thus a way of speaking: "This speech (whispering) constitutes my literature," and the reader must hear this whispering through the mute signs of the written or printed word: "One must hear the voice, even while reading." It is not necessary for this utterance, for this voice, to be very articulate: a writer must merely hear and re-echo the "uninterrupted noise in his soul." A writer does not write down ideas, but tunes: "One cannot jot down any thought, but only that one which is musical."

These ideas seem to be very close to the surrealist doctrine of "spoken thought," and to the symbolist attempt to reduce poetry to "the condition of music." Rozanov, however, is not a verse, but a prose writer; not a poet, but an essayist. Thus his view that writing is akin to musical composition has a very special meaning. For Rozanov the musicality of a writer is not so much a quality of his talent, as of his soul; it is a psychic power, rather than an artistic virtue. The musical poetics of Rozanov is based not on an esthetic but on a psychological interpretation of the notion of originality: a literary work is musical when it is the product of a peculiar personality, or, in Rousseau's terms, when it is dictated by its author's *génie,* rather than by his *esprit.* The automatic grace of literary creation is thus a mystery to the creator himself: "The secret of authorship consists in the constant and involuntary music in one's soul. If it is not there, a man can only make a writer of himself. But he is not a writer. Something is flowing in his soul. Eternally. Constantly. What? Why? Who knows? — least of all the writer."

VIII

Despite his hatred for the printed word, Rozanov sought an escape from the sense of his solitude not only in writing but in publishing as well. He often considered his books as means for his own rescue, or at least as cries for help: "I have been writing (am writing) with a deep longing to break the ring of loneliness. . . . It is really a ring, which I have been wearing from my birth. This is why I shout: here is what is here, let everybody know about it. . . . Likewise, someone drowning at the bottom of a deep well would shout to people over there, on the land." Yet Rozanov did not write merely to express this mood of solitary desperation, or to relieve it. He wrote for the same reason he lived: writing was for him another way to feel. Tears do not exclude laughter, but both tears and laughter exclude reflection and thought. Rozanov saw this himself: "I merely laugh or weep. Do I think in the proper sense? Never." Laughter is malicious when thoughtless; and this may suggest that sometimes Rozanov wrote to amuse himself at the expense of others, including his readers, or, in other words, that he indulged in the rather bourgeois inclination to *épater le bourgeois:* "Only for this I had to write *Solitaria:* to put my tongue out at the reader."

This is enough to prove that Rozanov's literature, though a typical literature of the ego, is not a literature of confession. Rozanov does not confess, as Saint Augustine does, in order to repent, or, like Tolstoy, to teach and preach. He may even be more honest and sincere than they are, simply because he reveals of himself what he wants to, and nothing more. He does not claim to confess everything, or even anything important; nor is he unconsciously led to reveal himself as more sinful, and therefore more interesting and less ridiculous, than he really is. He may choose to depict what is lowest and meanest in himself: still, he chooses. He freely admits having hidden many aspects of his personality, even to having lied about himself, and the page where he makes this admission gives an impression of higher sincerity through its candid cynicism:

It is surprising how I managed to accommodate myself to falsehood. And for this odd reason: what business is it of yours what precisely I think? Why am I obliged to tell you my real thoughts? My profound subjectivity (the pathos of subjectivity) has had this effect: that I have gone through my whole life as though behind a curtain, immovable, untearable. Nobody dares touch that curtain. There I lived, there with myself I was truthful. . . . And it seemed to me that no one had anything to do with the truth of anything I said on the other side of the curtain.

This is why Rozanov's work cannot be compared to the *Confessions* of Rousseau, although, undoubtedly, there is an ideal connection between these two men. Rozanov was therefore right when he said: "They failed completely to notice what is new in *Solitaria*. They compared it to Rousseau's *Confessions,* while first of all I am not confessing." Rozanov did not write either to defend or to exalt himself, which is what Rousseau, like any confessing man, wished to do. A confession is always a public statement, a social fact. As such, it never aims, at least intentionally, at scandalizing or showing off. A confession is a kind of dialogue between the conscience of the man confessing and the conscience of mankind, and it addresses itself to the large or small community to which the man confessing professes to belong. That the people supposed to be listening may keep silent is a matter of no importance. Like the Catholic sacrament by the same name, confession involves a series of questions and answers. The man who confesses expects to be judged, although he may try to influence that judgment. What he wants most is to be heard and to be understood, to be excused and forgiven, to be welcomed back, like a lost sheep, into the fold.

This is true even in the case of Rousseau, whose confession is dictated not by pride alone, but by self-pity too. Despite his own challenge to the reader to dare (or not to dare) to consider himself a better man than the confessing author, Rousseau addresses his fellow men while experiencing a feeling of contrition or repentance, when some sort of conversion is taking place in his soul. This is why any literary confession makes an appeal to the experience of other men, or at least invites each one of its readers to relive on his own account the ordeal of the confessing man. Every confession signifies the end of a crisis, and the beginning of a new path. But Rozanov is an inveterate monologist and an unregenerate sinner, indifferent to good and evil, "lukewarm" rather than cold or hot. He is unable to think consistently even about himself; he does not care about the opinion of others; he hates any public gesture or word; he neither repents nor changes his way; he refuses to teach and preach: how can a man of this kind confess?

A confession, in other words, implies that respect for social and ethical values which Rozanov failed so conspicuously to possess. We have already seen that he denied to any man the right to judge the things he had said "on the other side of the curtain," or to call him to account for the most intimate side of his Self. Yet Rozanov went even further, and refused to recognize the authority of public opinion even in less private matters than this. When facing public issues, he felt that he had the right to lie and to deceive and this is why his ideology cannot be taken so seriously as most critics have done.

This brings in the question of the sincerity of his activity as a journalist and a publicist. While performing these tasks, Rozanov played roles similar to those of an orator, of an advocate, of an official, even of a priest: after all, he was an active and responsible contributor to a conservative, semiofficial periodical, where he acted sometimes as a mouthpiece, and where he defended, on the political and on the religious plane, some of the most unpopular and hateful measures of the tsarist government, and the very foundations of Russian Caesaropapism. Yet let's hear what he had to say about those callings which were to a great extent his own:

In the idea of prostitution — the fight against which is hopeless — enters, inevitably, "I belong to all," i.e., that which also enters in the idea of a writer, orator, advocate, official in the service of the state. Thus, on one hand, prostitution is the most social of phenomena, to a certain extent, the prototype of sociability. . . . And on the other hand, there indeed enters into the essence of an actor, writer, advocate, even of a Father who officiates for everybody — the psychology of prostitution. . . . "Funeral or wedding?" asks the priest of a caller, with an equally smooth, vague smile. . . . A scholar, insofar as he is published, a writer, inasmuch as he is printed, are certainly prostitutes. Professors are most certainly *prostitués pécheurs.* . . . Essentially, the most intimate I give to all, is a notion utterly metaphysical. . . .

It was perhaps this leaning for spiritual prostitution that made a journalist and a publicist of a man who cared so much for private life and the intimacies of the Self. This very paradox explains why this free-lancer, who was at times almost a professional newspaperman, was all the same affected by a bourgeois hatred for newspapers: "Newspapers, I think, will pass away just as did the eternal wars of the Middle Age, women's *tournures,* etc." This scorn for the profession which provided his daily bread is not so contradictory as it may seem. At any rate, contradiction is the very staple of Rozanov's thought, and this is why his work gives the impression of a continuous recantation or palinode. Even so, he often managed to reconcile the opposite demands of his profession and of his calling: even when writing about current affairs, he tended to look at them as if they were individual cases, *scènes de la vie privée.* One could say that he used to write "leaders" or editorials from the point of view of the city desk.

Clearly a man like him could not become a prophet, which is the destiny of everyone who starts with a public confession of his sins, as Tolstoy did. And in truth Rozanov was never a prophet, despite what he once said of himself in a page worth quoting in full. This page opens with the repetition of a simile which Rozanov applies often to himself. This simile, by which Rozanov compares his destiny to the lot of a "wanderer," or a "pilgrim," aims at pointing out the spiritual restlessness which troubled this sedentary bourgeois:

Essentially I was born a pilgrim — a pilgrim preacher. So in Judaea a whole street used to start prophesying. Now I am one of those: one of the men in the street (average men) and yet a prophet (without the mission to change, for instance, the destiny of the people). Prophecy in my case has no reference to Russians, by which I mean that it is not a circumstance in our people's history, but it is my private concern, and it refers only to myself (having no significance or influence); it is a detail of my biography.

The statement is highly revealing, although at first it sounds but a confirmation of the commonplace thought: *Nemo propheta in patria*. This is even truer when the prophet's fatherland is a town or a village alone. Yet a local prophet, the prophet of a street or a borough, is a contradiction in terms. Prophesy is not individual, but collective, not private, but public, not local, but universal: it looks for strife and truth; it is far more an act of heroism than of holiness. How could a prophet be a man saying of himself: "Always in life I was a spectator, not an actor. . . . I didn't want truth, I wanted peace"? Yet, if not a prophet, this man was a seer: not of the coming of the Lord, but of the everlasting presence of the Soul.

IX

It is easy to imagine the kind of attitude which a man like this would take toward public affairs, in the field of politics. Like Flaubert and Baudelaire he did not care for political opinions, and he cared even less for political convictions, which might be defined as "the conscience of the political intellect." [10] The attitude of Rozanov toward political convictions is not merely one of indifference, but even of scorn and contempt: "And what about convictions? I simply spit on them. . . . It is not our tongue which is our convictions; it is our boots which are our convictions. . . ." No wonder that political opportunism and cynicism was a habit with him, a habit which he boasts of: "I changed even convictions like gloves." This instinctive dislike applies not only to the convictions of men belonging to other parties, but also to the ideas of the conservative and reactionary circles he belonged to: "Why am I so angry with the radicals? I don't know myself. Do I love the conservatives? No. What's the matter with me? I can't make it out."

As a matter of fact, his changes of mind in regard to what his fellow re-

actionaries would have called the "devil's party" are even more interesting
and significant than his ambiguous and contradictory relations with the
men and the ideology of his own camp. There is no doubt that this Slavophile and obscurantist often condemns contemporary Russia on the very
ground for which she had been condemned by Westernizers and nihilists,
by the liberal and radical wings of the Russian Left. He frequently indicts
the Russian nation for its lack of organization and for its technical inefficiency, and often complains about the fact that in Russia even the lowest
specialists and technicians (for instance, pharmacists) are foreign born. His
national defeatism reaches the extreme point in that passage of the *Apocalypse*
where he declares that the conquest of Russia by Germany would have
been a good thing. There is no doubt that he would have approved of the
successful Bolshevik attempt to reorganize Russian society in practical and
material terms, according to the blueprints of an over-all plan.

But on the other hand, he praises the Russian way of life for the same
reason it had been glorified by Slavophiles and romantic idealists, or, as he
says, because of the Russians' love for dreaming and singing, because of
their willingness to pray and to weep. At this point it may be necessary to
add that, perhaps because he was essentially a city man, Rozanov did not base
this mystical view of the national character on the premises of that agrarian
populism which was so dear both to the Right and to the Left. Less than
anyone else did Rozanov idolize the Russian peasantry, or idealize the
Russian masses in general. It was Russia, and not the Russian people, that
became his hypostasis, and he treated her as if she were a real person, in a
sense far more concrete and literal than France was "une personne" for
Michelet.

Rozanov hated populism for the same reasons he hated radicalism, for
its equalitarian tendencies, for its ideological and mathematical thinking,
for its hostility toward the accidents of personality and the peculiarities of
the Self. His indictment of the radical Left is in this regard very similar to
the one already made by Dostoevski in that famous page of the *Notes From
Underground* where he attacks utopian socialism and revolutionary radicalism. Rozanov uses again Dostoevski's mythical image of the Crystal Palace,
not merely to reject its ideal, but to deny the belief that it will ever be built:
"There will be a lot of broken crockery, but there will be no new building
erected. . . . Revolution will fail because in the revolution there is no
place for the dream." And through another reference to Dostoevski, this
time to the plan of Shigalev as described in *The Possessed*, Rozanov claims
that the revolution will fail even when succeeding, exactly because it will

have no room for genius, for the exceptional personality, or merely for the individual souls: "The revolution will strangle them [the geniuses] in their youth, when they suddenly discover something in their souls." And the revolution will kill them with these words: "Oh, you are proud; you don't want to mix with us, to share, to be chums. . . . Oh, you have a soul of your own, not a communal soul. . . ."

Often Rozanov's attitude toward the revolution is ambiguous (as is Dostoevski's), and this is probably due to the equal and opposite reactions of the bourgeois mind, which may be seduced by Robespierre and Napoleon, which may waver between legitimism and jacobinism, which, as modern history has amply shown, and as Ortega y Gasset was the first to notice in his *Revolt of the Masses,* may be attracted by violence (i.e., Fascism) far more than was thought before. Rozanov is often attracted by both extremes at the same time: "One may both fall in love with terrorism and yet hate it to the very bottom of one's heart, without any insincerity at all. There are matters, per se dialectical, radiating (themselves) now one, now another light, seeming on one side one color, and on the other side a different color. We, the people, are terribly unfortunate in our judgments in the face of those dialectical matters, for we are terribly helpless." Yet, despite this, Rozanov seems often ready to judge radicalism, to condemn as hollow any form of political activism, to deny any sense to revolution and terrorism: "The revolution has two dimensions, length and width; but it has not the third, depth. And because of this quality it will never have a ripe, tasty fruit; it will never fulfill itself."

In view of all this, it is highly interesting to see what stand Rozanov took when the Russian revolution, for good or for bad, succeeded in fulfilling itself. This very stand is the simple theme of the *Apocalypse of Our Times,* where the revolution is accepted as something fatal, unavoidable, irremediable, and where the author still tries to find the causes, or origins, of that historical cataclysm. The responsibility lies for him with the Russian state, and with the Russian nation, especially with Holy Russia, with Christianity itself. This idea is announced by Rozanov in a note "To the Reader" at the beginning of the book: "There is no doubt that the fundamental cause of what is happening now lies in this fact: that in European society (including the Russian) there have been formed cultural voids caused by old Christianity, and that in these voids everything crumbles: thrones, classes, castes, labor, and riches." The book's very title was suggested by this sense of catastrophe, as well as by the author's paradoxical belief that Saint John's *Apocalypse* had been not merely a condemnation of the ancient Christian churches, but an indictment of Christianity at large: "The *Apocalypse* is not a Christian book. It is an Anti-Christian book; there is no doubt about this."

Christianity's failure in the social and collective field is for Rozanov the political consequence of its moral and religious failure in the field of family and sex. Christianity has been an unworldly and sterile, an esthetic and rhetorical religion, treating men as if they were almost literally lilies of the field: "Suddenly everybody has forgotten Christianity all at once — the peasants, the soldiers — because it does not give any help, because it did not prevent either war or the famine. It only sings, always sings. Like a songstress. We have listened and listened. And now we have stopped listening." Here reactionary and radical thinking seem to merge into a single stream. Once again Rozanov's patriarchal and paternalistic conception of political and religious authority finds itself in agreement with the revolutionary criticism of Russian autocracy and orthodoxy, with the radical attack against state and church. Like the radicals, he feels that state and church have failed in their mission because they have neither served nor helped the people, because they have not given them justice, peace, and bread. Christian society and the God of the New Testament have not kept their covenant with their tribe.

The strangeness of this agreement looks less extreme if we realize that it derives from the hatred which the reactionaries of Rozanov's brand and the radical Left feel in common for liberal thought. It is only fair to acknowledge that this disciple of Dostoevski is far less liberal than his master. After all, Dostoevski condemned the point of view of the Grand Inquisitor, which in his late years Rozanov seemed all too prone to accept. In his last book Rozanov cursed the Russian church and state not because they had not been modern, liberal, and progressive enough, but because they had not been as traditional and conservative, as feudal and medieval as he thought they should be. For Rozanov, state and church had failed because they had renounced the exercise of their unlimited authority, the authority of the father and the shepherd, over their children and their flocks. By reforming under the pressure of modern thought, they had betrayed themselves and their wards. Thus, even though against their wish, they had resubjected man to the curse of freedom, instead of restoring him to the blessings of obedience and slavery, to the security of peace and bread.

Like the Grand Inquisitor, Rozanov seems to think that Jesus was wrong in rejecting the three temptations of wielding authority, performing miracles, and supplying bread. Man is weak and meek, but when his needs are not satisfied, he becomes revengeful and ungrateful. He cannot stand freedom and free will, or, more simply, the liberty to choose between grace and sin: to this he prefers servitude and obedience, dreams and wishes. Curiously enough, despite the fact that Rozanov's position was identical with the position of the Grand Inquisitor, whom Dostoevski conceived of as a symbol of Rome, Rozanov never realized how much his own standpoint coincided with the theory and practice of political Catholicism.

All this may ultimately prove that, notwithstanding his ideological and sentimental changes of mood, reactionary thinking was in Rozanov natural and inborn. In a certain sense, he was a kind of Monsieur Homais of political obscurantism: his opinions were equally prejudiced and dogmatic, even if he was a skeptic and a cynic; and, what counts more, he was a Monsieur Homais endowed with talent, even with genius. He had all the passions and the prejudices of the reactionary bourgeois; he had the criminal vice of anti-Semitism, which was for him not only an official, but also a personal and deep-seated belief, never fully belied by his equally personal and sincere love for some aspects of Jewish life, and for all his Jewish friends. And there is no contradiction between his cult of authority and his instinctive bourgeois anarchism, which is but a different aspect of that cult: "There is one thousandth part of truth in anarchism: there is no need for the social, for the *koinón,* and only thus the individual (the greatest beauty in man and history) will grow. . . ." The state is a necessary evil because man is selfish in the wrong way, rather than in the right one: "Egoism is not bad. It is the crystal (firmness, infrangibility) around the I. And indeed, if all the I's were within a crystal, there would be no chaos, and consequently the state (Leviathan) would be almost unnecessary."

Rozanov's psychological anarchism is not so much a protest against society as against history. Once, after having claimed that he was endowed with religious and historical vision, Rozanov denied that very boast by this avowal: "Yet, I am only an ordinary man of the passing day, with all his weaknesses, with all his great antihistoric *I don't want to.* . . ." And it is quite significant that to express his refusal of historical reality he chose the very words with which Tolstoy's Ivan Ilich expresses on his deathbed his rejection of death. Rozanov proudly affirms elsewhere that he possesses what he calls an "ahistoricity of the soul": by which he means the untimeliness of his own thought, his inability to understand current affairs and the *Zeitgeist.* This "untimeliness" has nothing to do with the "intempestivity" of Nietzsche, which implies a denial of the present and an affirmation of future values. Rozanov's "untimeliness" is precisely the opposite and could be defined as a kind of historical "intermittence du coeur," a sort of delayed action enabling

him to understand significant happenings only after they have become part
of the past: "An event I realize as deeply as only very few do, but I realize
it three years later, months after I have witnessed it."

This feeling of estrangement from the *Zeitgeist,* this awareness of his
own historical asynchronism, led Rozanov to the decision to live as if the
category of historical time did not exist. "Hence the conclusion: live and
work as though there were nobody, as though you had no contemporaries at
all." Private life is again placed against public life, personality against history:
"A man without a role? The nicest kind of existence." Yet history is not
so easily disposed of, and it perpetuates itself within man's consciousness, if
in no other way, as a parasite of his personality: "History is perhaps a monstrous second person, swallowing people like its own food, not even thinking
of their happiness." Perhaps the destiny of man's soul is to be destroyed by
its own inward fire, so that it may show its warmth and glow, while the
task of history is merely to provide the bonfire for this: "Each soul is a
phoenix, and each soul must burn: and history is but the great pyre of the
burning souls. . . ."

X

Rozanov's religion is a religion without faith, hope, or charity: it is the
religion of desperation and loneliness, of fear and insecurity. Speaking of
himself as a man, he states, "I am not needed"; speaking of himself as a
writer, he wonders about his "fallen leaves," "Who needs them?" As a
believer, he conceives of religion as a prayer which will remain forever un-
heeded: "The essence of prayer consists of the recognition of one's profound
limitations. The prayer exists where there is 'I can't'; where there is 'I can,'
there is no prayer." He considers the Godhead as a shadowy reflection of his
own "pathos of subjectivity," as something even less real than the God whom
Joyce defined as a "cry in the street": "Is not God my mood?" And elsewhere: "My God is my peculiar one. He is only my God and nobody else's
yet. If He is somebody else's then I do not know Him, and am not interested
in knowing Him. . . ."

In brief, Rozanov's God is a private God, as his religion is a private one.
His faith does not greatly differ in kind from that of the old servant woman,
Félicité, in Flaubert's "Un coeur simple." Like her, he worships a parrot as
if it were the Holy Ghost. Rozanov is an Everyman who loves too much the
things of this world, even the vilest ones, and this is why he will never accept
the transcendental mystery of death: "I want to arrive at the other world with
the handkerchief with which I blow my nose. With not a bit less." Thus his

religion is, on the one hand, a direct expression of his own idolatry of private life, of his fetishism for anything, even common and trivial, which is connected with the Self; and on the other, an almost comical extension of the same cult: "So that God is (1) my intimacy, and (2) infinity, in which the universe itself is but a part." God and the church thus become for him both the collective and the universal equivalents of home life, of the nest: "But I should never be able to give up God: to me God is the warmest [place] . . . the church, the truly warm, the last warm place on earth." A religion like this does not care very much for such doctrines as those of the salvation of man and the redemption of the world. Rozanov does not want the resurrection of the flesh after the last judgment, but merely its daily deification here on earth. One could say that his own is the religion of the *diable au corps,* and Rozanov is right in affirming that the originality of his religious and metaphysical thought consists in the introduction of what Rabelais would have called "Gaster" into religion itself. "What *Solitaria* is about," he says, "is the Belly storming into the fortress of religion." Elsewhere Rozanov proclaims "the morality of the skin, the innocence of the skin, the chastity of the skin, the holiness of the skin." The skin is for him the soul of the flesh, and the flesh is the spiritual body of the skin. This is why "the skin is esthetic . . . the skin is the esthetic principle of man."

In other words, the soul of man is *anima* in the sense in which the word "animal" is derived from it; as such, it is more *sensitiva* than *intellectiva,* and more *vegetativa* than *sensitiva.* To this "vegetable psyche" he attributes all the notions of the Christian concept of the soul, to which he then adds all the modern connotations of the same concept. The "vegetable psyche" is the individual, the personal soul par excellence: there is nothing more personal than a soul-skin, or than a skin-soul, which, like any vital organism, may be perceived by our senses, and through its scent. Thus Rozanov bases his own religion on what he calls "the pathos of subjectivity," which in its turn rests on a purely vitalistic conception of the Self. The nemesis of all religions of the Belly is to end up in *taedium vitae,* which in Rozanov's case takes the form of a metaphysical, and yet unromantic, "spleen." All this implies a shameless and even arrogant claim, that the supreme realities of man's existence are "the facts of life," to be understood in the biological as well as in the sexual sense. Thus it is without cynicism that Rozanov may close one of his aphorisms with the statement: "Written in the W. C." Yet the supreme irony of Rozanov's philosophy is that he still believes that the soul purifies by itself its own scum, and that even when prisoner in the filthy cage of life it shines like the Phoenix, and sings like the Firebird.

XI

Rozanov may be considered as the last link in a chain of thought, in a series of attitudes and feelings, to which one could give the name of idolatry of the soul. His importance lies not only in the fact that he carried that idolatry to a point of extreme intensity, but that he developed it in complete independence from any objective, or even subjective, standard. It is only fair to state that nobody in modern times has so radically transformed the notion of the soul as Rozanov did, by changing its substance, by charging it with new meaning, by enlarging its scope. To understand Rozanov's contribution, one must therefore trace briefly the history of the modern idea of the soul.

The definition of man as the soulful animal, as the animal endowed with a vital principle which is not only biological, but psychological as well, is the Christian discovery par excellence. The Roman Catholic tradition, authoritarian and paternalistic, saw the mission of the church and the priesthood, of religion itself, as an overseeing of souls: as the apostles had been the fishermen, so the priests were to be shepherds of souls. Consequently, the Roman Church valued very highly the religious or ethical components of the psyche, or at least those elements which could be brought under its control; the other elements were to be restrained or kept in check. The instrument of this restraint was the sacrament of confession, through which the repentant soul could both express and repress what was sinful within itself. The absolution granted by the confessor was the seal of this control, a manifestation of the indulgent authority of the "oversoul" of religion on the individual psyche, on the "undersoul" of man.

The Protestant revolt proclaimed not only the dignity, but also the independence of the soul, by which it meant its individual manifestations, the peculiar qualities of personality. It is true that the personal soul was still conceived primarily as spirit, and identified with its higher faculties, either as a manifestation of divine grace or as a realization of the ethical will. In other words, what was valued was either its inborn faith or its predestined virtues, which would lead the soul toward uprightness in life, and toward bliss after death. Protestantism did so by replacing religious authority with self-examination, and confession with introspection. But it was only through the eighteenth-century concepts of the natural goodness and the perfectibility of man that Jean Jacques Rousseau, a Protestant who had abandoned the faith he was born in, stripped that notion of all its traditional religious and ethical attributes, and saw the highest value in the soul per se: that value consisting in nothing else but its being a soul. Even when considering religious and ethical values as some of the components of the soul, Rousseau would treat them as secondary, with no other validity but that which the soul would grant them. In brief, what we witness in Rousseau is the triumph of a godless mysticism of the soul, which had been made possible by the religious currents called pietism and quietism. Protestantism and Protestant sympathies had been the necessary background for such a development, while Rome had constantly fought those ideas, since the Catholic Church had always been critical and skeptical of pure mysticism.

Thus, the soul could no longer accept any God it was unable to contemplate directly within its own mirror; as for the highest ethical value, that faculty or power called will, it suddenly lost any importance exactly because the Calvinist Rousseau took literally the dogma of predestination, and mixed it with the myth of the natural goodness of man. The result was the idea not only of the irresponsibility, but of the absolute innocence of the soul: a soul is good even if the individual does not act, or even if he commits evil deeds. This was the beginning of the modern degeneration of the ancient conception of the will, which after Rousseau took in Schopenhauer the paradoxical meaning of instinct, and became a blind cosmic force, transcending history and the destiny of man. Nietzsche translated into his own terms the idea of Schopenhauer, replacing the power of the will with the will to power, which is nothing else but the same blind natural force, now transplanted from the macrocosm into the microcosm of man.

Rousseau was not so much interested in the idea of the soul, or in the individual souls of his fellow men, as in his own soul, the soul of the man Rousseau. He felt therefore that what distinguishes one's soul from the souls of others is not its active faculties, its conscience or will. What really distinguishes a soul from another is psychological originality, which he named with a term of esthetic origin, *génie*.[11] By *génie* he meant the eccentricity, the nonconformity, the novelty, the irreducibility, the idiosyncrasy of each personal being. Every person was felt by him to be a new Adam, without precedent not only among men, but even within the universe itself. The ingredients of psychological originality were recognized by Rousseau in passions and sentiments per se: not inasmuch as they become social or unsocial acts, springs of actions, virtuous or not, as in the tragedies of Corneille and Racine, but merely as passive and yet self-sufficient elements of psychic life. This explains the expression *belles âmes,* which are very different from the *grandes âmes* of the seventeenth century, and even more, from the *beaux esprits* or *esprits forts* of the eighteenth.

For Rousseau the *belle âme* is the *summum bonum,* and this *summum bonum* consists exactly in the idiosyncrasies of the soul, in its "reveries." Introspection becomes therefore self-contemplation and self-adoration; narcissism changes from a vice into a virtue. How much this conception has affected the modern mind is shown by the frequency with which modern poetry has taken up, again and again, the myth of Narcissus. But modern poetry reflects within this myth its own idea of the poetic mind rather than its vision of the soul, and sees in Narcissus the poet and the artist rather than man in general, not without a sense of guilt. But the novelty of Rousseau's position lay in his scorn for intellectual pride, which is the relevant fact in his irrationalism: an irrationalism which otherwise would be, in itself, far less extreme than it is generally felt to be. Rousseau replaces not only ethical pride, the consciousness of being morally right, but also intellectual pride, the consciousness of being intellectually right, with the mere consciousness of having, or rather, of *being,* a soul.[12] After having liberated the concept of soul from the shackles of the will, he liberates it also from the shackles of the mind. The result, or residue, is what he calls "heart": and this reduction of the soul to the common denominator of sentiment, this semantic change, according to which heart becomes the synonym of soul, is one of the chief traits of bourgeois psychologism.

As a matter of fact, nobody made this conception as literally bourgeois as Rousseau did. He was the "great commoner" of modern literary psychology, and this is the reason why, from a certain point of view, he never completely abandoned, along with the ethical and intellectual values he destroyed, their sentimental and esthetic equivalents. In other words, the beauty of the soul was for him tied up with its goodness. In this, he followed old-fashioned standards of value, especially the traditional equation of the good, the beautiful, and the true. By giving the romanesque name of St.-Preux to his hero, he meant to say that the soul of a commoner could be more beautiful and noble than the soul of a gentleman. This newly acquired nobility of the bourgeois soul involves the ennobling of everything within it. Yet this is not a case of *noblesse oblige:* no feat or deed is required to reaffirm the privilege of being what one is. This explains why the inspiration of Rousseau is essentially pastoral: in the golden age, or in the natural state of the soul, everything is perfect and innocent, good and beautiful, noble and young. Life is self-contemplation and self-satisfaction: to prove its worth the soul does not need to act, nor to face any ordeal or test. In Rousseau's pastoral dream, the psyche of the bourgeois seems to acquire forever what one calls breeding, or the ease and grace with which the nobleman carries his body and his soul.

This, of course, does not apply any longer to a soul like Rozanov's. Between Rousseau and Rozanov there has been both romanticism and realism, and if we take into account the romantic element, one could almost say that Rozanov recaptures Sénancour's idea of the soul, rather than Rousseau's. In a sense, Rozanov is a naturalistic Obermann, pondering his own thoughts in a solitude created by social, rather than metaphysical, alienation. If we take into account their cultural differences, one could say that Rozanov is a more modern bourgeois than Rousseau, a bourgeois soul which has been flourishing, or withering, during the decline of its class. Finally, we cannot forget that Rozanov was only a disciple of a major prophet, his great master, Dostoevski.

Dostoevski, too, had been interested in the bourgeois, in the common, in other words, in the modern soul. The first outcome of this study was the *Notes From Underground,* and the portrayal of the "underground man," whom the author considers, as he states in a prefatory note, but one of the recent historical variations of modern man. Dostoevski saw that for a man of that kind his whims and wishes count more than his will, that self-consciousness is far more important than conscience itself.[13] But Dostoevski differed from Rousseau and his disciples (for instance, from Schiller, whom he loved and knew well) because he saw that the psyche of modern man could not be naïvely reduced to the simple standards of the *belle âme* or *schoene Seele.* This means that he treated modern man and his soul more impersonally and objectively, both from without and from within; and, when he used introspection in order to unravel the mystery of that soul, that introspection was critical too. Instead of an apology or a complacent confession, instead of cynicism and exhibitionism, he gave us a dramatic account of the internal conflicts of the modern spirit, which are nothing but one of the many forms taken by the everlasting civil war between ethical and nonethical impulses, between conscience and consciousness, between the psyche and the soul.

If in his early work this conflict is merely pathetic, in the great novels it becomes tragic, and it is worth while to remember that Dostoevski loved Racine, and that each one of his masterpieces is literally a tragedy of the soul. In those psychological tendencies in which Rousseau had seen the natural goodness of man, he saw the original sin; those which for Rousseau had been the idyllic virtues, became for him the vices, the tragic flaws of the soul. From the purely psychological standpoint, he progressed farther than Rousseau; he enlarged the soul of man to a vast *terra incognita,* and to a new Ultima Thule: to a Cymmerian night never explored or even reached before him. He penetrated into the depths of the soul even more than was done later by depth psychology, and, as a poet, he was both frightened and fascinated by them. In a certain sense, he was more afraid than proud of having discovered not only how deep but how wide the human soul is, how large is the living space it needs. As he said himself, with the words of Dmitri Karamazov: "Man is too wide, and ought to be restricted."

Rousseau had discovered paradise in the psyche, and Dostoevski had added to that the discovery of hell in man's soul. Rozanov differs from both Rousseau and Dostoevski because he was able to discover many earthly paradises in the psyche, and several limboes, too: or, if we want to go on using Dantean terms, also a few Ante-Purgatories and Ante-Hells. There he found also many larvae, and many monsters, but especially insects, bugs, and cobwebs. He made Rousseau's bliss far more snug and worldly by reducing it to bourgeois comfort; he made far more daily, common, and mean the torments and tortures of Dostoevski, lowering them to the level of those "vile tales" which make the prose of life even coarser. He brought to extreme limits the vulgarization or proletarization of the soul; or, in religious terms, he recognized among its components matters and substances which, before him, would have been defined as the least spiritual possible.

In this sense he became, rather than a possible patient of Freud, one of his peers. But Freud, the master of clinical psychology, was at least in part a positive and scientific mind, indifferent to any judgment of value, skeptical of any metaphysics. He was also a physician, a healer, trying to heal the body through the mind. But Rozanov was a strange kind of mystic, who, despite his anti-Christian stand, could never forget the dualism between God and the world, the mind and the body, the soul and the flesh. And he never wanted to heal or to redeem that dualism. As a matter of fact, he tried not to solve that dualism through a synthesis, but to perpetuate it in a sort of syncretism. His "scandal" consisted in this, that he not only gave a positive value to the least spiritual ingredients of the soul, but that he reversed the traditional judgment, and considered them its best parts.

From this point of view, he reversed even the last esthetic remains of Rousseau's idolatry of the self. For Rozanov, a soul is valuable not because it is "beautiful" but merely because it is a soul, even though it be ugly, vulgar, and filthy. In this sense, he was far more of a Christian than Rousseau: to that extent, the changeable Rozanov always remained faithful to himself. In *The Legend of the Grand Inquisitor* there is a brilliant page about *Crime and Punishment,* where the crime of Raskolnikov is seen not in the murder itself, but in his treatment of his future victim as if she were not a person, but an insect. Perhaps the tragic quality of that novel lies in its power to compel the reader to share the point of view of the criminal protagonist, and to find with him that the old pawnbroker woman is a disgusting being not only physically, but spiritually as well. Yet Rozanov is willing to recognize that even the pawnbroker woman has, and is, a soul. Rozanov is able to discover the signs of the spirit even in the most monstrous being. Better than any modern reader he would have seen the spiritual dignity of such a creature as the man-insect of Kafka's *Metamorphosis*. Taking another example from Dostoevski, one could say that Rozanov would have understood even that strange desire of the Devil, as stated to Ivan Karamazov, to be reincarnated in the fat and old body of a pious and stupid merchant's wife.

What could be called Rozanov's panpsychologism is made possible only by his own paradoxical narcissism. As we have already stated, Rousseau had looked at his own soul without intellectual pride, yet he had replaced the pride of the mind with the pride of the heart. But in Rozanov's narcissism, even if there is plenty of *amour de soi,* there is no trace of *amour propre* left. Narcissism is for him the human passion par excellence, and, as such, it does not need even the ingredient of vanity. His egoism does not try to transform itself, like Stendhal's, into egotism. For him self-adoration and self-contemplation are not only an inalienable right, but the unavoidable duty of even the most mediocre, of even the ugliest, being. With Rozanov narcissism becomes, so to speak, democratic and demagogic; it is the universal suffrage, the general will of the soul. This is possible because every psyche is endowed with the sense of its own peculiar value: because every soul possesses its own aristocratic distinction, it own kind of eccentricity, its own peculiar brand of originality and novelty.

This is another of the many paradoxes of Rozanov, who, in a highly original dialectic, reintroduces into the soul those romantic values which seemed to be alien to his bourgeois and plebeian conception of the soul itself. And he does so by assigning those privileges to every soul. Nobody except Rozanov would have fully understood the import of the remark made by Baudelaire in his essay about Balzac, according to which all the characters of the *Human Comedy,* even janitors, are endowed with genius. And it is only the ability to recognize the individual genius of any strange soul which makes friendship, or psychological understanding, real and possible. This ability is an intuitive gift, and consists in the discovery of the "elective affinities" of different souls.

If Rozanov had used the term "elective affinities," he would have used it in its literal meaning, implying a natural, almost physical, rather than spiritual, kinship. We must remember that Rozanov's psychology is not spiritualistic, but vitalistic, and this vitalism has a strong physiological emphasis. In one of his declarations of vitalistic faith, Ortega y Gasset once stated that his conception of the value of life was more related to the criterion of biography than to the criterion of biology. In the case of Rozanov, such a relationship would have to be reversed. Rousseau and the romantics were satisfied with saying that passion is the life of the soul. Rozanov goes even further, and introduces into psychic life not only sentiments, but sensations too. In other words, for him the body is also one of the domains of the soul. Every individual body has its own kind of peculiarity and personality, like every individual soul. And, for him, only the men and the groups that possess a stronger sense of the *realia* of the flesh have a high feeling for the *realiora* of the spirit.

This conception has nothing to do with the pagan dictum: *mens sana in corpora sano*. Rozanov does not care about either physical health or spiritual well-being. For him, as for Dostoevski and Nietzsche, the maladies of the flesh and the diseases of the mind may even become the sources of what is highest and richest in life and man. He cares even less for hygiene. When he says that "the spirit is the perfume of the body," he would not feel offended if someone would object that for him it may even be its smell.[14] In other words, by way of conclusion, one could say that for Rozanov the original soul is no longer the *belle âme;* the eccentric soul is no longer the dandy, or the satanic, titanic, or Byronic hero. The original and eccentric soul is now the average, the common, the vulgar human being: not even the *bohêmien* or the outcast, but the bourgeois and the paterfamilias, the family man. In this sense, his teaching agrees completely with the Russian literary genius, whose notion was to bring to consummation the democratization of the modern literary hero, especially in fiction.

Only now may we understand why for Rozanov the most important components of the soul are the least spiritual, why for him the soul is also, even primarily, sex. This places him in a tradition to which both Rousseau and Freud may belong. The position of the former implied a spiritualization of sex, while the position of the latter involves a sexualization of the spirit. Both positions can be found in Rozanov, for whom the soul is sex, and the sex is soul. These identifications are reached through a process which can be explained, better than by the system of Freud, by the system of his pupil and rival, C. G. Jung. The process consists of reducing everything psychological to the common denominator of *persona,* as Jung describes it: "In the psychology of the unconscious, there rules the principle that each relatively independent part of the soul takes the character of a person, i.e., personifies itself, as soon as it is granted the opportunity of its self-realization as an autonomous element. . . . Where an autonomous part of the soul projects itself, there an invisible person is born. . . ." [15] This happens with Rozanov not only with sex, but, as Jung says, with every "independent part of the soul." And this is why the *animus* in Rozanov's soul is not merely dreaming of an *anima,* but becoming, in the Jungian sense, an archetypal *anima* itself.

It is for the same reason that Rozanov adds the ingredient of religion to his dialectic of the sexual soul. He adds not only his own private brand of religion, but also the public one, the faith of the body politic, of the commonwealth. Public faith generally tries to repress, or to control, what Freud calls *libido.* Rozanov's sexual mysticism tries to transcend or reconcile that conflict. This is achieved not on the plane of observation, but of dream or myth. It is that dream or myth which becomes the chief inspiration of his writings. Yet, even in his manner of living and way of thinking, Rozanov succeeds in preventing the conflict from ending in a crisis or in a catastrophe. He resolves that conflict into a kind of bourgeois compromise, made possible by the routine of living, the habits of man, the warmth and the peace of the nest. In this domestic arrangement, the soul ceases to be the mistress of man, but becomes his motherly wife, or only the maid in the house, even though it sometimes may reveal itself as *la folle du logis.* Man becomes the domestic animal par excellence, and, as such, he forgets that truth once uttered by Tolstoy, according to which of all the tragedies of human life, the worst is "the tragedy of the bedroom."

XII

Despite his mysticism, Rozanov thus seems to be more the disciple of Rousseau than of Dostoevski. We have already seen that there is little similarity between Rousseau and Rozanov as writers. It is equally true that there is little resemblance between the two as men. To prove this point with a single example, it may suffice to say that Rozanov would never have put his children in a foundling hospital. But one fact remains: without Rousseau's precedent, that kind of idolatry of the soul which is that most characteristic trait of Rozanov the writer and the man, would have been absolutely impossible. Only after having stated this debt, however, do we have the right and the duty to emphasize their differences. The most important is that Rousseau is still a classicist, and, in spite of everything, a Calvinist — in other words, esthetically, a purist, and morally, a puritan. He may lay bare the bounds of the soul, but he does not expose with equal complacency the wounds of his body. Even when revealing his psychological anomalies, he must first find a mode of expression not conflicting too much with the prevalent esthetic and ethical norms. From this standpoint, the differences between them are essentially historical and cultural in character, and they could be summed up by saying that Rozanov is a Rousseau who had passed through the experiences of modern psychology and biology, of vitalistic and intuitionistic philosophy, who has experienced the pathetic disorder of the late romantics and the cynical immoralism of the decadents.

In literary terms one could say that the bridge separating Rozanov from Rousseau is what in modern writing takes the name of realism or naturalism. Even if Rozanov is not a novelist, the work of this man, who considered himself a disciple of Dostoevski, cannot be understood without the precedent of modern fiction. Rousseau was a novelist, too. Yet, in spite of his contributions to the most important genre of modern literature, he wrote before the tradition of modern fiction took shape. In a certain sense, he made that tradition possible, and from many points of view his *Nouvelle Héloïse* could be considered the first novel in the modern sense of the word. Yet that novel, like Rousseau's literary work in general, is still dominated by that kind of inspiration which the French call *romanesque,* i.e., by sentimental fancies, rather than by observation or introspection of psychological facts. That novel, as everything Rousseau wrote, is essentially an erotic idyll.

Perhaps because of the mere fact that he was a modern writer, and that he was born in the country of Dostoevski and Tolstoy, Rozanov was able to give us, in nonfictional form, the equivalent of fictional psychology. Fictional psychology, especially in some of its most recent manifestations, has been defined by Ortega y Gasset as not merely a scientific, but an imaginary structure, or, as he says, a hypothetic construction.[16] In this sense, Rozanov is really the peer of the great and visionary masters of modern fiction, of a Proust or a Joyce. As is the case with contemporary fiction and with contemporary psychological realism (or surrealism), he gave us not so much "slices of life" or "slices of the soul," as glimpses of a probable life, or of an eventual soul. In a certain sense, more than with life, he experimented with dreams. And his dreams were his experiences, too.

It was Valéry who saw in the novel an analogy not with reality (of which the novel had been described as a mirror) but with the world of dreams.[17] Dreams are essentially lyrical, and this may explain the lyrical temper of the modern novel. And it is this lyrical temper which marks the essential difference between Rozanov and Dostoevski. In the highest moments of his inspiration, Rozanov reaches the heights of ecstasy and prayer. Yet he lacks the pathetic, tragic, and sublime inspiration of his master. The Rousseauian idyll of the soul had been transformed by Dostoevski into the ethos and pathos of tragedy. This never happens in Rozanov. When he fails, his vision seems to degenerate into an unconscious comedy, into an involuntary farce. In his spiritual drama we read the signs of pity and of fear, but of a pity and fear that are never sublimated by their own catharsis. As we have seen, he was aware of this. He knew that triviality knows no sublimation, and carries within itself the nemesis of comic laughter. We call it a nemesis merely because in Rozanov's world comic relief is not supplied by the author, at least not intentionally. The ridiculous springs forth in his work from the shock which the impact of reality produces upon the unreality of his dreams: it comes from without, not from within. Yet Rozanov redeems himself in another way, by changing paradoxically the bathos of life into a pathos of his own.

When our author wants to free himself from the oppression of what might be called his excessive Rozanovism (which his contemporaries called sometimes Smerdyakovism or Peredonovism), Rozanov has no other way out than to offer himself, as an easy victim, to the sense of humor of his reader. To be effective, the reader's sense of humor must not be afraid to be cruel and must raise itself to the sense of the grotesque and the absurd. The reader will find a certain comic relief in Rozanov's familiarity with the secrets of sex, in his bourgeois pettiness and softness, in his passive resistance to the realities of history and society. But it is exactly when the reader finds Rozanov ridiculous and absurd, that he is ready to recognize how much this author's work and personality are human and pathetic. Only then may he understand the value and meaning of what Rozanov felt, thought, and wrote; only then may he appreciate the message carried by his life and his books. Only thus may he finally understand, in spite of Rozanov's feeling of his own uselessness, for what purpose a man of this kind was needed.

Rozanov was needed because, after the Human Comedy of society, someone had to write the Human Comedy of the soul. A few writers, from Kierkegaard to Dostoevski, had already written the tragedy, or the Divine Comedy, of the spirit. A few others, like Rousseau and Amiel, had written idylls, or elegies, about it. Rozanov was the first to treat man's soul as many other writers had treated man's body. To do so, he had to be the kind of man he was. He had to be, so to speak, a healthier and more vulgar Barbellion, with more robust instincts, and with the added disease of lust.

This is why, of the many parallels made, the one between Rozanov and Nietzsche is the least valid of all. It was Merezhkovski who called Rozanov a Russian Nietzsche, and the comparison has been repeated uncritically, and too often. Merezhkovski naturally had in mind the common bond of their antagonism toward Christianity. We have already pointed out some of the similarities between their attitudes in this regard. But Nietzsche's polemic against Christianity is antireligious, while Rozanov attacks Christianity from a religious standpoint. Nietzsche's polemic is from without; Rozanov's, from within. Both exalt the body, but Nietzsche, in spite of his naturalism, which was essentially mythological, does not really believe in the body, as Boris de Schloezer has cleverly noticed. The bodily and the physical are merely esthetic allegories, or intellectual symbols of his cultural views: external projections of his Apollonian ideal of a new mental life.

On the other hand, the earthly, the bodily, and the physical are always understood by Rozanov in the most literal and material sense: they are his Dionysian entities and values. Both Nietzsche and Rozanov defend egoism, but Nietzsche's egoism is but a variant of romantic individualism; it is a spiritual, not a barbaric or instinctive, *culte du moi*. Rozanov's egoism, is, rather, a psychological and physiological force. Nietzsche wanted to be the "physician of culture," while for Rozanov culture is an incurable disease, which needs not the treatment of a skilled practitioner, but the drastic operation of a surgeon. It must be extracted like a cancer from man's body and soul. Nietzsche was the prophet of the superman; Rozanov, even more than Dostoevski, of the "underground man." Nietzsche exalts private and solitary life only that it may become the germ of a future and better social life, a chapter in human history, a first stage in the metamorphosis of the species, while Rozanov is a Zarathustra who withdraws into the nest.

Of all the negative judgments on Rozanov, the most severe is naturally the one pronounced by Leo Trotski. It is worth quoting, because it sums up, bringing them to the highest pitch, all the accusations shouted against him from the housetops of the radical intelligentsia, of the revolutionary or progressive Left:

The truest and most consistent thing in Rozanov is his wormlike wriggling before power. A wormish man and a writer, a wriggling, slippery, sticky worm, contracting and stretching according to need, and like a worm, disgusting. Rozanov called the orthodox church unceremoniously — in his own circle, of course — a dung heap. But he kept to ritual, out of cowardice and for any eventuality, and when he came to die he took communion five times — also for any eventuality. He was underhanded with heaven as with his publisher and his reader. Rozanov sold himself publicly for pieces of silver. His philosophy was in accordance with this and was so adapted. He was the poet of the cozy corner, of a lodging with all comforts. Making fun of teachers and prophets, he invariably taught that the most important thing in life is the soft, the warm, the fat, the sweet. The intelligentsia in the last few decades was rapidly becoming bourgeois and was leaning very much to the soft and the sweet, but at the same time it was embarrassed by Rozanov as a young bourgeois is embarrassed by a loose cocotte who imparts her knowledge publicly. . . .[18]

From what we have already said, it is easy to see that these harsh words contain many truths, and are in the main justified. Yet, from another point of view, Trotski is unjust and wrong. According to the dictum of Marx, he thought that the business of philosophy (or of culture) is, like the business of revolutionary politics, to change the world. But he could not understand that before changing the world, one must change man. To change the world is of course the aim of every political utopia, especially of those modern utopias which the history of our time has shown to be capable of realizing themselves. The only utopias which seem to be condemned to remain such are those which admit of the possibility, or even of the necessity, of changing man. Rimbaud, Nietzsche, and the Kirillov of Dostoevski[19] dreamed of this. Rousseau took the line of least resistance; it is Marx, or the Marxist, who is the real heir, or disciple, of Rousseau. Rozanov could not follow Rousseau on this path. Like Dostoevski before him, he tried to show that any philosophy of social change is vain when it does not take into account, along with what can be changed, what can never be changed in man. In this sense, Dostoevski and Rozanov showed, better than anybody else, the factors of permanence and inertia, the ahistorical element of the human soul.

The opposition between the two heritages of Rousseau, the heritage of socialism on one hand and of individualism on the other, cannot be easily healed. This is only natural. What interests us is a different problem: whether it is possible to reconcile the Dostoevskis and the Rozanovs with the democratic ideal. The case of Rozanov, even more than the case of Dostoevski, shows how difficult it is to find a common ground for that ideal and the philosophy of personality. The validity of Sartre's position, which is the position of the existentialists of the Left, lies in the attempt at finding that common ground. The democratic ideal has been able to absorb easily both humanism and humanitarianism. But it is very difficult for it to cope with religious humanism, and, even more, with the mysticism of the Self.

After all, the teachings of these doctrines amount to saying that life is traditional and conservative, as nature is, and that man's existence, as such, is nearer to nature than to history, as Tolstoy tried to show in *War and Peace*. In recent times modern thought has maintained, with greater intensity than before, that it is life which must adjust itself to history. This applies also to the most valid attitude in contemporary democratic thought, to what could be called liberal progressivism. Perhaps the time has come to revise that tenet. Democracy must become something more than democratic politics and government: it must become also the active defender of the nonpolitical from the political, the seeker after a social redemption of private life, and of man's soul. Is it too wild to hope that it might now be the turn of history to adjust itself to the life of man? Is it too much to hope for the advent of a new civilization which will reconcile history and existence, private and public life, the family man and the political animal, the fireplace and the marketplace, the anthill and the nest, the relativity of the *Zeitgeist* and the absoluteness of the soul? If so, even Rozanov will be considered a prophet, although he was no more than a victim and a witness of the condition of man.

NOTES

1. Nikolay Strakhov (1828–1895), a literary critic with nationalistic sympathies, who in different periods of his life was a friend and a collaborator of both Dostoevski and Tolstoy.

2. This is how the English translator rendered the Russian title of this book, *Uedinennoe,* which the French translator rendered as *Esseulément* (see note 3 below). Its meaning could be perhaps better conveyed by the musical term, "solo."

3. This is perhaps the place to list the translations which have made available to English and French readers the best of Rozanov's work, at least in part. Some of the most important pages he ever wrote may be read in English in the books edited and translated by the late S. S. Koteliansky. The first is entitled *Solitaria* (London, 1924), and contains the whole of *Uedinennoe,* large selections from *The Apocalypse of Our Times,* and excerpts from Rozanov's correspondence with his friend and biographer E. Hollerbach (Gollerbakh). The volume opens with a very abridged version of the latter's biography, *V. V. Rozanov,* published originally in Russian at Berlin in 1922. The second book is a selection from *Fallen Leaves, Bundle One,* and was published under this title, with a Foreword by James Stephens (London, 1929). The French translators, Boris de Schloezer and Vladimir Pozner, inverted the order of preference chosen by Koteliansky in his selection from Rozanov's writings; in their one-volume collection, entitled *L'Apocalypse de notre temps précédé de Esseulément* (Paris, 1930) they cut the latter considerably, while giving the text of the former almost completely (only the last two installments are omitted).

4. Most of the critical pages devoted to Rozanov by such *émigré* writers as those mentioned above may be read in the surveys of modern Russian literature they compiled for the benefit of Western readers. Such is the case with Prince D. S. Mirsky's *A History of Russian Literature* (New York, 1949, pp. 418–424); with Vladimir Pozner's *Panorama de la littérature russe contemporaine* (Paris, 1929, pp. 47–65); and finally with Nicholas Arsenjew's *Die russische Literatur der Neuzeit und Gegenwart* (Mainz, 1929, pp. 226–240). One of the best essays, if not the best, on Rozanov published in any foreign tongue is perhaps Boris de Schloezer's introduction to his French translation of *L'Apocalypse de notre temps,* cited above.

5. In this essay I have too often quoted from pages never translated before. This is why in most cases I have given my own version of Rozanov's text. For the quotations from *Uedinennoe* and other related fragments, I have, however, used Mr. Koteliansky's

renderings in the *Solitaria* volume (see note 3 above). Even in this case I have made slight changes in the translated as well as in the original text. I have considerably abridged many of the statements quoted, and I have always avoided reproducing in full the typographical vagaries affecting the original editions of Rozanov's works.

6. Chekhov's story "The Man in a Case" is better known in English as "The Man in a Shell," as its title was translated by Constance Garnett.

7. The curious reader may find a far fuller definition of the notion of *poshlost* in Vladimir Nabokov's *Nikolai Gogol* (Norfolk, Conn., 1944), pp. 63–74.

8. Smerdyakov, the bastard son of Fyodor, and the halfbrother of Dmitri, Ivan, and Alyosha, is perhaps the shadiest of all the characters inhabiting the dark world of *The Brothers Karamazov*. Peredonov is the protagonist of one of the most morbid Russian novels, Fyodor Sologub's *Petty Devil* (1907). By a strange coincidence, Peredonov is a provincial teacher, as both Rozanov and Sologub once were.

9. This, as a matter of fact, is one of the many thoughts of the "underground man." See *Notes From Underground*, part I, section XI: "But there are other things which a man is afraid to tell even to himself, and every decent man has a number of such things stored away in his mind. The more decent he is, the greater the number of such things in his mind" (quoted as translated by Constance Garnett).

10. The definition is taken from Chamfort's *Maximes:* from the maxim describing conviction in general as "la conscience de l'intellect."

11. See especially the *Lettre sur les spectacles,* passim.

12. The romantic conception of personality is based on the same principle, although it emphasizes the exceptional individual rather than the common man. Nothing is more significant in this context than Von Justi's statement, at the beginning of his biography of Novalis, that Novalis was one of the first men of whom one could say not that "he had genius," but that "he was one."

13. Any reader of *Notes From Underground* will realize this, despite the semantic ambiguity created by the fact that in Russian, as in other Western languages, there is only one word, *sovest,* to indicate the two different notions of "consciousness" and "conscience."

14. Other Russian writers had conceived of psychological originality in terms of personal smell. It will suffice to recall the words of the provincial Hamlet who is the protagonist of a famous story by Ivan Turgenev: "Have your own smell, your individual smell, that's the answer" ("Prince Hamlet of Shchigrovo," in *A Sportsman's Sketches,* translated by Charles and Natalia Hepburn, New York, 1950).

15. This passage is taken from C. G. Jung's essay on the psychology of the figure of "Kore," included in C. G. Jung and Karl Kerényi's *Einführung in das Wesen der Mythologie.*

16. See José Ortega y Gasset's *Ideas sobre la novela,* translated into English by Helene Weyl in *The Dehumanization of Art, and Notes on the Novel* (Princeton, 1948).

17. In his essay on Proust, which can be read in *Variété,* V (Paris, 1948).

18. This critique of Rozanov can be read in its entirety in the English translation of Leo Trotski's *Literature and Revolution* (New York, 1925: pp. 44–45).

19. Kirillov, although a secondary character from the viewpoint of the plot, is the most demoniac of all figures in Dostoevski's novel *The Possessed.* He kills himself to prove man's absolute freedom, which for him consists in a denial of the fear of death as well as of the fear of God.

A Correspondence from
Opposite Corners

B

ETWEEN 1919 and 1921, during the years of the civil war, the Soviet government was afraid of the effects of foreign intervention and rather sensitive to shifts of public opinion abroad. The new regime was also painfully aware of the obvious fact that the leaders of the old-fashioned intelligentsia, after having flirted for years with a vague and dreamy revolutionary ideal, after having created their own brand of the radical-populist myth, were now disappointed and dissatisfied. They were reacting with outspoken indignation against the hard facts of revolutionary reality, or were remaining disdainfully aloof in the fight which the party was waging, with the claim of establishing the dictatorship of the proletariat. The first steps undertaken by the Soviet government toward what was to be called the cultural or literary policy of the regime (later, at least in that respect, *quantum mutatus ab illo!*) were dictated by a spirit of prudence and compromise, by tactics of expedience and opportunism, by the methods of nonintervention and appeasement. This policy at first even took the form of granting generous help and special privileges to the members of that class, dubbed with the rather amusing name of workers in letters, sciences, and the arts.

The policy was strongly supported by Gorki, who used for that purpose the prestige of his name, and even subordinated, to the fulfillment of the program, his ideological acceptance of the regime, toward which he had felt so doubtful and dubious at first. It was through Gorki and his project of publishing a collection of classical masterpieces, entitled "Universal Literature," that many of the older and younger writers got paid for their work as editors and translators and were more or less able to weather the storm. The living conditions of the Russian intellectuals remained, however, difficult, even tragic; and the Soviet government decided to open for their benefit a few comfortable dwellings of dispossessed aristocrats, industrialists, and merchants. These buildings were transformed into sanitariums where artists, writers, scholars, and scientists — old, weak, or sick — could be given an opportunity either to improve their physical conditions and to recover their health, or merely to work or rest in peace. In the summer of 1920, in one of these sanitariums recently opened in Moscow, two extraordinary patients, already acquainted with each other, the poet, scholar, and thinker Vyacheslav Ivanov, and the historian, philosopher, and critic Mikhail Herschensohn, spent the period of their treatment living in the same room. From their meeting and sojourn together, the work originated which is the object of this study, and for the understanding of which the reader must first be supplied with some information about the personality, background, and career of each of its authors.

At the time of that meeting, Vyacheslav Ivanov was fifty-four years old, having been born in Moscow in the year 1866. As a young student at the University of Moscow, he had shown so much promise in the field of classical scholarship that he had been sent to study under Mommsen at the University of Berlin. His thesis, in Latin, about some of the most practical aspects of civic and communal life in ancient Rome, had shown so much learning and such thorough archaeological training that it seemed to open for him a brilliant academic career in the West. But the reading of *The Birth of Tragedy* and the later works of another deserter from the field of classical philology, Friedrich Nietzsche, led him to the literary and philosophical study of Hellenism, especially of the meaning and origin of the Dionysian cult. This interest in religious history brought him back to modern Russian culture, which, at the end of the past century and at the beginning of ours, was absorbed in questions of faith and mysticism, in strange and eclectic creeds, in the attempt to build a kind of syncretic religion, and was then indulging in mythical and allegorical, in heterodoxical and heretical beliefs. In brief, Ivanov turned to the problematic metaphysics of Dostoevski, to the liberal Christianity of Solovyev, to the erotic mysticism of Rozanov, to the "religion of the Holy Ghost" which was to be developed later by Bulgakov and Berdyaev, and, last but not least, to the pedantic and vulgar, literary and naïve Manichaeanism of Merezhkovski. Less inclined than his contemporaries to believe that Orthodox Christendom was the highest achievement of Christianity, Ivanov was on the other hand ready to accept literally and determined to prove, with more learning and imagination than they, their belief in the dogmatic statement of Tertullian, that Christianity is not only above history, but also that it has always existed, even within history itself. Even the Di-

onysian cult was for him an announcement of the coming of the Redeeming
Son.

All these thinkers were also literary men, and Solovyev was, like Ivanov,
a poet. As a matter of fact, the mystical allegories of Solovyev's verse were
to be more influential than the systematic doctrines he had expounded in his
philosophical works. His poetic adoration of Sophia, a pale and vague in-
carnation of the *Ewig-Weibliches,* of the feminine component of the Divine
Substance, was going to be the dominant inspiration of the school, or rather
sect, of poets, who affirmed themselves after 1905. These poets were recognized as the second generation of Russian symbolism, and later were to be
called the Russian symbolists *tout court,* while the poets of the first generation (Balmont, Bryusov, and *tutti quanti*) were instead to be considered the
Russian counterpart of the European Decadence. The symbolists merited
their name because they were a more exact historical equivalent of the symbolist movement as it had developed in France and in the West, and also because they were "symbolists" in the permanent and traditional meaning of
that word.

Vyacheslav Ivanov became not only a disciple of the philosophy of Solovyev (who before his death in 1900 had seen the early verse of his young
admirer and had recommended its publication), but also a poet and a symbolist. After his return to Russia in 1905, Ivanov settled in St. Petersburg,
opening his famous "tower," a house in Tavricheskaya Street, making of it
both a literary *salon* and the *cénacle* of the school. The differences between
his poetry and the poetry of the two younger masters of Russian symbolism,
Andrey Bely and Alexander Blok, could be briefly summed up as follows:
Ivanov was a more cultivated artist and a less genuine poet than Blok, a
more classical and less experimental writer than Bely, a less literal and less
naïve writer than either of them. For a while he shared some of their vaguest
and wildest dreams, passing, at the epoch of the "little revolution" of 1905,
through a period of mystical anarchism, longing for a social crisis which
could be at the same time a moral palingenesis and a spiritual apocalypse.
It was to literature, however, that he devoted his best efforts. Between 1903
and 1912, in addition to his "classical" tragedies, his excellent translations,
his suggestive critical, philological, philosophical, and religious essays, he
published five important collections of poems. The mystical and metaphorical
inspiration of his poetry, his predilection for classical themes, his sibylline
and oracular style, his learned and archaic diction, often filled with ancient
Slavonic words, the liturgical solemnity and ornamental richness of his verse,
all those qualities for which Leo Shestov gave him, not without irony, the

epithet of "Vyacheslav the Magnificent," are revealed even by the titles of his books of poems: "Pilot-Stars," "Translucidity," "Eros," "Cor Ardens," "The Tender Secret," and so forth.[1]

Such had been the career of Vyacheslav Ivanov up to the moment of his meeting with Mikhail Herschensohn, and of his sojourn with him, under the same circumstances, in the same room. But since the knowledge of the turning points of his future development may have some bearing on the study of the work which is the object of this essay, it is perhaps worth while to acquaint the reader with the later phases of Ivanov's *curriculum vitae*. In the fall of 1920 he went to Baku, where he remained for four years as professor of classical philology at the local university. There he published his magnum opus on the Dionysian cult and wrote perhaps his most human and poignant lyrical masterpiece, the "Winter Sonnets." This work is a sequence of twelve pieces for which he chose the form, rare in Russian verse, of the Italian sonnet, and where, using the symbol of winter, with eloquent simplicity, in direct images and in intimate, almost private terms, the poet expressed the feeling of cosmic and human tragedy, with which he was already viewing the historical tragedy of the Russian revolution. In 1924 he emigrated to Italy, where he has been living ever since, having recently crossed the advanced landmark of eighty years of age, surviving the crisis of the war and its aftermath, perhaps smiling at the false news that reached the Russian circles in New York of his own death.[2] During the last twenty years, he has been living by teaching the classics in private schools, and writing and publishing essays in Italian, German, and French. But he has not abandoned his poetry: one of his most important lyrical works, the philosophical cycle *Man,* appeared in the complete and original text, after having been reworked for almost a quarter of a century, only a few years ago. The most significant event of the later phase of his life has been his conversion to the faith of Catholic Rome, which took place in 1926, and which had been anticipated shortly before by the appearance of his "Roman Sonnets." [3]

Mikhail Herschensohn (or Gershenson, in a more exact transliteration of the spelling in Russian script of his surname) was three years younger than Ivanov, having been born in 1869, of a Jewish family, in Kishinev, the capital city of the province of Bessarabia. Like Ivanov, he had studied classical and Greek philosophy at the University of Moscow, but he had been unable to follow an academic career because of his race and creed. Like Ivanov, his interests turned from classical antiquity to modern Russian culture, where he showed a marked preference for its few representatives of the tradition of romantic and idealistic liberal thought. From 1900 to 1914 he wrote a series of outstanding historical works and biographical essays, devoted to such figures as Pushkin and Griboedov, Chaadaev and Ogarev. In 1909 he was one of those writers who contributed articles to *Vekhi* (Landmarks), a collection of critical and polemical studies on the role played by the radical intelligentsia in Russian history and culture.[4] During the First World War and the early period of the revolution, Herschensohn wrote a few more formal and ambitious philosophical works, in the vein of what would now be called religious and optimistic existentialism. When he died in Moscow in 1926, he left an immense number of letters, printed only in part (merely a few to his brother), which promise to be — when it is possible to publish them in their entirety — his literary masterpiece, and perhaps one of the most important historical documents left to posterity by his generation and epoch.

This uncommon gift for letter writing, for a more intimate and private kind of communication, and this predilection for the psychological and biographical essay, give us a clear indication of what kind of writer and man Herschensohn was, and emphasize the contrast between his nature and Ivanov's. In spite of the fact that Herschensohn considered Carlyle as his master, and that he was called the "Russian Macaulay," as a biographer he resembles rather Lytton Strachey, not because of any anecdotal predilection, since he is essentially interested in the intellectual and sentimental portrait of his model, but because of his earnest concern for personal traits, his curiosity in seeking for individual peculiarities, his deep and yet discreet insight into the secrets of private life, his keen intuition of what might be called the originality of the soul. That is, of course, an essentially Russian trait, and it shows how this historian and biographer was a worthy compatriot of the great masters of Russian psychological fiction.

Summing up the characters of these two men, we see on one side a poet and scholar; on the other, a biographer and letter writer; in Ivanov, a lofty passion for the metaphysics of history and culture; in Herschensohn, a love of intimate detail, a great interest in the daily chronicle of life. The former hides in the liturgical aloofness of the priest of poetry, the hierophant of culture; the latter shows the lively enthusiasms of a man interested in political ideas, in social ideologies, in radical thought. The poet reveals the impassioned and archaic solemnity of a mind equally versed in the philosophical and religious lore of the ancient East and the eternal West; the biographer betrays the inquietude of a modern man, troubled by the question of the day. The Jew, with his Talmudic strain, with his zest for life, and with his human warmth, is psychologically more Russian than the Slav, who, having spent so many years of his life in distant lands and in remote ages, confesses to his friend, in the very document that is the subject of this study (Letter XI), that he is only "half Russian." Ivanov, so much more deeply and widely cultivated, is on the other hand too much a learned Slavophile to be the more cosmopolitan of the two; furthermore, he belongs, rather than to the republic of letters, to the Brahmin caste of the chosen ones, the happy few. It is still very easy to find individuals to whom Herschensohn may be compared within the tradition of Russian culture: he resembles Herzen very much; he is a Herzen and a Westerner of his time. As for Ivanov, in spite of his deep understanding of spirits like Pushkin and Tyutchev, Dostoevski and Solovyev, we cannot find any adequate spiritual peer of his in Russian culture: discarding the national and political implications of this parallel, and recalling that Ivanov is not the lesser poet of the two, one could say that the German Stefan George is, among his literary brethren, the figure he resembles most.

The sojourn together of two men like Ivanov and Herschensohn, the meeting of two minds like theirs under the impact of such a historical emergency as the Russian revolution, could not but be an excellent opportunity for exchanging ideas, for an intellectual discussion of the validity of culture and its chances of transcending through its epiphanies the tragedy of history itself. The conversation of the two men could not dwell on any other object, and this prevented them from devoting the greater part of their time to their private meditation and speculative quest. Both immediately realized that their views were diametrically opposed, and this made their dialogue more difficult, but even more necessary. They were still trying to find a common ground for their fears and hopes, doubts and beliefs, when one day one of them proposed to the other that they exchange their ideas through the medium of the written, rather than the spoken, word. The other accepted this proposal, adding that from their written dialogue there would perhaps come out a "correspondence between the opposite corners" of the same room.[5]

Ivanov wrote the first of his six letters on June 17, 1920, during an absence of his friend, who found it, at his return, on his desk; Herschensohn penned the last one on July 19. These letters, covering a period of a little over one month, take no more printed space than a fifty-page pamphlet. They were published under the title of *Perepiska iz dvukh uglov,* or "Correspondence Between[6] Two Corners," at Petrograd, in 1921; a reprint of the original edition appeared in Berlin the following year. In Russia, for obvious reasons, the book did not receive the attention it deserved; as for the circles of the Russian *émigrés,* they were too busy, like all exiles at the beginning of their exile, with the pettiness of the everyday chronicle of political events for them to take seriously such lofty and impassioned meditations about history itself.

Abroad, even the first translation (into German) of the *Correspondence,* which appeared in 1926, passed almost unnoticed, although Ernst Robert Curtius commented upon it, with his usual alertness. The French translation appeared in a Catholic literary review, and one year later was reprinted in book form, with a preface by the philosopher Gabriel Marcel, now an existentialist of the moderate, religious wing, and with an important exchange of letters between Vyacheslav Ivanov and Charles Du Bos. The Italian translation, which was particularly important because it was prepared under the supervision of Vyacheslav Ivanov, who made also a few changes in his own text, followed soon.[7] The letters of only one of these two correspondents (Ivanov) have recently been brought to the attention of an English-reading audience,[8] and I hope that, together with them, the present essay will contribute to the acquaintanceship, on the part of the American public, with a work which is one of the most important cultural documents of our epoch.

II

This investigation will begin by a detailed analysis of the *Correspondence,* by means of a logical rather than a critical résumé, and by making use, in the words of their authors, of the passages which seem the highlights of this lofty dialogue. The very first sentence of Ivanov's opening letter must have made a strong impression on his friend. "I know," says Ivanov to Herschensohn, "that you are overtaken by doubts about man's immortality and the person of God," and he proceeds by affirming the presence within man's soul of a "luminous guest" who is like the promise of our future rebirth, a guarantee given by God the Father to all his sons (I). In his reply Herschensohn, after accepting the principle of personality as the supreme value, as the only reality, confesses candidly his temperamental dislike of metaphysics; and he adds that, in the present human and historical condition, his instinctive and fundamental distrust involves something more solid and substantial than metaphysics alone, that is, culture itself. Under the impact of present experience, culture seems to him not merely useless, but harmful:

For some time I have been finding oppressive, like an excessive load, or too heavy clothes, all the intellectual conquests of mankind, the entire treasure of notions and knowledge, of values collected and crystallized by the centuries. . . .

Such a feeling began to trouble my soul a long time ago, but it has now become customary with me. It must be a great happiness, I think, to dive into the river Lethe, cleansing one's soul within its waters, clearing away the remembrances of all religious and philosophical systems, of all wisdom and doctrine, of poetry and the arts, and land again naked on the shore, naked as the first man, light and merry, freely stretching and raising one's naked arms, remembering of the past but one thing, how one felt burdened by those clothes, and how one now feels easy and free without them. . . . Our elegant clothing did not weigh upon us as long as it remained unsoiled and unspoiled, but since during these years it has been torn and now hangs in rags from our shoulders, we would like to take it off our body and throw it away (II).

In his answer, Ivanov does not defend reason, the usual object of hatred on the part of instinct, and one which seems to him deserving of hatred, although on other grounds; he rather defends the spirit, not culture alone, but that ultimate and primordial kind of culture which cannot be conceived outside religion, because it rests on religion and is nourished by it. Herschensohn is reproached by his friend for thinking of culture in the usual modern terms; it is for this reason that culture is, to him, slavery to the letter instead of being freedom of the spirit:

That state of mind now dominating and greatly torturing you, that excruciating feeling of the intolerable load of the cultural inheritance weighing on your soul, is essentially due to the fact that you experience culture not as a living treasure of gifts, but as a system of the subtlest restrictions. No wonder, since culture has aimed at being no more than that. But for me it is the stairs of Eros and a hierarchy of venerations (III).

Herschensohn replies by referring to Ivanov's "work in progress" (a translation of Dante's *Purgatorio*), and by expressing a feeling of nostalgia for the "harmonic" civilization of the Middle Ages, but turns immediately back to the present, asking a rhetorical question:

How, in such circumstances, can we trust our reason, when we realize that reason itself has derived from culture and, naturally enough, bows before it, like a slave to the master who has raised him? . . . I am not judging culture, I merely witness that I suffocate within it. Like Rousseau, I see in my dreams a condition of bliss, of perfect freedom, where the unburdened soul lives in an Edenic thoughtlessness. I know too many things, and this load tortures me.

Herschensohn's criticism of culture, as well as of the body of knowledge it implies, seems here dictated by the desire to escape from history, by the wish to live in the individual passions of the moment: "As for that knowledge, I have no use for it when I am in love or in sorrow." An attack follows on philosophical idealism, which Herschensohn accuses of having destroyed the immediate sense of reality and of having reduced the experience of life to a ghost: "That century-long illusion has passed away, but how many awful traces it has left behind!" After the attack on modern culture, there follows the attack on modern civilization and its technology, on the *embarras de richesses* of modern industry, which in itself is merely a consequence of that "cultural inheritance weighing on our personality with the pressure of sixty atmospheres" (IV).

Ivanov's reply is still inspired by his belief in the syncretism of religion and culture, by his definition of religion as a kind of transcendental culture:

It seems to me that you are unable to conceive of the permanence of culture without one's substantial fusion with it, without one's merging within it. As for myself, I believe that our consciousness must at least partly transcend culture itself. . . . The man believing in God would not consent at any price to consider his faith as a part of culture: this is what I believe, although I am convinced that every great historical culture springs forth from a primordial religious fact. A man enslaved by culture (such is the conception of modern thought) will instead consider his faith as a manifestation of culture, whatever his definition of faith might be. . . . Only through faith is man able to transcend the "temptation" of culture. . . . The dream of Rousseau sprang forth from his disbelief (V).

The dream of the *tabula rasa,* says Ivanov, is not the dream of a new culture, or of a life liberated from it: it is the dream of a new morality, or of the destruction of traditional morality, even of morality itself — in other words, an attempt to erase from the soul of man the traces of original sin. Herschensohn replies by denying the possibility of a coexistence of culture and faith: "But it is not of this that I wish to speak. . . . I do not know or wish to know what man will find beyond the wall of the jail he is going to leave, and openly acknowledge my indifference toward 'the work of preparing freedom's roads.' . . . I merely *feel* . . . an urgent need of liberty for my spirit and conscience" (VI). Herschensohn ends by comparing himself to a Greek of the sixth century, oppressed by the complexity of his pantheon of gods, and to an Australian aborigine, tired under the weight of his totems and taboos.

In the following letter we find the first discreet hint, on the part of Ivanov, that his friend's viewpoint is due to Herschensohn's desire to share in the cave of his soul the collective and historical experience now taking place outside its walls: "Perhaps the last of Faust's temptations ought to become for you the first: the enchanted dream of the canals and the new world, the illusion of a free land for a free people." It is the revolutionary illusion that leads Herschensohn, in Ivanov's judgment, to think that culture is an abandoned temple, a ruined city, or simply an empty shell. Ivanov sees that Herschensohn's denial of culture had been dictated by his wish to merge, morbidly, unconsciously, and passively, into the stream of historical contingency. It is the convulsive force of contemporary events, Ivanov tells his friend, that makes him feel that culture is a static weight, though it really is a dynamic power: "not only a monument, but also an instrument of spiritual initiation" (VII).

But Herschensohn has no use for that monument or instrument: "The revelations of truth which descended on our forefathers have changed into mummies"; modern man is tyrannized by objectivized and abstract values, which may be classified into "fetish-values," that is, the traditional taboos of morality and religion, and into "vampire-values," that is, the bloodless totems of metaphysical and philosophical abstractions. "It may be that the last war has been but a hecatomb never witnessed before, forced upon Europe by a few intelligible values allied to each other through their priests." It is to real, personal, immediate, everlasting, and metacultural values that man must return. "When around a simple prayer one has built an immense structure of theology, religion, and church," Herschensohn says, we need a religious revolution, such as the Reformation; and when similar structures have been built also in the field of social life, we need a political revolution, such as happened in France in 1789. A similar house cleaning or clearing of the air is taking place at the present time: "Now a new storm is shaking the world: the individual right to work and property forces us to go out, into the open, into the free air, from century-long complications, from the monstrous complexities of abstract social ideas" (VIII).

Ivanov's answer is an argument *ad hominem:* "Yesterday's values are now shaken from their roots, and you are one of those who feel joy in this earthquake"; but it is also a keen criticism of his friend's presuppositions about the acultural or anticultural essence of the Russian revolution. Ivanov sees in it not merely a mystical, popular outburst, but the plan of a new civilization, of a new culture to be built: "The anarchistic current does not seem to predominate within it" (IX). Herschensohn feels that he has been touched on a sore spot and reacts by accusing Ivanov of treating him as a physician treats a sick man, unaware that his diagnosis is wrong. He too finds a weak spot in the armor of his friend, whose great learning, in spite of his transcendental religious beliefs, leads him to historicism, that is, to an attitude which implies a justification rather than a judgment of culture. And he takes upon himself again the task of the judge: culture was created by man as an instrument to make it possible for him to live better in his environment, but now the instrument is so complicated and heavy that it has become harmful.

"The deer developed horns as a means of frightening his enemies and defending himself, but in some species they have reached such dimensions as to prevent him from running through the woods, and the species is dying. Is it not the same thing with your culture? Are not your values those horns?" (X). Perhaps the proletariat will destroy those horns; perhaps it will adapt them to changed conditions; perhaps it will create better organs for the new men.

In his answer, Ivanov recognizes that the controversy has reached a dead end, that from now on it will be only a repetition of opposite statements. He sees that there is no meeting ground for his "humanism and mysticism," and for the "anarchic utopianism and cultural nihilism" of his friend (XI). Herschensohn, discovering signs of bad humor and even of bad temper in their dialogue, concludes it with an apparent compromise, postulating a new culture, different from the old one, which is only "a daily habit . . . not an intellectual nourishment" (XII). The correspondence can go no further; and Herschensohn, defining himself as a stranger and a pilgrim searching for the promised land, while Ivanov feels at home on the native soil of history and culture, ends by saying that their brotherly souls will find, in the house of the Father, a common abode.

III

It is difficult to conceive of a loftier discussion, of an exchange of ideas on a higher plane, of a polemic about history more detached from the superficial passions aroused by current events, and at the same time more concerned with the absolute and essential reality underlying the facts that take place before one's eyes, within the relativity of time and of human things. The war and the revolution, Russia and Bolshevism, are hardly mentioned, or referred to only a few times; still, their presence is deeply and constantly felt, and the sense of this presence has a direct bearing on what each of these two speakers says, thinks, or feels. The *Correspondence,* however, needs not to be praised, but to be appraised. What one must try to achieve is a critical interpretation of this text, and to extract from it useful lessons for all, valid conclusions for the present manifestations of the same crisis, still torturing the West and the world.

The position of Herschensohn is easier to deal with, and even to find fault with, and this task of faultfinding is expertly performed by Ivanov himself. Ivanov is right when he maintains that Herschensohn's viewpoint is not new: that a similar palingenesis, beyond culture or without it, with identical intellectual and ethical implications (the longing for a simplification of life, for the regained paradise of primitivism, for an escape from any tie and any bond) had already fascinated Leo Tolstoy, who, as Ivanov tells his friend, "must naturally attract you" (XI). Even before, the same dream had possessed the soul and mind of Rousseau, in whom Ivanov recognizes a decadent *avant la lettre* (V). In this, too, it is easy to agree with him, since Rousseau's ethical, political, and social ideal is nothing but the projection into the future of a retrospective utopia, of an Eldorado dimly seen in a distant time, discovered by looking backwards into the darkness of the past. Ivanov is equally right when he implies that a "transvaluation of all values" succeeds only in achieving the destruction, or at least the dethronement, of the values of the past, but that it always fails to transform them into new values, or to create values of its own. Any transvaluation of this kind is another symptom of decadence of the nihilistic or cynical type, and Ivanov is again in the right when, after the names of Tolstoy and Rousseau, he brings in, to explain or rather to judge the viewpoint of his friend, a far more dangerous and suggestive name — the name of Friedrich Nietzsche. "At bottom, the problem of Nietzsche is your own: culture, personality, values, decadence, and health — above everything, health" (IX). We could add that, while Nietzsche aims at being the "physician of culture," at becoming its regenerator and healer, Herschensohn would rather be the priest performing the burial rites of culture, singing over its body a requiem for the peace of its soul. For, in spite of the fact that he says, "Let the dead bury their dead," we know that he, too, is one of the living dead.

Herschensohn is rather perplexed at this kind of criticism. His reactions are varied: now he denies, now he accepts, now he modifies or qualifies Ivanov's strictures. For instance, he answers the reference to Rousseau in a rather conciliatory way: "It seems to me that even Rousseau, who shook Europe with his dream, did not contemplate a *tabula rasa*" (VIII). It is easy to accuse Herschensohn of many such inconsistencies and perplexities, or to admit that his dreamed-of palingenesis points at a cultural renaissance of its own. On the other hand, credit must be given to him for candidly recognizing, more than once, the absurdity of a denial of culture based on culture itself.[9] Yet, when all this is said, there is no doubt that the idea of the *tabula rasa* coincides with his utopia or promised land, with his ideal aim, with the object of his dreams.

To agree with Ivanov's criticism of Herschensohn's position, to accept the *pars destruens* of his argument, does not mean an approval of his positive viewpoint, an acceptance of the *pars construens* of his system. After all, the dream of the *tabula rasa* is dialectically the cultural equivalent of the socialist

ideal, as Dostoevski was able to demonstrate and anticipate in his *Possessed*.
On the other hand, provided that that ideal be realized without becoming
totalitarian, one must admit that it springs forth (and it is only on such soil
that it may flourish and live) from the human need for a terrestrial and historical justice: a need, to be sure, not easily satisfied by theological and metaphysical justice, the only kinds offered to us by religion and by historicism.
It is only in this sense that, against the cultural and religious consciousness
of Ivanov, against what he calls the "vertical line," in a given epoch of crisis,
in a given historical experience, man's conscience may have its good reasons
for preferring the solutions of intuition and sentiment, Herschensohn's "horizontal line." This means that the controversy is not merely a philosophical
one, as Ivanov seems to think, and as he felt it necessary to restate, many
years later, by defining the *Correspondence* as "a peculiar re-evocation of the
everlasting and protean dispute between *realism* and *nominalism*." [10]

That medieval dispute was a scholastic replica of the Platonic-Aristotelian
alternative: were ideas, that is, the names of things, the only real essences, the
only authentic values contained in those appearances, in those non-values
that are the concrete objects? Or were those ideas only names, *flatus vocis,*
mere conventional or practical labels, deprived of any existence of their own,
while reality belongs to solid objects and to concrete things? The realist considered as true the first hypothesis; the nominalist, the second one. In such
a sense, there is no doubt that Ivanov is the realist, and Herschensohn the
nominalist, for the former considers culture, which is a collection of ideas,
of name-things, as the human equivalent of the Logos, which, as in religion,
is made flesh; while, for the latter, culture is the dead letter and life the
living spirit. Ivanov is of course nearer than his friend to Goethe, whom he
often quotes or refers to, but here Herschensohn restates as his own the poetic
truth of Goethe that "the tree of knowledge is gray, and the tree of life is
green." And, like Goethe, Herschensohn does not care too much either for
the eternal archetypes or for the *Ding an Sich*.

Yet, if Herschensohn were merely a nominalist, he would not take issue
with culture, exactly because he would consider it only a collection of labels, a
dictionary of names and nouns, a heap of dead or at least lifeless words. In
such a case, he would not feel it necessary or worth while to make such a
sweep of all the cultural traditions of the past, since human reality would
remain outside them: one does not fight phantoms or kill ghosts. But Herschensohn is a modern man, and he knows, or thinks, that names, labels,
ideas may not only be different from human realities, but possess a validity,
solidity, and vitality of their own, and be filled with such an explosive energy

as to act and react upon life, converting or perverting it. Herschensohn would agree with such different thinkers as Burckhardt, Benda, and Ortega y Gasset, for whom modern history and modern politics have been and still are a politics and a history of ideas, and of bad and harmful ideas at that. Herschensohn states as much when he says that the First World War had perhaps been a hecatomb forced upon mankind by ideas, that is, by the intellectual dogmas and the ethical creeds of the past.

In spite of the fact that Herschensohn's moral position and sentimental attitude differ very much from Sorel's and Marx's, to those ideas which he calls "fetish-values" one could easily give the Sorelian name of myths; and to those ideas which he calls "vampire-values," one could with equal justice give the Marxist name of ideologies. Sorel approves of social myths because of his Machiavellian sympathy for political activism; Marx, who naïvely expected that his so-called scientific socialism would not have any use or need for them, condemns ideologies as the intellectual weapons of the classes or of the social system he attacks. Unlike Sorel, we fear myths and hate ideologies, either of the Right or of the Left — for very different reasons from Marx's, and also because in this case we know better than he. One should agree therefore with Herschensohn's condemnation of myths and ideologies while differing from him in the awareness that the revolution in which he saw the dawn of a reborn human innocence is as guilty as any established society, or even more so, of creating or perpetuating "fetish-values" or "vampire-values," which enslave the soul and destroy the dignity of man.

Ivanov stands on solid ground when he tells Herschensohn that Bolshevism is also culture, even if it is a culture of its own, and that those anarchistic tendencies of which Herschensohn is so fond are absent from the revolution and seem alien to it. One could add that technology, the very technology which he condemns as harshly as he condemns culture itself, will be the most important economic and political business of the society of iron and blood that the revolution, in which he sees only "sweetness and light," will finally build. At any rate, as Ivanov rightly maintains, iconoclasm does not lead anywhere, not even to the city of Utopia, to that Erewhon which is a Nowhere.

On the other hand, Ivanov commits the opposite sin, the sin of spiritual and cultural idolatry. His idolatry of religion and historicism leads to an essential indifference to the tragedy of history, to the social condition of man. Yet one must accept the principle inherent in his position, that it is not through the iconoclasm of culture and history that man will be able to build a better house or a better life for himself. On the stage where the tragedy of history is performed, man rejects the intervention of a *deus ex machina,* which is Ivanov's theatrical trick; but he refuses also that too easy catharsis which Herschensohn naïvely offers in his belief that it will compensate for the catastrophe, for that unhappy ending which always involves grief, death, and bloodshed. One feels rather skeptical and doubtful of those who wish, like Herschensohn, to merge themselves mystically and morbidly into an elementary and telluric force, merely because it may clear the air in the old, dusty, and unhealthy dwellings of man. One must equally dislike the purely symbolical interpretation of Ivanov, and the too literal acceptance by Herschensohn, of the truth contained in Goethe's *Stirb und werde,* which after all is a command for man to act and to live.

On one side, Ivanov's defense of culture and religion, within and without history, *pro et contra,* for or above man, and, on the other side, Herschensohn's desire to throw away culture in order to be better able to embrace mankind (suffering — who knows? — either the pangs of childbirth or the agony of death), prove that the real issue at stake in this text is a question of vital importance not so much for the intelligentsia as for the intelligence of the West. The real theme of the *Correspondence* is not the antinomy of realism and nominalism, but the antithesis of two ideals: the humanistic and the humanitarian. It matters very little that Ivanov is a religious humanist, since, despite his affirmation of the supremacy of religion, he certainly yields to the temptation of culture, even though he condemns it. Thus his judgment against the humanist, already quoted, applies to the judge himself: "A man enslaved by culture . . . will consider . . . his faith as a manifestation of culture, whatever his definition of faith might be" (V).

As for Ivanov's attempt at a conciliation of the humanistic and religious traditions, it is nothing new. Heine, Nietzsche, and Renan had already praised the Catholic Church for having achieved that conciliation during the Renaissance, and condemned the Reformation for having broken that ideal relationship. From Marsilio Ficino and Pico della Mirandola up to Cardinal Bessarion, the European mind had often tried, as Ivanov tries, to create a synthesis of the two antiquities, the classical and the biblical, to harmonize paganism and Christianity, Plato and Jesus, Hebraism and Hellenism, the civilization of Rome and the West and the culture of Byzantium and the East. Such a synthesis is still essentially humanistic in character, and therefore unable to change the essence of humanism, the ideal of which had been already perfectly stated by a pagan writer of the third century, Aulus Gellius, in a famous passage of his *Attic Nights* still worth quoting: "Those who created the Latin tongue and spoke it well never gave *humanitas* the notion inherent in the Greek word *philanthropia.* They gave that word the meaning of what the Greeks call *paideia,* i.e., knowledge of the fine arts."

But the humanitarian, Christian or not, radical or mystic, follower of Tolstoy or of Gandhi, is interested in philanthropy, both the word and the thing. Sometimes he is interested also in the humanities, but only when he thinks that there is no conflict between them and humanity. In a few short periods of Western history, in the eighteenth and in part of the nineteenth centuries, the two ideals coincided, the former being considered as the cultural instrument and the intellectual counterpart of the latter. But this coincidence between the humanistic and the humanitarian ideal broke down during the second half of the nineteenth century, when a few spirits, in their reaction against rationalism, historicism, scientism, and positivism, forced the humanitarian ideal to cope with the problem of personality and to find other foundations for its faith.

The mission of modern culture has been to react against four historical kinds of reason: *Verstand,* or the *raison raisonnante,* that is, "mathematical" reason; *Vernunft,* or "critical" or "idealistic" reason; and, derived respectively from the former and the latter, "scientific" and "historic" reason. In other words, modern culture has reacted against Descartes, Comte, and Taine, and against Kant, Schelling, and Hegel. Such a reaction had been anticipated by Rousseau, and was to culminate in the work of Dostoevski: two men who were dear to the heart of Herschensohn, a humanitarian basing his faith upon sentiment, intuition, and instinct. Such is the meaning of his attack on philosophical idealism, on historic and ideal reason; after all, Dostoevski had already aimed his telling blows at mathematical and scientific reason, in the first part of the *Notes From Underground.* If it is superfluous to note that Ivanov had no use for mathematical and scientific reason, it is perhaps worth while to remark that many words and ideas have, in Herschensohn's attack against philosophical idealism, a Bergsonian ring.

The humanitarian of the rationalistic, practical, utilitarian kind (as Dostoevski had already noted, in the novel mentioned above) is active and positive, at least in thought; while the humanitarian of the sentimental, intuitive, and instinctive type, *à la* Herschensohn, is negative and passive in character: feminine and pacifistic, so to say. As a natural consequence, he is destined to be disappointed by that revolution he falls in love with, and which he greets, as Herschensohn does, in the name of personal freedom and the dignity of man — or, as he says, in the name of "the individual right to work and property" (VIII), as a liberation of all human faculties, as an opportunity for the self-development and self-expression of Everyman. He was dreaming of a Crystal Palace where there could be room also for the dissident and the heretic, for private life and individual idiosyncrasies, not only for the will, but even for the whims of man. If he had understood the dialectic of Dostoevski, the ironical inventor of that myth, he would have seen that in the Crystal Palace there is no room for this. The humanitarian must find out this truth by himself. The mystical humanitarian awakens only when he survives his dream, and then he is not only disappointed but crushed, because, unlike his more logical rivals or mathematical colleagues, he is unable to rationalize the cruel reality now oppressing him and his fellow men. Herschensohn was perhaps fortunate in being spared by death from witnessing the awful metamorphosis of the figure of his dream into a new Leviathan.

Exactly because of the blindness of his irrational hopes about the kind of future which the present will bring forth, Herschensohn's iconoclasm becomes a new idolatry, and Ivanov is right in condemning it. On the other hand, as already hinted, there is an idolatry in Ivanov too, the idolatry of the eternal, which is very often only the apotheosis of what is merely old. The iconoclast, as Ivanov rightly implies, is a decadent; yet the idolater is a decadent, too. The cultural idolatry of Ivanov and the cultural iconoclasm of Herschensohn have the same origin: both come from Nietzsche, who is the common spiritual master of their generation and of both men, even if both disciples later discarded him. Nietzsche condemned decadence, although he was a decadent himself, and this is what both Ivanov and Herschensohn do. This point is proved merely by quoting and using the beautiful definition of decadence given in this text by Ivanov himself: "What is decadence? The awareness of one's subtlest organic bonds with the lofty cultural tradition of the past, but an awareness tied up with the feeling, both *oppressive* and *exalting,* of being the last of the series" (VIII). It is that oppressiveness which leads the decadent Herschensohn to the blind and mystical acceptance of a new series, the series of a resurgent barbarism, replacing the traditions and beliefs of a tired and dying civilization; it is that exaltation which impels the proud Ivanov to keep faith with the cultural values and the spiritual creeds of the old series, and later to accept as his own the creed of the most dogmatic and canonical, ancient and permanent church of the West, Roman Catholicism, the most compact system of revelations ever devised by man.

Thus, in spite of the fact that both Ivanov and Herschensohn are, as the former accuses the latter of being, two "monologists" (IX), in spite of the fact that they stand, as Herschensohn says, "at the opposite ends of a diagonal not only in our room, but also in the spiritual world" (II), a dialogue between them is, up to a certain point, still natural and possible, owing to their common decadent background. It is decadent to believe that the only choice left to man lies between cultural traditionalism and religious conservatism on one hand, and revolutionary messianism on the other. It is a symptom of decadent psychology to feel that man's fate at this stage in history offers no alternative but being, as Herschensohn and Ivanov equally are, prisoners in a kind of Platonic cave, which resembles more than they think the corners of those squalid St. Petersburg flats where Dostoevski's heroes — or better, victims — live, suffer, and die. Both in their room and in their minds, like Dostoevski's "underground man," Ivanov and Herschensohn are cornered, as were their younger brothers of the lost generation after the First World War, as are we, too, members of another lost generation, unstable and unsafe survivors of so many social and political floods. Their discarded master, Nietzsche, was more right than they when he prophesied the advent, in a not too distant future, of what he cynically calls "war's classical age." We are even more oppressed and cornered than they are, because we feel more remorse for the past and more fears for the future of man.

This is why we have no right to dismiss either one of them with a curt *medice cura te ipse*. And yet we cannot afford to share the traditional faith, the metaphysical beliefs, the pre-established harmony of Ivanov; nor are we able to indulge in Herschensohn's desire to merge with the present, with those physical bodies which are called parties or masses, or even less, with that mystical body which is called revolution, or what you will. The Western reader is likely to prefer Ivanov's position, or at least to be won over by the greater consistency of his stand. Ivanov has the more powerful intellect of the two, and also the more virile and logical mind, able to avoid the contradictions, paradoxes, and anticlimaxes of the position of Herschensohn — which is that of a man of culture who, by denying it, hopes to save his soul. And if I think that Herschensohn's testimonial is the more important and poignant of the two, it is merely because his illusion is candid and fresh, and also because we have been lucky or unlucky enough to see it shattered before our own eyes. Only because we were young enough to become such eyewitnesses are we able to recognize that the obscure dialectics of Herschensohn's ideal involves not merely the "great betrayal" of culture, or even a betrayal of the revolution in Trotski's sense, but man's treason to man.

On the other hand, we are equally dissatisfied with any brand of ecclesiastical culture or of cultural religion, with intellectual mysticism, which is always fated to become an intellectual superstition, and like all superstitions, to end unconsciously in a kind of worldly and universal skepticism. The utopian and anarchistic messianism of Herschensohn is, of course, a religion, too, but not in the literal and positive sense of a sect or a church; and at bottom one should sympathize with his unconcern, or even disdain, not for the religious or the divine, but for theological and metaphysical problems, for the golden chains of revelations and dogmas, canons and myths. For this we are ready to forgive his confession of a medievalistic nostalgia, and even the final, eucharistic appeal to his friend. The important fact is that we agree with him that Jacob's ladder, the vertical line of transcendence, even if it may become the stairway of individual ascensions, is, like contemplation and prayer, unable to save us. We think that the only way to save our souls is to save our world. This is exactly what Herschensohn is asking for, but his horizontal line is different from ours.

We want a horizontal line able to take into account the irregularities of history, the accidents of geography, the idiosyncrasies of psychology, the peculiarities of life, and the absurdities of man; we reject his *tabula rasa,* that *tabula rasa* which, through that very culture, those very values he wanted to destroy, may be created only by the steam roller of revolution, by the juggernaut of the totalitarian state, or by the most radical and nihilistic leveler ever invented by man, the atomic bomb. Even in this case, we owe our attitude not to insight, but to hindsight, and therefore we feel as if we had no right to reproach Herschensohn for having failed to foresee what we have seen. But the vertical line of Ivanov may also be the one along which both the Ivory Tower and the Tower of Babel are built; in a certain sense, it is also the line along which the atomic bomb may fall. Idolatry of culture implies also the idolatry of science and, in the long run, of technology; and transcendental, not less than immanent, historicism is only a metaphysical justification of all of history's acts and deeds, and therefore also of the atomic bomb. At all events, not everyone is able, like Ivanov, to find a shelter in the Vatican, which was at least spared by aerial bombs.

What we are looking for is a conciliation, a synthesis, of the vertical and horizontal lines, between respect for what is transcendental in man and respect for what is immanent in society, in history, in the world. It is our duty to remember that the vertical line of humanism is a good corrective for the horizontal line of humanitarianism. While the humanist may care only for the happy few, the humanitarian may very well love mankind only in the general and in the abstract; sometimes, by looking at the masses, at the forest of men, he loses sight of the tree, of that suffering and thinking reed which is man. Only too often, as Dostoevski says in *A Raw Youth,* " 'Love for humanity' is to be understood as love for that humanity which you have yourself created in your soul." In other words, almost as easily as the humanist, the humanitarian may become the Narcissus of his own idea. If humanism is too easily satisfied with being merely humane, humanitarianism may frequently become inhuman, antihuman, too. Even more than the modern humanist, the modern humanitarian is too easily inclined to be a mere anthropologist.

Man's life must be built in extension and depth, on the cornerstones of the Others and of the Self; only in such a shelter, temporary or not, will man no longer feel that his back is against the wall. We want a house where we shall never feel cornered; we refuse to be overwhelmed either by the waves of the future or by the waves of the past. This means that we are not ready to discard, as Herschensohn advises us to do, the theoretical, practical, and ethical wisdom of our Western and Christian past; and on the other hand, we are not resigned, as Ivanov is, merely to conserving that tradition. We want to respect both values and life, or, in political terms, to enjoy the fruits of those ideals of spiritual freedom which are the legacy left to us by Ivanov and his peers; but we also feel a longing for that ideal of justice which, in spite of so many deviations and errors, is still the truthful message carried by Herschensohn to us. Liberty and justice are but different names for the vertical and the horizontal lines, which we want to see united again into a symbol of redemption, into the sign with which we shall conquer. In this year of our Lord, the son of man, either *homo sapiens* or *homo faber,* does not want to be crucified on any other cross.

NOTES

1. "Pilot Stars" (*Kormchie zvezdy*) was published in St. Petersburg, 1903; "Translucidity" (*Prozrachnost*), in Moscow, 1904; "Eros," in St. Petersburg, 1907; the two series of "Cor Ardens" (both consecrated to the poet's grief at his wife's death), in Moscow, 1911 and 1912; "The Tender Secret" (*Nezhnaya tayna*), in St. Petersburg, 1912.

2. Vyacheslav Ivanov died in Rome on July 16, 1949, after this essay was written.

3. The dates of publication or composition for the most important poetic works of Vyacheslav Ivanov's later period are the following: "Winter Sonnets" (*Zimnie sonety*), published in Ilya Ehrenburg's anthology, *Poeziya revolyutsionnoy Moskvy* (The Poetry of Revolutionary Moscow), Berlin, 1921; "Man" (*Chelovek*), published in Paris, 1939; "Roman Sonnets" (*Rimskie sonety*), written in Rome, 1925.

4. This publication appeared in Moscow, 1909. In this book, the former Marxist, later a Western liberal, Peter Struve, the religious thinkers Bulgakov and Berdyaev, on the left wing of orthodox theology, and, finally, Herschensohn himself, attacked the shallow and superficial thinking of contemporary Russian revolutionary ideology, its cultural and spiritual nihilism.

5. This testimonial is given (without revealing the author of the statement) by a friend of Vyacheslav Ivanov, O. Deschartes, in her introduction to the Italian translation of the *Correspondence* (see note 7 below).

6. Literally, "from."

7. The German translation, *Briefwechsel aus zwei Ecken,* appeared in the little-known organ of a mystical group, the review *Die Kreatur,* I:2 (1926). The observations of Ernst Robert Curtius on the *Correspondence* are contained in an essay entitled "Humanismus als Initiative," which was included in his book *Der deutsche Geist in Gefahr* (Berlin, 1932). After having appeared in *Vigile,* I:4 (1930), the French translation was published in book form under this title: *Correspondance d'un coin à l'autre, précédée d'une introduction de Gabriel Marcel et suivie d'une lettre de Viacheslav Ivanov à Charles Du Bos* (Paris, 1931). The Italian translation has the following title: *Corrispondenza da un angolo all'altro. Traduzione . . . riveduta da Venceslao Ivanov. Introduzione di O. Deschartes* (Lanciano, 1932).

8. While this essay was being prepared for publication, the letters of Ivanov alone had appeared in English, under the title "Correspondence Between Two Corners of a Room," in the third issue (Winter 1947, pp. 4–22) of the international review *Mesa,* edited and published in this country, at Pennsylvania State College, by Herbert Steiner. Unhappily, the issue was printed in a very limited number of copies, and a new edition of the *Correspondence* was required for this reason alone, without speaking of the need to put before American readers the letters of Herschensohn. After this article was finished, a complete edition, under the title *Correspondence Between Two Corners,* was brought out by the *Partisan Review,* IX: 951–965, 1028–1048 (1948). The *Mesa* translation of the Ivanov half of the *Correspondence,* made by Miss Eleanor Wolff, is very good; I preferred, however, to keep my own renderings of quotations from Ivanov, owing to a desire for terminological consistency and stylistic coherence between the passages and statements quoted from both the authors of this text. As for the *Partisan Review* translation, made by Mr. Norbert Guterman, it appeared too late to be of any use to me; at all events, it would have been of little help, because the translator failed to take into account the changes that Ivanov had introduced into the text of his own letters through his revision of the Italian translation of the *Correspondence.*

9. As for instance in Letter VIII, where, confessing that he is listening with enchantment to the siren voice of culture speaking to him through the words of his friend, Herschensohn asks himself the rhetorical question: "Am I not myself one of her sons?"

10. In his letter to Charles Du Bos, published together with the French translation of the *Correspondence* (see note 7 above).

Isaak Babel in Retrospect

Now, when the American reader has at his disposal the whole body of Babel's narrative writings,[1] may be the time to reassess what is probably the best work of fiction that has ever appeared in Soviet Russia, one written partly within the framework of Soviet literature and partly outside of it. The best way to proceed is perhaps to relive first its author's *curriculum vitae,* which, in the light of the historical experience in which he was actor as well as victim, is both tragic and exemplary.

Isaak Emmanuilovich Babel was born in 1894, in Odessa, of a family of small Jewish merchants. He spent his childhood in Nikolaev, where, as his stories relate, he fully experienced what the life of a Jew under tsardom was really like. From his youth he must have asked himself the question which in "The King" he puts in the mouth of his hero, the gangster Benya Krik: "But wasn't it a mistake on the part of God to settle the Jews in Russia, for them to be tormented worse than in Hell?" In "The Story of My Dovecot" he re-evokes his own early struggle and toil to be admitted into a Russian school, inaccessible to all too few Jewish boys because of the *numerus clausus;* in the same tale and in "First Love" he recalls the murder of his grand-uncle Shoyl during the pogrom of 1905, as well as the humiliation of his father, whose kneeling down before a Cossack officer did not spare his shop from a looting mob, nor himself from ruin.

The work of Babel is often autobiographical, but never pathetic, and only indirectly does it reveal the most intimate secrets of the author's psychology and personality. Yet, from the reading of his tales, we easily discover that the writer was deeply affected by a sense of alienation from the world. That sense was rooted in the three curses of his life, which were race, poverty, and his calling as an artist. Perhaps the spectacles on his nose and the books under his arm estranged him from the world at large even more than his being a pauper and a Jew. Babel shared all his life that feeling of loneliness so characteristic of the prerevolutionary intelligentsia, with its unrequited and all too mystical love for the Russian masses. At the same time, as a denizen of the ghetto, or of the worst urban slums, he deeply felt as an added curse, for both the man and the artist within himself, his inability to commune with nature, to experience within his heart and mind all the lively and lovely things that organic life creates for the joy of man.

Babel's isolation is to be seen also in his attitude toward Jewish culture itself. When his family returned to Odessa, he failed to follow the trend dominating the Jewish cultural life of that prosperous and turbulent city. While Vilna was the capital of Yiddish writing, expressing the life of the "pale" in the vernacular language, with a prosaic realism, full of self-pity and irony, Odessa was the moral center of Zionism, and had generated a school of poets returning to the messianic and prophetic traditions of old, singing of the newly promised land in the sacred and symbolic accents of the ancient tongue. Thus his city really deserved the sad praise sung for it by one of the many rabbis we meet in Babel's masterpiece: "Odessa, a god-fearing town — the star of our exile, the involuntary well of our distress. . . ." But Babel refused both Yiddish and Hebrew, and chose instead Russian, the idiom of the goyim. He did so not merely to escape from the ghetto, but to turn, through Russia, to Europe and to the West.[2]

In those years he had discovered his masters, who were not only Tolstoy, Chekhov, and Gorki, but also Rabelais, Flaubert, and Maupassant. It was the same urge, the urge to know a broader and nobler world, that led him to settle in Petersburg toward the end of the First World War. The city was then closed to Jews not settled there, and Babel lived in the capital illegally, without means of his own, and with great hardships, in order to start a literary career. His first stories appeared in print in 1917, under the aegis of Gorki, in the review the latter was then editing, *Letopis* (The Chronicle). They had a *succès de scandale,* and got the young writer an indictment for obscenity, but the trial never took place, because of the fall of the tsarist regime. In the meantime Babel had been drafted, and the February revolution caught him while he was fighting the Germans on the Rumanian front.

Babel saw in that great upheaval the first communal experience in which he could share, the first social and historical reality of which he could finally become an active and integral part. After October, although not a party member, he served enthusiastically the new communist order in varied missions and tasks, and was finally attached, first as a civilian, and later in uniform, to the "mounted army" led by Marshal (then General) Budenny in the Polish campaign and in the Civil War. He edited for that army *Krasny Kavalerist* (The Red Trooper), a propaganda sheet, and fought with it on the western and southern fronts. Then, after a few years of silence, he started writing again. "It was only in 1923," he stated later, "that I learned to express my ideas clearly and at not too great length." So he wrote down his impressions of those two campaigns in the form of sketches, which, as they were published, provoked the indignant protest of Budenny, who saw in them a libel against the troops under his command. In 1924 Babel collected about thirty of those sketches in the book known as *Red Cavalry* (or rather, "The Mounted Army," as the Russian title *Konarmiya* really means), which revealed to the Russian public that a new and gifted writer had been born.

Shortly afterwards he published the slim collection *Tales of Odessa,* which, however, passed almost unnoticed. In the meantime Russian social and political reality had been rapidly changing, and Babel did not feel any longer in tune with what was going on, on other fronts as well as the literary one. He was already considered a "fellow traveler," according to the sense which that term had been given by Trotski in his book *Literature and Revolution*. It was for writers like him that, after the introduction of the new literary orthodoxy represented by the dogma of "socialist realism," Gorki coined the formula of "revolutionary romanticism," so as to justify those mild heretics who still looked back with nostalgia to the tragic and epic years of the civil war, instead of looking forward and celebrating what the regime was now building on the ruins of the past. The changed atmosphere made it difficult for Babel to write anything important or new, although he tried his hand at a novel, and wrote a rather interesting play, *Sunset,* dealing with the same hero and the same milieu he had already treated in the *Tales of Odessa.*

Soon after this, Babel practically ceased to write, as he confessed, rather ambiguously, in a speech he gave at the 1934 Writers' Congress. At that time he was still free to travel abroad, and he went for a while to Paris, where, as he had already tried to do in his youth, he did some writing in French. Upon his return home, his creative vein dried out, and he published nothing but an augmented and revised one-volume collection of all his short stories, which appeared in 1934. Significantly enough, several political and historical allusions, dealing with the revolutionary role of Trotski, were expunged either by the author or the censor from this text. Babel's signature appeared in print for the last time in 1937; one year later he was arrested at the peak of the purges of Trotski's followers, supposedly for no other crime than an imprudent joke about Stalin, and he was sent to a concentration camp, where he died in 1939 or 1940. According to one version, he succumbed to disease or hardships; according to another, he was shot. In either case, what spelled his doom was that revolution in which he had so desperately willed to believe, and thus he died in the same alienation in which he had lived. Whatever happened to Babel the man, we know that the writer was officially condemned to death. After his disappearance, his works were proscribed, and his name was condemned to public oblivion.[3]

Red Cavalry, which remains Babel's masterpiece, is a book hard to describe to those who are unacquainted with it. When we read its pages, we see all the western and southern marches of Russia: Volhynia, Podolia, and the Ukraine pass fleetingly by. We ride, in a cloud of powder and dust, amidst bursts of fire, and rattling of sabers, from the flat fields of Poland to the green slopes of the Caucasus. In the distance, among the felled trees and the burned huts, we watch, as they pass before us, the men and women, old and young, who are both the victims and the spectators of our endless raid. Jews in the cities and peasants in the villages look with unseeing eyes at the horsemen and their mounts, both of Cossack blood, that are trampling on their land and their lives. Sometimes, all of a sudden, a horse gallops by without his master, whom a Polish or "White" bullet has nailed forever to the wet mother earth. Some of the riders may turn their heads to salute the lost comrade, but the mounted army will never stop or slow down its relentless race toward war and death. And while riding along, we glimpse on the open skyline the giant shadow of the Russian masses on the move, and we wonder whether their march is an ordeal or a quest.

The reader will never forget the figures who appear fleetingly in the pages of this book. We shall mention a few of them. The mounted army's chief officer, the former tsarist "noncom," Semen Budenny, who smokes and smiles while threatening to shoot anyone who yields or turns back. The youthful giant Savitski, with his legs as handsome as a girl's in his shining boots. The red general Pavlichenko, still smelling of milk as he did when he was a herdsman, who could tame buffaloes and elephants as well as goats and sheep. Konkin, the former ventriloquist, shooting prisoners as if they were clay pigeons. The young officer Kolesnikov, who knows how to do honor to his luck when the fortunes of war raise him to an exalted command. Dyakov, who was once a circus performer, and under whose will and skill a dying nag may still perform like a thoroughbred.[4] And Afonka Bida, with his shrill feminine voice, who weeps over his dead horse and who raids the countryside for days and nights, in order to get himself a new mount as good as the old one.

On the other side there are all the meek and the weak, the poor and the humble, whom for their mischance we shall meet on our path: Apolek, the Polish wandering artist, a heretic and a mystic, portraying peasants, publicans, and country wenches in the saintly figures he paints on the walls of a Catholic church; his German friend Gottfried, the blind musician with white mice as pets; and numberless Jews, among whom there stands out the old Gedali, the Dickensian owner of a curio shop, who is unable to distinguish between counterrevolution and revolution, because he does not know where in the latter the good ends and the evil begins, and who dreams of another, impossible International, one made only of men of good will.

Unlike Gedali, Babel seems to know where the good ends and the evil begins. For him, the revolution is good, and the counterrevolution is bad. He may hope or believe that sooner or later we shall have another International, this time made only of decent people; but he thinks that in the meanwhile we must be satisfied with the Third, and pay for both the present and the future with sweat, tears, and blood. As his hero Benya Krik will later say in the *Tales of Odessa,* in the story entitled "The King": "There are people already condemned to death, and there are people who have not yet begun to live." And many must die so that others may begin to live. By bowing to what one might call either historical necessity or revolutionary expediency, Babel ends by accepting as valid and just the ordeal of war: war taking victims from both enemies and friends, from the strong as well as from the weak. Thus one of the main antinomies of this book is the everlasting conflict between the army and the militia, between the volunteer and the professional soldier, between the man for whom war is an occupation or a calling and the man for whom war is an act of either freedom or necessity. A man with a faith like Babel's will fight out of a sense of ideological duty, and thus will treat any kind of military struggle as a civil war. But for the Cossacks of the unit to which he is attached, the enemy is always an alien or a stranger, and war itself is a job. Strangely enough, the realization of this contrast stirs within the soul of Babel what one might call an inferiority complex, and he feels his own unworthiness before all those martial murderers for whom killing is a natural habit, or a simple routine. Thus he defends the slaughter and the slaughterers from those who fear and condemn them: "She cannot do without shooting . . . ," he tells Gedali, "because she is the Revolution. . . ." Without being born a killer, he not only joins the killers, but wishes and tries to become one of them, "imploring fate to grant *him* the simplest of all proficiencies — the ability to kill *his* fellow men. . . ."

It is with a sense of great humility that he accepts as fully deserved the reproach of weakness leveled at him by those who are soiling their hands while "busy shelling and getting at the kernel for *him*." And he trembles in every vein when a Cossack sees through his chicken heart, all too full of worries, especially with the concern "to live without enemies," all too empty of bravery, even of the simple courage to cut short the torments of a comrade mortally wounded, with a violent and yet merciful death. Thus, in order to gain the friendship of the Cossacks, he beheads a poor goose, and propitiates them with his offering of the slaughtered animal for their evening meal: yet, at night, after the sacrifice, his heart feels stained by the blood he has shed. Despite this, the attitude of Babel toward the Cossacks remains that of an unrequited lover, while at the same time he turns his pity toward the victims of the slaughter, whoever they are, although in the main they are Jews like him. Often he even admires the moral strength of the meek and the weak, as when he says, speaking of the Jews of Galicia and Volhynia: "Their capacity for suffering was full of a somber greatness." The very man who accepts war as the apocalypse, and revolution as the palingenesis, of history, rejects the daily crimes and commonplace misdeeds they imply: "The chronicle of our workaday offenses oppresses me without respite like an ailing heart." Babel is thus of the devil's party, and knows it. His unavowed comradeship may go not to his war companions, but to their victims, and he certainly feels misplaced among the slaughterers whom he wishes to imitate, and cannot help but admire and love. Yet, although unable to fully identify himself with the murderers, he still remains with them, even if only as an outcast.

Mr. Trilling, who has written a penetrating essay about Babel, tries to explain his inner conflict in terms of the contrast between Jew and Cossack, claiming, however, that the writer has tried to reconcile that contrast within his mind and soul: "Babel's view of the Cossack was more consonant with that of Tolstoy than with the traditional view of his own people. For him the Cossack was indeed the noble savage, all too savage, not often noble, yet having in his savagery some quality that might raise strange questions in the Jewish mind." There is some truth in this, but not the whole truth. If the conflict could be reduced only to such terms as those, then its reconciliation would be a purely literary one. Mr. Trilling is undoubtedly right in mentioning Tolstoy in connection with this book. Yet the Tolstoy who has directly influenced *Red Cavalry* is not the youthful author of *The Cossacks,* but the old and classical master of *Hadji Murad,* as we could easily prove by examining Babel's style, and by listing all the reminiscences, especially in the form of images, that the reading of that late Tolstoyan tale has left embedded in the pages of this book. The difference between *The Cossacks* and *Hadji*

Murad is not merely that in the latter the Cossacks are replaced by Caucasian Tartars, but that its characters are evoked in heroic rather than in sentimental terms. While in his earlier work Tolstoy looks at Luka and at his fellow Cossacks in the idealized light of a Rousseauistic vision, in his later one he represents Hadji Murad and his followers with objective simplicity, in an epic, not nostalgic, key. It seems to us both evident and significant that Babel's imagination had been influenced by *Hadji Murad* more than by *The Cossacks:* yet from another viewpoint, the inspiration of *Red Cavalry* is rather mixed, and this makes it nearer to *The Cossacks* than to *Hadji Murad*.

What we mean is that both *Red Cavalry* and *The Cossacks* have been written out of a dual mood, out of their authors' double allegiance to opposite attitudes and values. In the case of Babel's book, one could say that the writer has made his own the antagonism between Jew and Cossack, or, as we prefer, between the killers and the killed. In brief, there are two main strains in this work, and neither of them dominates fully its atmosphere or its structure. The first strain is epic in quality, but, despite its power, acts within the book in a fragmentary and spasmodic way, or, in literary terms, as a rhapsody. Babel's epic breath is genuine, but, as in all moderns, rather short. Thus Babel fills the intervals between warlike episodes with a pathetic strain, which is antiheroic in character. Many critics have maintained that the book is based on a contrast between epic and lyrical values. We would say, rather, that the lyrical element appears in and results from only the juxtaposition of the heroic and pathetic ones. Mr. Trilling must have guessed this when he states that even when recording "violence of the extreme kind," Babel responds to the brutality so recorded "with a kind of lyric joy." In such moments, Babel reconciles within himself the man and the artist, in a reconciliation that is truly poetic, rather than merely literary.

The supreme manifestations of such a reconciliation are to be found in those crucial images through which Babel sums up an entire episode, or closes it. Think of the vision of the newly elected brigade commander, bowing his head under the burden of his responsibility, and yet standing out against the whole horizon while marching toward either glory or death: "And suddenly on the earth stretching away far into the distance, on the furrowed, yellow nakedness of the fields, we could see nothing but Kolesnikov's narrow back, his dangling arms, and sunken, gray-capped head." Think of the scene where the Cossacks ride calmly across the plain, with no other accompaniment but the tune and the words of an ancient ballad: "The song floated away like smoke." Think finally of the vengeance of Prishchepa, who first cruelly punishes all his fellow villagers who pillaged the property of his parents, executed by the Whites, and then ends by burning down his family hut: "The fire shone as bright as Sunday."

Babel submits to this kind of poetic transfiguration only what he has once seen with his own eyes, and feels still alive in his own soul. His imagination, which is strikingly original, prefers to operate at the level where mere invention can be dispensed with. Despite this, in *Red Cavalry* or elsewhere, he never writes autobiographical pieces in the narrow sense of the term. The character using the first person singular in his tales is more of a spectator than an actor; at any rate, he is never a central figure. That character is often identical with the writer himself, and yet he is not so much a person as a point of view. The vision conveyed through his perspective is often static; what the writer tries to recapture is the tension of being, when time seems to stand still, rather than the ever changing and daily drama of man's life. Many critics misjudged this quality, and this led them to accuse Babel of a lack of psychological depth or complexity. Perhaps they failed to realize that in his chosen medium, a short story as brief as a sketch and as tight as a prose poem, there is room for sudden epiphanies, but not for searching and slowly unfolding insights. We forget all too often that while the novel can be musical, the short story is plastic and visual in essence. And Babel works like a painter, representing on a flat surface and in a small space all the massive and colorful variety of reality. Like an old painter he yields to other figures the center of the scene, while tracing his own self-portrait in one of the corners of the canvas. The immediacy of his vision seems to suggest that he always writes under the shock or impact of the event; yet at second sight we realize that he represents the event itself as if it were detached in both mood and time. In his work rage is controlled by order, and the emotion is recollected in tranquillity. This is why these tales look at first as if they were only vignettes, but this impression is immediately corrected by the sense of their perfection, of their finicky polish and finish, which justifies up to a point the Soviet critic who defined them as miniatures. Yet, although many-colored and vivid, their moral contrast is as simple and elemental as the chromatic one between white and black, and this is why they remind us, more than of anything else, of Goya's engravings about the horrors, and even the splendors, of war.

Red Cavalry is not the whole of Babel's literary heritage. The *Tales of Odessa*, although inferior to *Red Cavalry*, as well as posterior to it, could perhaps serve as a better introduction to his work. While *Red Cavalry* is epic and lyric in character, the *Tales of Odessa* are picaresque and picturesque.

They do not deal with the world at large, which is the world of history, but with a narrow and peculiar milieu, the Jewish quarter of Odessa, the so-called Moldavanka, of which the author gives us the glorified annals. The main characters of this book are rogues, mainly smugglers and racketeers, and its single hero is Benya Krik, "gangster and king of gangsters," but above all a passionate man, since "passion rules the universe." One could say that this little collection is a kind of *Beggar's Opera* in fictional form, with the difference that Benya Krik is a more human, and less cruel, MacHeath. This representation of Jewish popular life, with its allusions to Jewish folklore, with weddings, funerals, and feasts, goes against the grain of Yiddish writing, since, unlike the latter, Babel treats the denizens of the ghetto as romantic heroes and as plebeian caricatures at the same time. Here pathos merges into a kind of sympathetic grotesque, producing an art which reminds us of the engravings of Hogarth, or of the prints of Callot.

If "The Story of My Dovecot" lies halfway between the world of *Red Cavalry* and the *Tales of Odessa,* the piece entitled "Guy de Maupassant" occupies a place of its own within the canon of Babel's work. Inspired perhaps by Chekhov's "Mire,"[5] this simple narrative in the first person, certainly autobiographical in character, begins by re-evoking the author's illegal stay, and his bohemian way of life, in Petersburg. To make a little money, the protagonist accepts a position helping a rich Jewish lady with no literary abilities to translate into Russian the whole of Maupassant. The high point of the tale is the dramatic contrast between the plush vulgarity of her person, house, and milieu, and the noble and comic naïveté of her literary ambitions. This awkward situation is handled with great irony and pity, which redeem even the sexual climax of the story, when the two co-translators consummate an embrace in the propitiatory presence of Maupassant's ghost.

No story better testifies to the maturity of Babel's talent than this one. It is therefore only fitting that it contains the whole of his *ars poetica,* so to speak, in a nutshell. The author expresses his views about style, and his ideals of writing, in two statements, which are not merely personal asides, but observations naturally and directly related to the subject matter of the story, which is the translator's (or the writer's) task. Here is the first: "A phrase is born into the world good and bad at the same time. The secret lies in a slight, almost invisible twist. The lever should rest in your hand, getting warm, and you can turn it once, not twice." And here is the second, which is a development of the first: "I began to speak of style, of the army of words, of the army in which all kinds of weapons may come into play. No iron can stab the breast with such force as a period put at the right place." Babel's sympathy for Flaubert and his school justifies Lionel Trilling's claim that at least the first of these two passages has been dictated by an obsessive concern for *le mot juste*. Yet, if we look deeper, we shall find in both passages echoes of ideas that Tolstoy developed in *What is Art?* There is in that treatise an all too neglected page, where Tolstoy says that all art is merely a matter of a "wee bit" less or of a "wee bit" more: of avoiding or omitting here and there a little something insignificant in itself, but the absence or presence of which spells success or failure. What Babel has added to this theory is a series of dynamic and material images, mechanical and military in content. Yet they suffice to change into a skillful craft, or into a cunning strategy, what Tolstoy had conceived as an intuitive process or a tentative quest. In the same manner, Babel seems also to accept the Tolstoyan theory of artistic communication as a contagion of feeling, although even here he replaces the notion of contagion with a surgical, or even murderous, metaphor. And it matters very little that Babel seems to reduce the sorcery of words to the operation of a well-placed graphic symbol, of a mere sign of punctuation, which is, however, able to pierce our mind, as well as our soul. Perhaps the miracle of his art lies in this power to touch and wound, rather than to calm and soothe, through the magic of words. If this is true, then the best epigraph for the whole of his work was given by the author himself, in the very phrase by which he tried to define Maupassant's writings in this story named after him. We certainly can repeat for Babel's tales what he said of the stories of his French master: that they are "the magnificent grave of a human heart."

NOTES

1. Isaak Babel, *The Collected Stories,* edited and translated by Walter Morison, with an Introduction by Lionel Trilling (New York: Criterion Books, 1955).

2. In the years after the revolution, the Jewish community of Odessa was to produce a small pleiad of poets in the Russian tongue, the best known of whom are Vera Inber, Ilya Selvinski, and Edvard Bagritski.

3. After this article was written, there were reports in the American press that this silence had been finally broken. It seems that Babel's name is reappearing in print, that his rehabilitation is in the making, and that his works will soon be published again.

4. In the light of what we shall say later about Tolstoy's influence on Babel, we may remark at this point that this scene, closing the story entitled "The Remount Officer," is highly reminiscent of the famous racing episode in *Anna Karenina*. Both this episode and that scene culminate in the single, identical detail, of the pitiful glance which the dying mare turns toward her master and torturer.

5. Thus Constance Garnett translated Chekhov's original title (*Tina*).